LESSONS AND LEGACIES III

LESSONS AND LEGACIES III

Memory, Memorialization, and Denial

Edited and with an Introduction
by Peter Hayes

NORTHWESTERN UNIVERSITY PRESS EVANSTON, ILLINOIS

Northwestern University Press
Evanston, Illinois 60208-4210

Printed in the United States of America

ISBN 0-8101-1665-0 (cloth)
ISBN 0-8101-1666-9 (paper)

Library of Congress Cataloging-in-Publication Data

Lessons and Legacies III: memory, memorialization, and denial / edited by Peter Hayes
p. cm.
Includes bibliographical references.
ISBN 0-8101-1665-0.—ISBN 0-8101-1666-9 (pbk.)
1. Holocaust, Jewish (1939–1945)—Congresses. 2. Holocaust, Jewish (1939–1945)—Historiography—Congresses. 3. Holocaust, Jewish (1939–1945)—Influence—Congresses. I. Hayes, Peter, 1946– .
D810.J4L4 1991
940.53′18—dc20 91-14707
CIP

The paper used in this publication meets the minimum requirements of the American National Standard for Information Sciences—Permanence of Paper for Printed Library Materials, ANSI Z39.48-1984.

With deep love and appreciation
for instilling in us the values
of love of family,
we dedicate this volume
to our parents

Helen and Jules Abramson
and
Eileen and Milton Altman

Earl and Sharon Abramson

Contents

Theodore Zev Weiss
President, Holocaust Educational Foundation

Foreword

IT IS A GREAT PLEASURE, ONCE MORE, TO THANK THOSE WHO HAVE made the publication of another volume in the Lessons and Legacies series possible. The essays assembled here constitute a selection of those presented at the third Lessons and Legacies Conference, which was held at Dartmouth College in November 1994. The Holocaust Educational Foundation is extremely grateful to President James Friedman for his vigorous commitment to the conference and for the superb work of its two principal organizers, Professors Michael Ermath and Leo Spitzer of the Department of History. Thanks to these individuals and their many helpers in Hanover, the conference not only took varied and stimulating form but also became an integral part of Dartmouth's intellectual life. Words cannot convey our appreciation for their accomplishment and for our pleasure at being part of an educational experience in the broadest sense.

As was true regarding earlier Lessons and Legacies Conferences at Northwestern University and subsequent ones at Notre Dame and Florida Atlantic Universities, the sessions could not have occurred without the generous support of many patrons. I am particularly indebted to our board for supporting and fostering this very important undertaking of the foundation. One of our most devoted board members and a close personal friend who gave me much encouragement and counsel, Mort Minkus, died in 1994, and a special tribute was paid to him at the opening banquet of the conference.

Once again, we thank Professor Peter Hayes for the time and energy he put into editing this work. Of course and as always, I drew strength for this project from my lifetime partner Alice and my children, Deborah, Danny, and Gabi, who have become as much a part of the Lessons and Legacies family as they are of mine.

With the Dartmouth Conference and the publication of this volume and its predecessors, the Lessons and Legacies series has established itself as a major forum for Holocaust study and research. The Holocaust Educational Foundation is proud to have fostered this ongoing initiative and to present this collection of the scholarly results.

LESSONS AND LEGACIES III

Peter Hayes

Introduction

THIS VOLUME, THE THIRD IN A GROWING SERIES, DEPARTS SLIGHTLY from the format of its predecessors but shares their preoccupation with both the past and, so to speak, the present of the Holocaust. Indeed, at the center of all the essays collected here are issues of process: of how such disparate entities as academic disciplines, interpretive frameworks, nationalities, sites, media, popular attitudes, and even judicial mind-sets have coped with the challenge to understanding and memory that this subject poses.

That challenge is the theme of Elie Wiesel's affecting introductory piece, "Looking Back." In it he dwells on the ambiguities, even contradictions, inherent in the scholarly study of such a cataclysm. Two of these concern Wiesel in particular: the imperative of expanding our recollection of a phenomenon that to him remains forever only incompletely recallable; and the double nature of looking back, an act that can teach but also transfix. Wiesel's brilliant evocation of Lot's wife reminds us that looking back is a virtually irresistible human impulse, but that it entails the risk of paralysis, of our becoming petrified by the emptiness of loss. Researchers, Wiesel concludes, must run that risk with only the hope, not the rewarding certainty, that knowledge will positively affect human behavior.

The essays collected in Part I, "Disciplinary Reflections," focus on the ways five fields of study have kept (or can keep) thinking about the Holocaust dynamic, that is, the ways they can open new perspectives on it or sharpen older ones. In typically lucid and concise fashion, Christopher Browning clarifies several of the recently most vexed questions about historical writing on the Holocaust: the terminology historians should employ, the causal chains in which they should locate what occurred, and the inherently interpretive and meaning-laden nature of their search for evidence. Alan Steinweis, in a similarly clear-eyed piece on Jewish studies, warns against the multiple intellectual losses that flow from teaching and writing about the Holocaust as if Jews only happened to be caught up in it or, conversely, as if they were its only targets. While Gerald Markle finds the contributions of sociology to Holocaust study wanting to date, he suggests that this need not be so. If sociologists were to take their leads from such nonmembers of their guild as Primo Levi, Hannah Arendt, and Gershom Scholem, they could better do justice to two of their discipline's essential callings: the identification of regularity in human behavior, and the obligation to instruct about the contemporary world. Hearkening in similar fashion to his own field—philosophy, with its mandate to confront the "right questions" about human life—John Roth calls upon philosophers to recognize the failure of their previous answers to impede the Holocaust. He exhorts them to overcome the aversion to detailed historical study that causes them to skirt the subject. Finally, Jeffrey Peck's probing essay challenges Holocaust scholars to recognize the distinct "avenues of entry" to the subject that literature and literary commentary provide, as well as literature's limits, and to make use of as many of these avenues as possible in teaching and research.

The more traditionally structured essays of Part II, "The German Context," take up an issue that has figured prominently in much of the heated scholarly criticism of Daniel Goldhagen's best-seller, *Hitler's Willing Executioners:* the degree to which the horror of the Holocaust ought to be read as the linear projection of the German past. Michael Berkowitz and Karl Schleunes offer distinct takes, one focusing on culture, the other on politics, on the relationship between what preceded and followed the divide of 1933 in Germany. In a contribution attentive to both perpetrators and victims, Berkowitz reminds us not only that German culture was hardly an undifferentiated entity but also that Jewish Germans often rightly perceived that it was not, and that their cultural grounding helps explain the distinct impact that exiles and survivors from Germany had on the societies and intellectual spheres of Israel and the United States. Karl Schleunes deftly makes the case for the revolutionary nature of what the Nazis wrought, emphasizing its "complete inversion of political and social values." How that inversion interacted with the routine ambitions and operations of a particular commercial institution is the theme of my own detailed examination of the role of the Deutsche Bank in the persecution of Jews. Contra Goldhagen, I conclude that "situational" and "functional" motivations, not ideological oneness of mind, propelled the mounting complicity of much of German society in the crimes of the Third Reich.

The eight essays in Part III approach "Memory and Memorialization" via diverse routes. A concern with tendencies in Holland to avoid self-questioning about the Holocaust unites Henry Mason's comprehensive survey and Debórah Dwork's illuminating inquiry into policy toward Jewish children concealed during the German occupation. Harold Marcuse and Michael Marrus take up the problems of physical commemoration at camp sites, with Marcuse's description of the partialities of successive official efforts at such an undertaking at Dachau serving to buttress Marrus's argument for leaving the remnants of Auschwitz-Birkenau as "unrestored" as possible. The next two essays deal with the potential of film as a medium for Holocaust memorialization. Nathan Cogan reports on his documentary about the sole survivor of his father's family in Lithuania. His account raises far-reaching historical and methodological issues concerning recollection and narrative—and the response of viewers to both. Scott Denham's contribution, accompanied by a valuable bibliography on German and Austrian discussions of *Schindler's List,* explores the degree to which Spielberg's filmic treatment of horror both ripped open old suspicions and soothed contemporary citizens of Central Europe. Finally, Judith Doneson, discussing the increasing role of the popular media "in translating the destruction of the European Jews to the American people," and Lawrence Baron, analyzing popular awareness of the Holocaust, both come to reassuring conclusions about their subjects. Doneson urges us not to lose sight of the manifest beneficial impact on the consciences of "ordinary men" of even flawed media programs on the Holocaust. Placing the gaps in public knowledge of this subject alongside other examples of the state of mass historical awareness, Baron finds that "Holocaust education has been relatively successful" in the United States, particularly in view of the comparatively recent onset of such pedagogical efforts.

If the contributions to Part III suggest general progress over time in educating and sensitizing national cultures, monument planners, and media interpreters to the complex issues the Holocaust raises, the essays in Part IV remind us of the limits to such successes. Deniers continue to well forth from disparate generational springs, according to Jonathan Petropoulos, each having distinct driving impulses and hence requiring different responses. And occasionally, as in the instance described by Geoffrey Giles, sanitized versions of Holocaust deniers' arguments find expression in judicial pronouncements in Europe. Scholars may have greater grounds for optimism about the results of their labors than Elie Wiesel allows in his opening essay, but they can hardly afford to relax their efforts.

All in all, these essays demonstrate the vitality and variety of current scholarship on the Holocaust and the continuing urgency of the issues associated with it. They stand as a call to scholars and students alike to remain constantly aware of the interaction between knowledge of the past and conduct in the present, of the implications of "looking back" for looking forward.

Elie Wiesel

Looking Back

I HOPE YOU WILL NOT ACCUSE ME OF TRYING MERELY TO PLEASE THE feminists, but I have a very special feeling for a woman in the Bible who has no name. Probably the only one. This is the wife of Lot. Lot was the relative of Abraham who tried to prevail upon God to save Sodom from the fire. He did not succeed, and so the angels came to destroy Sodom, and other angels came to save Lot and his wife and children, the whole family. Nepotism at its best. Now, Lot and the family were ordered not to look back, and everybody obeyed except his wife. And she was punished, by being turned into a pillar of salt. Why was she dealt with so harshly? After all, it was the natural thing to do, to look back for the last time. To look back for a minute. To see the flames, or maybe even, with some luck and grace, to see her house before it burned down, to see the neighbors, their families, the children. It is natural to look back, and it is unnatural not to look back. For me, the villain in the story is Lot, not his wife. So why are we so harsh with her?

Now, as I am sure many of you teachers and students must know, in antiquity looking backward was severely judged. When Orpheus began rescuing Eurydice from the Land of the Dead he received a warning. And because he chose not to heed it, he lost his beloved forever. What did Lot's wife lose? For the moment, let us say that looking back is inevitable for some people, dangerous for others, and a question mark for us. Can one imagine what went through the mind of Lot's wife as she looked at the fire that engulfed her home and the homes of her neighbors? Was she wondering why her city was so harshly punished? Because of the sins of the population? What about the children, who by definition are always innocent? And yet she must have wondered why her children were spared.

These doubts and self-interrogations can easily be placed in the context of our inquiry. Who among the survivors from Treblinka and Majdanek was not afraid of looking back, afraid of losing his or her sanity, or faith, or will to live?

There is a novel in which the hero meets a madman in his town. And the madman simply explains his madness in this way: he says, "Can you imagine? Can you imagine that the city which was ours is what it is now, devoid of Jews? I must be mad. I am insane. Because I walk in the streets, I look in the windows, in the shops, in the houses, and all the people whom I knew are not there. That means that I must be mad." Therefore, to look backward means fear, the kind of fear that Kafka so well explained in all his stories and novels, the fear of the emptiness, fear of the knowledge that, outside, it is emptiness that is waiting. One is afraid to look back so as not to face the emptiness.

Inside the black hole of history that we know now Auschwitz was, prisoners preferred not to look back. Inside Auschwitz they were afraid to evoke the vanished families. All they recalled were superficial things. What did they talk about there in the camp? About meals they used to eat, physical pleasures. Religious people would recall visits to the rabbi's court or cantorial performances, but not occasions involving siblings or parents. Why? They were afraid, afraid of bursting into tears, of weeping. I never spoke to my father about home: we were afraid. We were afraid that if we started to weep, we would not stop. And so in our endless conversations, we prisoners did not refer to our parents, our sisters, our brothers. It took me fifty years to really speak about my relations with my father and my mother and my little sister. For fifty years I could not. I just published my first volume of memoirs (*All Rivers Run to the Sea,* Knopf, 1995), and in it I finally convinced myself that I had to do that. So I wrote, and I know you can imagine how difficult, how impossible, it was to speak about them.

Ask psychologists and they will tell you that it is part of human nature to repress memories of pain and agony. It is easier not to reopen certain wounds, for they are too real, too profound, they hurt too much. For us today, however, the opposite has become true. We want to remember more and more. We do not want to forget anything. Quite the contrary, we look everywhere, we listen to every word, even to those words that reverberate only in our own consciousness or even in our dreams. We want to remember.

Does this mean that inside Auschwitz the prisoners did not remember? They did. Their memory remained active and open. Except that inside and for some time afterward, their memory did not find expression in language. Men and women remembered everything but lacked the strength to speak about it. In their sleep they relived their past, which seemed more enchanting and real than when the past was present. But they kept their dreams to themselves, and their fear of their silence, their inner longing for death. What were the prisoners' dreams? Of home. In the morning when they woke up, it was doubly tragic because awakening brought not only the interruption of sleep and immediate contact with a cruel, bitter, and tragic reality, but also it took them away once more from home.

What do we dream these days, these nights? Survivors will tell you that recently we dream more and more frequently and more deeply of the war, not of now. From the moment we go to sleep, we find ourselves inside the kingdom of night. And when we wake up we feel better. Because now we are in touch with a different reality.

But after the war, survivors had problems expressing themselves, although they tried. In truth, many survivors wanted to testify, wanted to share their memory. They were burning with desire to tell the tale and bear witness on behalf of those who were left behind or who had left them behind. But they felt incapable and perhaps unworthy of accomplishing their task. Because they could not find readers or listeners, they lacked the proper words, words that could perhaps express the infinite dimensions of solitude and fear, despair and agony. I have said it and I repeat: it is not because I could not speak that people did not understand; I could not speak *because* people could not understand. And therefore, many survivors locked themselves up in their private memory, knowing that they had become its prisoners, knowing that their memory was only theirs, because no one else could penetrate it.

It is for the survivors that I wrote my first narrative testimony, *Night*. Or as I called it in Yiddish, "And the World Was Silent." I wanted to tell my peers, my colleagues, my friends, that although there are no words, we must invent them. Although there is no possibility of communication, we must create it. Although only those who were there inside will ever know what it meant to be there, we must believe that it is given to us to move others closer to the gate.

What you are doing—you teachers, professors, and students—is, of course, a great source of hope to us. Often we worry about what will happen after we are all gone, after the last survivor is gone. What will happen? I have asked this question, and I am sure every other survivor has asked this question. And you answer: not to worry too much, because you are there. I cannot tell you how gratifying it is to see how many young teachers there are, and for those of my age to know that we have successors, that we have heirs, that now you will do what we tried to do and often could not. For I confess to you I could not teach what you are teaching. When few were doing so some twenty-five years ago, I tried for a year or two. I had to. But it was difficult. It is because of my awareness of the difficulty that you are facing that I have such respect for you.

It was not easy in the classroom, I remember, to teach about Treblinka and then see the students go on to Biology 101 or literature or anything. By the way, they often did not move; they stayed. And either/or: either everyone wept or we all remained silent. We read poems written by children, as surely you sometimes do. Sometimes when you read and study the arguments, the silly, brutal, vicious, ugly arguments offered by the most ugly of our enemies, the deniers, I can imagine the anger that invades all of you teachers and students, and yet you must continue. So it is good that you are here and that you are teaching.

But remember that memory has always been for us not only a challenge but a commandment. The fact is, there were witnesses during the upheaval, there were historians in the ghettos, there were chroniclers in the death camps. Just think about it. The problem for them was not only one of consciousness but of conscience. Where to look first, whose name to retain, whose anguish to record? There were so many stories, so many events, so many episodes of humiliation and courage, faith or despair. Which ones deserved to be transmitted to future generations? Which ones deserved to enter history? Which ones deserved to enter the classroom?

Emmanuel Ringelblum, who was the historian of the Warsaw ghetto, had at his disposal one hundred researchers, one hundred of his so-called Oneg Shabbat club. And they all had their own areas of responsibility; they covered all aspects of life and death in the ghetto.

One Rabbi Huberman wrote of only the religious side; others covered the medical side. But every area, every zone of activity in the ghetto was recorded by these one hundred historians.

What about other ghettos, where simple and ordinary men and women happened to become witnesses? They, too, fulfilled their tasks with commitment and sincerity and compassion. In Y. L. Peretz's hometown of Zamosc, a simple baker wrote the first page of the tragedy that befell his community. A simple baker who had never read a poem in his life went up to the attic and wrote a poem describing what he had seen in the marketplace where Jews first were killed. In other places, adolescents improvised themselves into living vehicles of testimony.

But what about those communities, especially in Eastern Europe, that perished without leaving a trace of blood in our collective memory, without leaving a single survivor? I do not envy the historians who have to deal with this problem. They must because they believe in justice and they have to do justice to our memory. Where do they find the documents, the testimonies, the testaments of those who had no time or chance to write?

But then, remember again, the assault of the enemy was directed not only against the Jews but also against their memory. Heinrich Himmler made that clear when he addressed a group of SS superior officers during the war, in Posen (Poznan) in 1943. Speaking about their role in the Final Solution, he said that theirs was a page of glory that would never become known. Here he was not entirely wrong, since he and his acolytes pushed their cruelty to its limits and beyond, and thus deprived their victims of a language to communicate the suffering and the pain and the ordeal and the murder to which they had been subjected. Not only were the victims made to endure hunger, thirst, isolation, pain, despair, humiliation, agony, and death, but then they found no adequate words to tell the tale. Their experience became like God's name, ineffable. Their first defeat could have been the loss of their ability even to store the past as a clue for the future. Can memory exist and function without words? The killers saw themselves as gods whose language was different from ours, whose life was more valuable than ours, whose memory was a substitute for ours. The SS was a kind of religious order. We know now that the example they took was—of all things, of all people—that of Ignatius Loyola. For them, we the victims, the prisoners, were not worthy of seeing their faces. The prisoner had no right to look into the eyes of the SS man.

In a novel, there is a story of a community that was being wiped out, one family after another being shot in a mass grave. Only one young man remained, a student of the yeshiva. He was the last, and when the SS officer fired his gun at him, for some reason the young man did not die. In his anger the SS man fired again, but the young man did not die, so the SS man approached him and asked, "Why don't you die?" The young man replied, "I cannot, I am the last." The SS officer responded, "Young man, you are so crazy. You think that now you will live, you will survive, and you will tell the story. You think you possess the truth? Your truth is the truth of a madman. Nobody will believe you." What should that young man do with his memory if no one was ready to receive it? His memory was from the outset under such assault that even he could have doubted its power and validity.

If memory is, and I think it is, the substance of the human being, I believe one must measure its vulnerability as well as its impact. Because I remember, I realize that one may grow weaker by virtue of his or her humanity. During those years of fire and fear, it was not humanity that made the victim strong, physically strong, it was something else, quite the opposite. Humanity became an obstacle to life. But because I remember, I realize that memory, if kept alive, will eventually be stronger than the enemy. Is that not why memory is subjected to such a variety of assaults today?

Our task remains to serve as the custodians of memory. But the problem was and remains: how does one activate its mechanism? How does one make sure not to divert it from its original, noble mission? When we deal with human beings, they are, to me, the beginning and the end of my quest. The agony of one child, the despair of one mother, the silent prayer of one dreamer, they contain the truth. They contain the substance of truth, their words must be remembered, for they are an intrinsic part of the memory of the dead. But there we face another problem: how does one share memories that lie beyond the realm of knowledge? We remember only what our memory retains. What about things we neither recall nor grasp? In other words, how does one control memory? Can memory be controlled at all? Can one dominate memory, or must one be dominated by it? To be more precise, when is the memory of truth truthful? Can it be limited and still remain truth? God alone remembers everything about everyone. God alone could be our true witness. As in all of our endeavors, we are limited in our capacity to remember what transcends the human condition. Perhaps what we can and must do is not allow the enemy to impose his memory of our suffering onto history. That would add to his victory over the dead, for their tragedy would be told by him and not by their heirs and friends.

But then, perhaps memory needs to be assaulted in order to react, to be energized, motivated, and strengthened. Does a society need war in order to long for peace? Must human beings experience suffering so as to appreciate serenity and happiness and harmony? This is quite possible, though not to be recommended, for if the assaults are too heavy, frequent, and painful, memory may, in self-defense, take refuge in numbness. The enemy of memory is numbness. The enemy of memory is apathy.

Why is the Holocaust so important for education? Why do I believe that it must be taught in every school, including every professional school? Because it helps to sensitize students. If the Holocaust does not sensitize people, what will? You read those chronicles, those poems, those stories, those documents, those tales, and you know what it means to be human in an inhuman society. And you know what humanity is all about and then you are sensitive not only to the past but also to the present.

The perils, the threats looming over memory have various origins and methods. Some are unavoidable for they are rooted in the passage of time. As much as we wish we could recall every episode in its every detail, we are aware of the depressing fact that survivors are not computers but human beings. Their faculty to remember will tomorrow no longer be infallible. Oh, they will recall major aspects of their personal story, but secondary ones may be dissipated in the process. Do I remember the color of the sky the day before the selection in Buna? Could I quote verbatim what the pious scholar of Riga—or was it Kosovo?—whispered to me one Friday evening as he returned from the soup distribution empty-handed? And if I do not, who will? I do not know what to do about things that we do not remember anymore. I was recently back in my hometown and there were houses where I know my friends lived, but I no longer remembered the numbers of the houses. Fifty years. Another example, an example that is so recent: what about personalities in the world who all of a sudden reveal a past that was not to their glory, to their honor? Why did it take fifty years, and how can one be sure that now, fifty years later, what we think is true is really true? Maybe it was worse.

Memory implies personal witness. Said Jeremiah, "*Ani hagever*—I am the man who saw it happen," and his authority is derived from the words "*Ani hagever*"—I am the man, I was there. What arguments are being used today to deny us that authority? Those outsiders who pretend to know more than the victims themselves say—and, of course, all of them are our adversaries, our opponents, ideologically or otherwise—that we did not really suffer that much. Others say, "Look, you are not the only ones who suffered, others also have suffered." The antisemites used to add that not only did Jews not suffer but they made others suffer. How do they justify their unwillingness to accept our word as truth? One justification can be found in the different, if not contradictory, narratives and statements by survivors from the same ghettos and the same camps, often describing the same events. Small, quasi, insignificant discrepancies. Did this or that selection take place early or late in October? At 3 or 4 A.M.? Was it conducted by Mengele himself or by one of his associates? Was Mengele's mustache blond or brown? Did he smoke a cigarette that night or a pipe? Did transport *x* or *y* stop in Cracow or Katowice? Not every survivor had a photographic memory. And when faced with the enemy, of course, a survivor often had other things to think about—parents, friends—than the dress of the officer or the color of his belt.

In the sixties there were trials in Germany. After the Eichmann trial, which I attended, came the Auschwitz trial and the other camp trials. I did not go to the Frankfurt trial of the Auschwitz SS, but I remember reading about it and studying documents. The defendants used to come into the courtroom laughing. They were all laughing. They would see the pictures and laugh. They laughed when, say, a witness, a survivor of Auschwitz, would give an answer about the color of a belt. What does one do with their laughter? It is quite possible that two men or women do not recall the same visual image from the same spot. Still, they told the truth, and their truth had to do with something other than a simple visual statement.

There are base, nasty, mean, indecent individuals who use these unavoidable mental traps to negate the substance of Jewish memory. Their number is small, and some are not nameless. I hope I will be forgiven for citing a personal experience. The critic Alfred Kazin recently wrote an essay on what he owes to Primo Levi and me. Primo Levi and I were very close friends. Three days before he committed suicide, he called me and we had a long conversation. During the war we were together in the same camp, in the same barracks. When Kazin writes about what he owes us, he says with incredible arrogance that he doubts my description in *Night* of the three prisoners who were hanged. Indeed, he says he would not be surprised if anyone told him that I imagined that incident. I used to know Alfred Kazin, and I am sorry that our paths ever crossed. He is one of very few people of whom I can say that. How dare he, an American Jew, who discovered the tragedy of our people very late, from other people's testimony, deny the validity of a survivor's testimony? He doubts that two adults and a young boy were hanged in Buna. I wonder what a man named Jack Hendeli from Salonika and now Jerusalem thinks of Kazin's outrageous statement, what a man called Freddy Diamond from Berlin and now Los Angeles feels when he reads Kazin's unconscionable remarks. Freddy's younger brother was one of the three. The other two were Natan Weisman and Yanek Grossfeld.

What does a witness do when faced with something as outrageous as that? If Kazin says this, why should not others? If he says this, why should Faurisson not say it? And he does. Why should Arthur Butz not say it? And he does. Why should all the deniers not simply say, "We do not believe you?" Which they say. There is much frustration in us when we think of what could happen when people with a certain reputation start saying, "Look, you were too close to the subject. You are not objective, you are sentimental. We do not believe you. We like you, we weep for you, but we do not believe you." What do survivors do then? That is part of the assault on memory, and I confess I do not really know how to handle it.

The deniers like Butz and Faurisson seem to be multiplying and gaining visibility, credibility, if not respectability. Twenty or more years ago, I think I was among the very first who began warning against their crazy theories. To me they are morally deranged, just as there are people who are mentally deranged. I went to Northwestern University then and opened a lecture series, joined later by three colleagues. Again and again we wrote articles about denial. Now we read books by others, magnificent books. But none of this seems to have an effect on the deniers. One thing I refused to do was to allow them to engage me in discussion. I would never grant them the dignity of a debate. They have tried to provoke me. During my Nobel ceremony, they staged a demonstration in the street. There they were outside, demonstrating. Who finances their ugly activities, who handles logistics for them? I do not know. But I do know they are rich and well organized and their goal is to destroy Jewish memory, just as ours is to preserve it.

One area where serious wounds have been inflicted by the assault on memory is the dilution of certain horror-laden words and symbols that are, as it were, copyrighted by Jewish destiny. The dilution is dangerous, the trivialization is dangerous; the mixing up and mingling brings nothing but confusion.

In 1994, I went back to both Birkenau and Buchenwald. Buchenwald for the first time in fifty years. I went there for all kinds of reasons, but mainly because of the impending fiftieth anniversary of the liberation of Auschwitz and Birkenau, which I was to attend. I wanted to see what was happening. At Birkenau for a few hours, I saw a few stars of David, which were appropriate, since 95 percent of the victims there were Jewish. Near the place called the Bunker—the gas chambers built for Jews, especially those from Hungary later on—I realized that the site was surrounded by huge crosses. Even after the problem with the convent a few years before, crosses hugging stars of David? I do not oppose the Christian community or religion. But I simply would like some show of taste, of respect. In those dark times, crosses were not meant to protect the Jewish people. Here they stood now as if they were there to caress, to shield the Jewish stars. Why? I do not know.

In Buchenwald, there were two camps, a larger one for the political prisoners and a smaller one for the Jews that was a kind of death chamber, a place Jews were brought to die. When we Hungarian Jews and other Jews from Auschwitz came after the evacuation, we were all put in the small camp. My father died there. Now there is nothing. Trees and grass, but otherwise nothing. Not even a sign, a plaque, saying "Here was the little camp." Worse, in 1945, after the Americans who liberated the camp had left, it was taken over by the Russians, who maintained the camp, in the beginning mainly for former Nazis. The Nazi party had been declared illegal by the Nuremberg tribunal, and its members criminals. The Russians put them in Buchenwald. The camp remained until 1950. I am sure that later they put other political prisoners there too. Many died, probably. And now they are building a memorial honoring the Nazi victims of the Russians. Really: at the same camp where there is now a memorial (that only recently was changed to include mention of Jews) to the victims of Nazism, they are now building another memorial to the Nazi victims of the Russians. How can one not be worried about the future of memory? This is an assault, a serious assault. Because the memory is diluted, it contains falsehood. The corruption of language leads to the banalization of its message.

I have always believed, and I still do, that the Holocaust is a unique event in recorded history. It is to me essentially a Jewish tragedy with universal implications and applications. Its universality lies in its uniqueness. Perhaps it could have happened to other people. But it did not. Yes, there were other oppressed peoples, and some such as the Roma ("Gypsies"), who were even condemned to death. Nevertheless, do not call tragedies that are atrocities a Holocaust. We should rebel against them, we should condemn them. The victims of those tragedies must be remembered by us and by everybody. But Auschwitz was different.

This goes for later atrocities as well. Cambodia itself must not be compared with Auschwitz. I went to Bosnia because I wanted to be there and help, but also because I read in the paper about "Auschwitz in Bosnia." No. If Bosnia was like Auschwitz, then Auschwitz was like Bosnia. Nothing ever was like Auschwitz. Auschwitz can be compared only to itself. How many are we today who still believe that?

Today our subject has become popular, which is good. Has it not been our goal to teach this event through history and literature so that it will be remembered until the end of time? As if obsessed, some of us have tirelessly given our hearts and souls to this task, which we consider sacred and imperative. What efforts have we not made? We have knocked at every door, used every key, explored every avenue, from the written word to imagery of exhibits, films, and classroom material. Logically, we ought to be pleased with the results and feel rewarded. People go to a film or visit a museum and emerge deeply moved. "Now we know," they say. Should we not receive a certain measure of satisfaction from such a reaction? Well, I do not. I have always hoped to hear the opposite, to hear that someone reads my book or another's, or goes to see an exhibit or a museum, and says, "Now I don't know."

You see, I still don't know. Oh, I read. I know what so many scholars are doing and how important it is. I repeat, I am grateful to them for the description of the role of the banks in what happened and the economic aspect of the crimes, for what Raul Hilberg did on the role of the railways or what Deborah Lipstadt is doing about the deniers. We know they are giving us so much information that is needed. But I wonder how it is being transformed into knowledge. Is it? I still do not understand. The more I read, the less I understand. There is something that always remains unsaid, unexplained. In other words, I imagine that what you know, I know. Where and when and how death claimed victory, in what manner, and who its victims were. But that is not enough. The *why* remains an open question. Why did it happen? Why did it have to happen? Why were the killers not stopped? Why did so many good people, influential writers, impeccable statesmen, statesmen who believed in good, why did they choose to ignore the systematic annihilation of Eastern European Jewry, including all men, children, women, Sephardim, Ashkenazim, tailors, philosophers, rabbis, assimilated Jews? Why? Why didn't the word of God stop the killers? They could have been stopped right away, in 1934 or 1936 if France had mobilized, in 1938 at the Anschluss, in 1939 with Poland. There were so many steps when it was possible to avoid the greatest tragedy, the greatest massacre in history.

I do not know. And yet people want to know. They are eager to acquire understanding. Why this fascination with an event dating back to the 1940s? When I was a child at home in my town of Sighet, fifteen or eighteen years after the end of the First World War, hardly anyone talked about it. I do not remember people talking about the First World War at home, even though my paternal grandfather was killed in the war, and there were people in every family who had fought in it. How different it is now. Why? Why is the interest in the Second World War so general, and why does it transcend nationalities and cultures and age groups? It is to our great satisfaction that young people today want to know more than previous generations, not only here but everywhere. Why? It is simply because the Holocaust will forever remain a watershed in humankind's history. There is a before and an after. Something happened. Somehow we crossed a threshold. The world is no longer the same. Humanity is no longer innocent. Whatever we had known must be checked again. About humanity, about society, about history, about God. The French historian Michelet said of the French Revolution, "If the ashes are still so warm, imagine what the flame must have been." If the ashes of the Holocaust are still so warm in our hearts, in our minds, just imagine, if you can, what the flame must have been.

In conclusion, all of these questions lead to one more, at least for me, since I come from a very religious background. It is not only humanity that for me is now a question mark, but God Himself. To illustrate the Creator's compassion for His creation, an ancient talmudic legend tells us that whenever a just person dies, God Himself in His incommensurate grief weeps. And when His tears fall into the great ocean, says the Talmud, they produce such unbearable sounds that they reverberate from one corner of the world to the other. I like the legend. But I fail to understand. I like the legend because it shows God as compassionate. But then . . . Six million men, women, and children perished in a tempest of fire and fury. Did God weep? Have His tears fallen into the ocean, or on deaf ears? Or is it possible that God wept and humanity was not moved? If it was not moved then, will it be moved now?

I. DISCIPLINARY REFLECTIONS

Christopher R. Browning

The Holocaust and History

AT THE OUTSET LET ME EXPLAIN THAT I CONSIDER MYSELF A historian of modern Europe who decided midway through my graduate studies to specialize in the history of the Holocaust—what at the time I termed the Nazi persecution of the Jews. My undergraduate honors thesis was in English history; my master's thesis in French history. In effect, I became a historian of modern Germany by virtue of becoming a historian of the Holocaust.

My research focus has been on perpetrators rather than victims and bystanders, with an emphasis on behavior that is situationally and institutionally produced, rather than psychologically disturbed, culturally conditioned, or ideologically motivated. My perspective has been universalistic rather than particularist, contingent rather than teleological. I see the Holocaust primarily as the conjuncture of rather recent or modern factors, not the inevitable culmination of millennial antisemitism. Ultimately, for me the study of the Holocaust is a voyage of personal discovery about the potential destructiveness of Western civilization, the nation state, and human nature.

I could not hope to "unpack" all of what I have just referred to in a few pages, so I wish to concentrate on three issues: first, the use of "Holocaust" and "genocide" as unique or generic terms; second, the Holocaust as modern or "barbarous"; and third, history and meaning.

Let me turn first to the terms "Holocaust" and "genocide." My colleague Steven Katz has recently published a remarkable book—the first of a projected three-volume study—on *The Holocaust in Historical Context,* in which he argues with great erudition that the Holocaust is a unique, unprecedented, singular event. Moreover, he argues that the Holocaust is the only genocide to have occurred so far in history, with genocide defined as "an actualized intent, however successfully carried out, to physically destroy an entire group (as such a group is defined by the perpetrators)."[1]

My colleague Robert Melson has also recently published a remarkable book, comparing the Holocaust and the Armenian genocide in detail and arguing also for treating Stalin's assault on the kulaks and Pol Pot's assault on urban, Westernized Cambodians as modern genocidal events.[2] He conceives of genocide along three axes or dimensions: the degree of killing, the degree of destruction of identity, and the geographical scope of the assault. The Holocaust's uniqueness, he argues, lies in its extreme position on all three axes, that is, intended total killing and total destruction of identity wherever the Nazi grasp could reach. But he allows for other less extreme or less total genocides as well.

Despite their substantive differences, Katz and Melson agree on two important matters. Both insist that the comparative method is essential to the historical study of Holocaust and genocide and—as Katz so clearly points out—that any conclusion for uniqueness must be the product of practicing comparative history, not a denial of it. Both authors also recognize that our definitions and concepts are scholarly constructs that may be more or less helpful, may provide more or less insight and clarification. They are not platonic forms to be discovered by pure reason, nor easily resolved disputes to be settled by uncovering more empirical data.

If usefulness is the historian's criterion in this regard, I would urge using the term "Holocaust" (with a capital *H*) to indicate the Nazi attempt to exterminate European Jewry, and "genocide" to indicate other, less total attempts to destroy the existence or identity of target groups. To define "genocide" in the exclusive way that Katz does, making it in effect synonymous with "Holocaust," would require us to invent yet another term to indicate the less extreme assaults on groups that Raphael Lemkin had in mind when he coined the term, before either he or subsequent scholars fully understood the unique nature of the Nazi assault on the Jews. To designate those genocidal assaults that resemble in significant ways the Nazi assault on the Jews, I would not oppose using the generic term "holocaust" (with a lower-case *h*).[3] To allow the term Holocaust a generic variant does not deny the uniqueness of the Nazi assault on the Jews, but rather affirms that it was an unprecedented, watershed event that has prompted historians to invent new terminology and concepts to denote kinds of human behavior we previously did not realize we had to deal with. To speak of a holocaust of the Roma ("Gypsies") in my opinion does not trivialize but rather honors the term. They were subjected to the same discriminatory legislation drawn up by the same bureaucrats, enforced by the same SS and police, and often shot by the same killing units or deported on the same trains to the same death camps and killed in the same gas chambers as Jews—though they did not hold the same pivotal position in Hitler's *Weltanschauung,* and a higher percentage of them presumably slipped through the grasp of the Nazi killing machine.

Steven Katz has made a strong plea against the use of imprecise definitions and concepts. But historians use vague and imprecise concepts all the time. We do not require a precise standard of social change to employ the term "social revolution," or a precise measure of economic transformation to employ the term "industrial revolution." Human affairs are multifaceted and our grasp of them incomplete. Living with imprecise terms is, I think, inherent in the historical discipline.

A second problem inherent in practicing history is sorting out elements of continuity and discontinuity. The Holocaust historian immediately confronts two questions in this regard. To what degree was the Holocaust the culmination of centuries of antisemitism? To what degree was it a product of modern or recent developments? Interpretive discussions of the latter question have become inextricably tied up with German historiographical debates in general and unjustly tainted, I would argue, by the *Historikerstreit* in particular.

Most notoriously, Ernst Nolte has tried to relativize the Holocaust as a mere copy of and reaction to the gulag, which in turn for him was the culmination of modern revolutionary and exterminatory politics since 1789. Detlev Peukert sees the Holocaust as a product of the modern "spirit of science" and evidence of the "pathology of modernization" virtually unrelated to traditional antisemitism—an approach that spurred Marion Kaplan to urge against creating a "*judenrein* Holocaust."[4]

Other attempts in Germany to study National Socialism as either a product of or contributor to modernization have also encountered harsh criticism. For instance, in their book *The Racial State,* Michael Burleigh and Wolfgang Wipperman denounce any attempt to study National Socialism as a manifestation of or reaction to modernity, for in such interpretations the "unique horrors of the Third Reich disappear within a fog of relativizing, sociological rhetoric" and "the crimes of Nazi Germany cease to be singular."[5] The Nazis, they argue, must be seen as barbarous, not modern.

My own view is that the historian of the Holocaust can no more avoid the question "Why in the twentieth century?" than the questions "Why the Jews?" and "Why the Germans?" Examining historical discontinuities—in particular the relationship of modernization, National Socialism, and the Holocaust—must not be made taboo because of Ernst Nolte's notions or Burleigh and Wipperman's claim that such an approach obscures the barbarity of the Nazis.

Concerning modernization and barbarism, two semantic points need clarification. First, modernization does not inherently mean progress or betterment, as Wipperman and Burleigh insist. On the contrary, it is precisely the experience of National Socialism and the Holocaust that has totally and irreparably severed the comfortable identity of progress and modernization. This, to me, is one of the invaluable lessons to be learned from studying the Holocaust.

Second, the denotative and connotative meanings of "barbarous" must be distinguished. The denotative historical meaning is precivilized, undeveloped, the antithesis of modern. This the Nazis were not. The common moral connotation is utterly without ethical restraint, or contrary to the presumed moral norms of Western, Judeo-Christian civilization. This the Nazis most certainly were. Events can be developmentally modern and morally barbarous at one and the same time. In short, the study of the relationship between National Socialism and modernity does not inherently imply a favorable moral judgment about National Socialism. Neither claims to the contrary nor "guilt by association" with the likes of Ernst Nolte must block such an avenue of historical study.

Finally, let us turn to the issue of meaning. Richard Rubenstein, whose provocative and insightful writing on the Holocaust I use frequently in class to good effect, once told me that as a theologian he takes the work of historians and gives "meaning" to it. He intended this statement as an acknowledgment of indebtedness, especially to Raul Hilberg, and not as a condescending claim to disciplinary superiority. But his statement does raise an important issue about disciplinary division of labor. Are historians the academic proletariat who, like miners, dig up the facts as mere raw materials that other disciplines, the true artists and skilled artisans, then transform into intellectually attractive and meaningful objects? Do historians work at a level below "meaning"?

I would be the first to admit that historians shy from the big questions, such as why there is evil in the world and where God was during the Holocaust. But that does not mean that they are merely excavating "meaning-neutral" facts about time- and space-specific events. As a historian, I surely do want to know when *Einsatzgruppe* C first received orders to kill Jewish women and children in Russia, and I also want to know when the first Silesian Jews were deported to Birkenau and gassed in Bunker 1. But there are many other facts that I am not going to spend time looking for, quite simply because for each historian some facts are more significant—more "meaningful"—than others.

The very method of selection in sorting through vast numbers of documents, the choice of foci of interest, and the construction of historical narrative all inherently involve, sometimes explicitly but often only implicitly, the construction and answering of what I would awkwardly call "middle-level meaning questions." How are killing decisions taken, disseminated, and implemented? How is killing behavior situationally and organizationally produced? Or more broadly, as I asked earlier, how is the long tradition of European antisemitism to be balanced with twentieth-century discontinuities in discussions of the origins of the Holocaust? These are interpretive questions—questions of meaning—that are not answered simply by digging up more raw materials, by researching for more empirical data. Yet these are the questions that historians of the Holocaust must wrestle with constantly. They are inherent in the practice of our discipline. Historians need not be embarrassed by the charge that they leave questions of meaning to others. They do not.

Alan E. Steinweis

The Holocaust and Jewish Studies

HOLOCAUST STUDIES IS CURRENTLY ENJOYING A RAPID EXPANSION IN American higher education. Most small colleges now offer at least one course on the subject, while it is not unusual for larger universities to offer instruction about the Holocaust across a number of disciplines. Several institutions have recently established or announced positions specifically for Holocaust specialists, financed at least partly by external endowments.[1] Such breakthroughs have been long in coming. For many years the academic world resisted recognizing the Holocaust as a field worthy of specific curricular attention. It is still the case that a bright college graduate wishing to pursue graduate study on the Holocaust, be it in history, literature, or one of the social sciences, must look very hard to find appropriate graduate programs.[2] But this situation is not likely to last much longer.

The expansion of Holocaust studies is taking place in an academic environment that is itself undergoing major reform. Faculties, student bodies, curricula, and course content are all growing increasingly diverse. Even if the drive toward so-called multiculturalism (whatever that term might actually mean) stalls, there can be little doubt that life at American universities will have less of a "Euro-American" orientation than in the past. This transformation presents both opportunities and dangers to the burgeoning field of Holocaust studies.

Diversification on campus has included the emergence of Jewish studies. Major Jewish studies programs have begun to flourish at large state universities on the coasts and in the Midwest, and even institutions that lack a distinct Jewish presence on campus have come to recognize the need to offer at least a course or two on Jews or Judaism as presented from a Jewish perspective. The efflorescence of Jewish studies has major implications for the questions of how

Holocaust courses will be conceptualized and structured, who will teach them, and in what academic units they will be based.

Until very recently, courses on the history of the Holocaust were offered primarily by scholars trained in German history, secondarily by those trained in other areas of Western history, and only rarely by the relatively few trained in Jewish history. Consequently, many such courses have had little Jewish content. The focus has been more on the perpetrators than on the victims. This by no means implies that instructors have intentionally slighted the Jewish victims; indeed, many have gone out of their way to address the experiences of the victims by including memoirs and diaries in assigned readings and by inviting survivors to class. Nonetheless, real constraints are imposed by teachers' insufficient training in Jewish studies. During the Holocaust, patterns of accommodation, defiance, and resistance were profoundly influenced by previous Jewish experience. Without a basic understanding of Jewish culture one cannot adequately teach about manifestations of spiritual and cultural resistance such as surreptitious Talmud study or clandestine ritual purification baths in the ghettos. One finds it similarly difficult to explain the factionalism within Jewish society that hindered organized Jewish resistance from coalescing sooner and more effectively. More generally, the Holocaust is historically significant not only because it involved the most systematic genocide in human history but also because it destroyed a distinct culture. Shouldn't students come away from their study of the subject with some knowledge of the destroyed culture, to supplement their knowledge of the causes and processes of destruction? Because most students in a Holocaust class will take no other courses on Jewish history during their college careers, this course presents the instructor with a unique opportunity to teach not just about Jewish death but also about Jewish life.

Despite the expansion of Jewish studies, at many colleges Holocaust courses will continue to be taught by professors who have not specialized in Jewish studies. It will therefore be important for these scholars to acquire the requisite background in Jewish history and culture. While many will do so on their own, I believe that supporting institutions, the Holocaust Education Foundation being the best example, can make a valuable contribution toward this end by sponsoring workshops, study tours, and conferences for nonspecialists devoted specifically to Jewish culture.

Such a retooling effort is not simply an expedient, to ensure responsible teaching of Holocaust history until such time as the Jewish studies field will have expanded to the point of subsuming Holocaust studies under it. Quite to the contrary, we must be aware of the potential dangers inherent to placing Holocaust studies entirely under the Jewish studies umbrella. Ensuring instructional expertise about the history and culture of the victims ought not to preclude expertise about the perpetrators. As an intellectual and moral enterprise, educating students about the motives and psychology of mass murderers is every bit as important as educating them about the victims. I would hope, therefore, that instructors who have been trained in a Jewish studies framework will also have sufficient access to resources that will assist them in rounding out their knowledge of German history, modern European racism, and other key areas.

To take this logic one step further, I would argue that Holocaust courses not automatically be given over to Jewish studies programs once the latter are in place. Obviously, the expertise and interests of specific faculty members at specific institutions will heavily affect such decisions. But I think it is important to avoid situations in which the assumption that a Holocaust course should be taught by a Jewish studies scholar squeezes out a more knowledgeable instructor whose training is in, say, German history. The Holocaust is too historically meaningful a subject to segregate into a single corner of the curriculum. It is also too universally meaningful to segregate into a specific segment of the faculty. I will be blunt here: scholars who are hired into Jewish studies programs to teach the Holocaust, among other Jewish studies topics, will most likely come from Jewish backgrounds. The more that Holocaust courses are taught by Jewish scholars based in Jewish studies programs, the more students will perceive the Holocaust as a specifically Jewish topic. Acknowledging that opinions differ, sometimes vehemently, on the legitimacy of this conceptualization, my own hope would be to avoid such pigeonholing. For one thing, it might undermine the perceived relevance of the Holocaust to non-Jewish students in the twenty-first century. For another, it might prove historically unfair to the non-Jewish victims of Nazi persecution.

This is neither the time nor place to recapitulate the "uniqueness" and "whose Holocaust" debates, which have generated immense literatures.[3] While my own view of the Holocaust tends to be Judeocentric, I think it is important to contextualize the Jewish Holocaust experience within the wider framework of German and European nationalism, eugenics, and biological racism. For the sake of historical veracity, and in the interest of conveying to students the interconnectedness of antisemitism and other forms of discrimination, this contextualization must go well beyond token references to Nazi programs that targeted Roma and Sinti ("Gypsies"), the disabled, gays, and other groups. Although the debates over how the Holocaust is best conceptualized have been and are fated to remain inconclusive, the healthy and fruitful scholarly dialectic has enhanced our empirical knowledge of the Holocaust. The institutionalization of Holocaust studies as a branch of Jewish studies might shift the balance within this dialogue. My concern is that the ground would shift not because of the discovery of new evidence or the persuasive power of an interpretation but rather because a particular perspective achieves institutional hegemony.

While it is always risky to make predictions, it might be appropriate to try to anticipate how students might relate to Holocaust education in the future. Several trends on the national and international scenes could increase the potential relevance of Holocaust history, but only if that history is conceptualized and taught with a broad view. The reemergence of antisemitism, in tandem with the rise of ethnic nationalism, in Eastern Europe, Germany, and Austria is the most obvious contemporary (and likely future) development that study of the Holocaust can illuminate. Less publicized, but just as real, is the flare-up of violent hostility toward "Gypsies" in that part of the world. Instructors who omit this connection, or give it short shrift, will be passing up a fine opportunity to use history to shed light on a phenomenon of our own time. Perfunctorily pointing out that "Gypsies" were reviled in the past, as they are now, will hardly accomplish anything pedagogically valuable. What is needed is an extensive discussion of who "Gypsies" are, why they have been persecuted, and how the discrimination against them was linked to that against Jews and other marginalized peoples. But such a discussion takes up valuable time in a finite semester or quarter, and would inevitably detract from the time devoted to Jewish aspects of the Holocaust. This presents a tough choice to an instructor.

Also of increasing contemporary relevance will likely be Nazi eugenics policies, above all the notoriously mislabeled "euthanasia" of the disabled. Recent events suggest that hereditarian explanations for social and economic inequality may now be making a comeback, after having been out of favor for several decades because of their associations with Nazism.[4] Although the eugenics movement of the first half of the twentieth century can be presented to students within the context of modern antisemitism, that approach, if used exclusively, would not sufficiently clarify the evolution of a movement that killed tens of thousands of non-Jewish Germans before the "Final Solution" was even initiated. There is a large and growing body of scholarship devoted specifically to Nazi sterilization and eugenically motivated murder;[5] but these topics tend to receive little attention in treatments of the Holocaust written from a Jewish studies perspective.[6] Without dismissing important conceptual distinctions between the "euthanasia" program and the "Final Solution," I do hope we can avoid a pedagogical approach that unduly minimizes the former in order to leave room for an intensive treatment of the latter. Aside from our moral obligation to the memory of these victims, we teachers need to consider with our students the lessons that the German experience with heredetarianism might offer to a society that is newly flirting with pseudoscientific biological racialism. In fact, when contemplating the stereotypes and mentalities that I, as a historian of the Holocaust, endeavor to undermine, I conclude that racialist assumptions are more common among my students than antisemitic ones. I therefore feel obligated, quite apart from considerations of historical context, to devote a good deal of my Holocaust course to Nazi eugenics and "euthanasia."

If Holocaust history is to remain the lively and creative field that it has proven so far, as reflected both in published scholarship and in stimulating pedagogy,[7] it must continue to draw on the talents of scholar-teachers from a variety of specialties. And if it is to remain morally compelling for students into the next century, it must be made relevant to the society and world in which they will live. Both these challenges can best be met by resisting the intellectual and institutional pigeonholing of the one subject matter that, better than anything else I can think of, should underscore the common humanity of all involved in the teaching and learning process.

Gerald E. Markle

The Holocaust and Sociology

AFTER ACCEPTING THE INVITATION TO WRITE ABOUT THE SIGNIFICANCE of the Holocaust to my discipline, I checked the online library catalog at Western Michigan University for the keywords "Holocaust and sociology." One reference, to Helen Fein's work, appeared on the screen.[1] Using "Holocaust and sociological" I got one more reference, this one to Zygmunt Bauman.[2] I know of a few sociologists who did not appear: J. Stanley Milgram, Nechama Tec, and Fred Katz, plus Ruth Linden's book, published in 1993.[3] But even with these additions, the list is not large. By comparison, "Holocaust and history" as keywords yielded 481 references, of which forty are from 1993 alone.

The sad truth appears to be that the Holocaust has not been terribly significant to my discipline, and my discipline has not been terribly significant to the study of the Holocaust.

Why is this so?

Remember Sherlock Holmes's famous case of the "dog that did not bark." Holmes solved this mystery because something did not happen: in this case, the silence of a dog which normally barked at a certain time every night was the important clue. The lesson here is that it is always easier to account for something which *has* happened than something which has not—in this case the inactivity of sociology in Holocaust studies.

Let me propose an algorithm to account for—to quantify, if I might—this nonbarking dog of a discipline. First, sociology, though philosophically unruly, has been dominated by positivists. Second, these positivists have sought to develop statistical models to explain social structural regularity—what happens to most people most of the time. And third, in such an attempt, history is declared irrelevant.

The gods of operationalization insist on measurement. We understand immediately, with a bit of help from Werner Heisenberg (a particularly interesting name to mention here!) that to measure something we must pretend that it stands still; that is, we conceptualize stasis, not process. Moreover, we must forsake social structural or cultural units of analysis, for such concepts resist easy measurement. Rather, our unit of analysis becomes the individual, albeit in the aggregate. Raul Hilberg's chapter organization in his book *Perpetrators, Victims, and Bystanders,*[4] demonstrates well this preference. This method looks for, even requires, regularity. Any one-time event, be it the French Revolution or the Holocaust, is set aside. In fact, the goal of this method—to declare an invariant regularity across time and space—is in fact nothing less than to transcend history and geography.

With a few exceptions, sociologists who study the Holocaust have complained of loneliness. They have confessed their discipline's failures. Yet, as the brilliant sociologist Alvin Gouldner notes, "Voluntary confessions should always be suspect." When people "complain about the bonds that enchain them," we should ask "whether their tone is one of disappointed resentment or of comfortable accommodation."[5]

Since the bulk of this paper is a critique, I should first make it clear that the positivist sociological program *has* contributed to our understanding of the Holocaust. Let me illustrate with an example of my own, a content analysis of articles on the Holocaust in the *Kalamazoo Gazette,* a small-town, Midwestern newspaper, during the period 1938 to 1945.[6] Figures 1–3 relate some of the findings. Somewhat surprisingly, the *Kalamazoo Gazette* published 245 articles on the Holocaust during these years. More than half were on the front page. Twelve percent were reports on concentration camps. Our conclusion? The regular reader of this small Michigan newspaper did have enough information on the Holocaust, though not presented in a convenient cognitive framework, to understand what was happening to the Jews of Europe.

Having complimented the method, and publicized my own findings, I want nonetheless to turn away from this entire mode of research. Let us leave positivist sociology behind and seek a *non-*

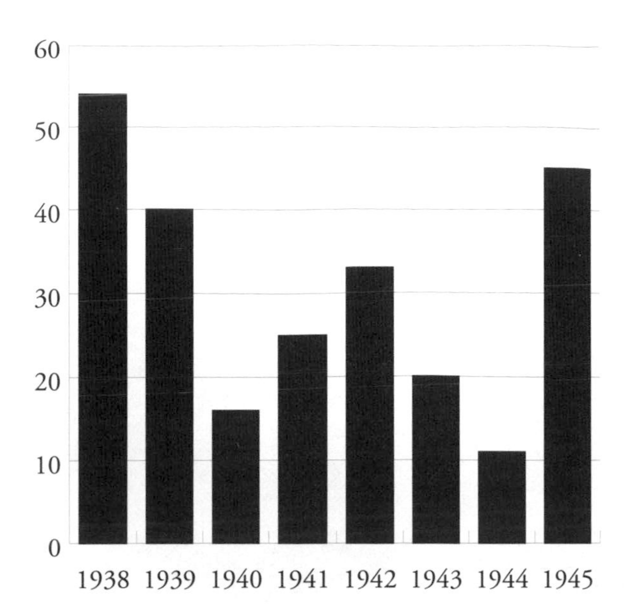

Figure 1. Number of *Kalamazoo (Mich.) Gazette* Articles about the Holocaust, by Year

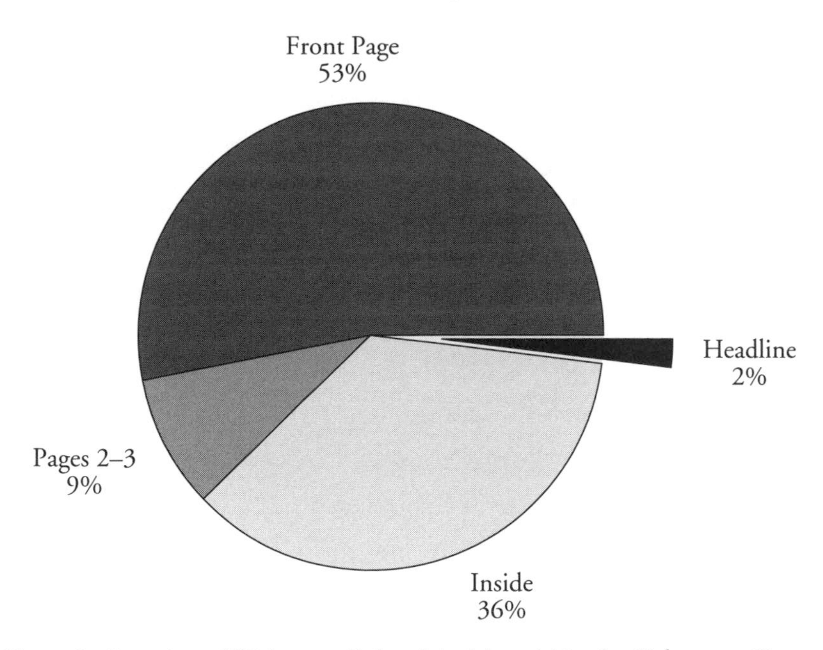

Figure 2. Location of Holocaust-Related Articles within the *Kalamazoo Gazette,* 1938–1945

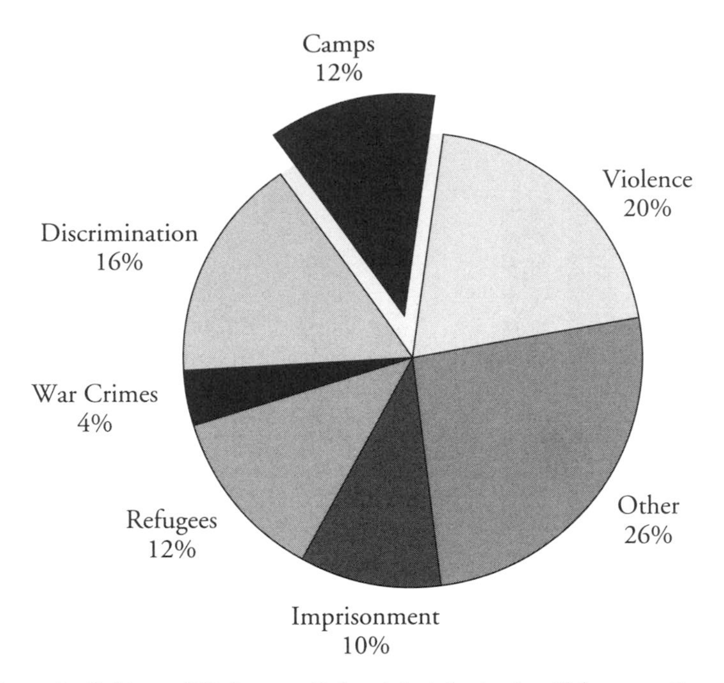

Figure 3. Subject of Holocaust-Related Articles in the *Kalamazoo Gazette,* 1938–1945

positivist approach to the Holocaust. This is, of course, not entirely new ground. Members of the Frankfurt school, particularly Theodor Adorno, began to write with some insight about the Holocaust in the 1940s. Perhaps it was the writings' translation across the Atlantic Ocean, perhaps their obscure style, but the work of these scholars has not had a great influence on contemporary Holocaust research.

Much more recently, Ruth Linden has pushed a nonpositivist reflexive method to its limits, though her goal—to use the Holocaust to understand herself—is different from mine. Some of the contributors to Saul Friedlander's 1992 collection (Vincent Pecora, for example) also write from a nonpositivist perspective.[7]

Zygmunt Bauman is probably the most noteworthy exception to positivist research; but he writes from the United Kingdom. The first chapter of Bauman's brilliant and difficult book *Modernity and the Holocaust,* titled "Sociology after the Holocaust," is more about the discipline than the genocide. Indeed, the chapter appeared before the book, as an independent article in the *British Journal of Sociology.* In it Bauman laid out the argument against, and then indicted, both the profession of sociology and its intellectual discourse. (It also was an important stimulus for my book, *Meditations of a Holocaust Traveler,* published in 1995.)[8] Bauman's most important methodological insight is captured in his remark that, for the sociologist, the Holocaust is "a window, rather than a picture on the wall. Looking through that window, one can catch a glimpse of many things otherwise invisible."[9] Here I hope we might see a division of labor between historians (painting the picture) and sociologists (looking through the window), not in the spirit of academic imperialism but rather as a cooperation of disciplines. Bauman's message for sociologists is that we must seek an analogical method and take it seriously.

Bauman's work leaves me, nonetheless, with two complaints. First, the book's conclusion, that studying the Holocaust might help us develop a sociological theory of morality, bothers me. Such an attempt seems naive at best, and a secular theodicy—which we should always oppose—at worst. Second, Bauman gives little credit to critical theorists, Adorno in particular, to whom he owes a great intellectual debt. In this sense, Bauman has ignored the wonderful dictum of Marc Bloch, that the task of the historian (might I substitute "scholar") is to organize a dialogue between the living and the dead.

But let me attempt to gaze through the window.

I am interested in constructing a sociology that would help us dare to be "tourists" of the Holocaust. My journey originates in what Karl Mannheim called the sociology of knowledge, crosses through the territory named social constructivism, and comes just to the border of postmodernism. Such a sociology begins by taking nothing for granted. We ask: How is society possible? What glue binds it together? How might it be torn asunder? This is a sociology that recognizes order and stability, to be sure. But order and stability are never givens and are never taken for granted. Moreover, this sociology also, and at the same time, envisions chaos.

I want to challenge the ways in which we typically think about the Holocaust: them versus us; then versus now; there versus here. I want to travel across time and space to bridge dichotomous, oppositional categories. It is not my intent to blame any group of people. To friends who reported that Nazism made them ashamed to be Germans, Hannah Arendt retorted: "I am ashamed of being human."[10]

What are the methodological implications of such a stance? We must recognize the importance of reflexive methods. Here perhaps I might invoke Heisenberg again. For it is impossible to understand observation without appreciating the observer. At the same time, the method demands that we treat the world with "strangeness."

Let me illustrate these methodological issues with examples from my book. I begin my book, and continue throughout, with reports of my own experiences as a "tourist" of the Holocaust. At first glance the term "tourist" seems a poor choice: shocking, trivializing to the point of being insulting. The irony was intentional, hopefully insightful. As I visited Holocaust sites, I did so as a tourist, and surrounded by other tourists. Yet I understood that I did not belong there. To claim that story as my own might have some distant lineal justification, but the connection was mostly vicarious. My intent was to somehow nest my own feelings within an outsider's historical and physical context. I wept but I also felt, and this for me was a key, an ineluctable strangeness. In the final analysis, I did not belong there.

My emphasis on knowledge and ideology as social constructions has methodological implications too. When Christopher Browning kindly read a draft of my book *Meditations of a Holocaust Traveler,* he commented that I had underestimated the role of ideology generally, and antisemitism particularly. I agree with him that ideology is always important, and in this case was a matter of life and death. But, following Karl Mannheim, I have trouble seeing ideology as *the cause* of anything. To me, ideology is—at least to a degree—a reflection of social structure, particularly vested interests. In this sense, ideology is a part of, rather than an independent cause of, tactics and strategy. So I give ideology less emphasis than other analysts. I try not to reify ideology. Talk is cheap.

How might this critique, this point of view, lead to a sociological analysis of the Holocaust?

Perhaps sociology is merely but one of the social sciences, but perhaps it is rather, as Pitirim Sorokin asserts, the "queen of the social sciences." I wish to invoke this queenly status as a basis for anointing two unlikely candidates as sociologists: namely, Primo Levi and Hannah Arendt. For I am convinced that these scholars pointed the sociological enterprise in the right direction for studying the Holocaust.

Primo Levi spent his life pondering the sociology of the Holocaust. It was Levi who wrote that Auschwitz was a "ferocious sociological laboratory."[11] It was Levi who understood the utility of "useless violence"—the bed-making ritual (to cite one brilliant example) as a "sacral operation" of "prime and indecipherable" importance.[12] What the Germans wanted, and what they got, was order and control amid chaos and death. It was Levi's great insight to conceptualize a "gray zone" within a concentration camp, "an incredibly complicated internal structure which contains within itself enough to confuse our need to judge."[13] I think of the entire Holocaust as a gray zone. The more I think about the Nazi genocide of the Jews, the more confused is my need to judge. The more I think about the general phenomena of racism, obedience, the alienation of modern life, the more is my ability to judge confused.

In *The Origins of Totalitarianism* and *Eichmann in Jerusalem,* Hannah Arendt presented an extraordinarily naturalistic and unreified version of the Holocaust.[14] Her understanding is based on notions of power, rule-following, and sanity—all nested within a conception of modernity—that are profoundly sociological. All of Western morality is reduced (appropriately) to the status of table manners. So much for morality. Eichmann's normalcy is certainly a disturbing finding. We are still trying to come to grips with the implications of his frightening sanity. The idea of the "banality of evil" may now be a catchphrase, but it contains, I am convinced, valuable insights into what sociologists call deviance and social control.

I want to conclude by borrowing freely from two other great scholars. Gershom Scholem did not approve of Arendt's treatment of Eichmann. His argument with her is not my concern here, rather his view of Eichmann's death. Scholem had opposed the death penalty for Eichmann, but not for the obvious reasons. Eichmann's death, he declared, was an "inappropriate ending" which "falsified the historical significance of the trial." The Jerusalem proceedings created an illusion by asserting a conclusion, he maintained. "Such an illusion is most dangerous because it may engender the feeling that something has been done to atone for the unatonable." But the hanging of one "human or inhuman creature," for Scholem, concluded nothing. Quite the contrary. One fears that "instead of opening up a reckoning and leaving it open for the next generation, we have foreclosed it." It is to our interest, he maintained, "that the great historical and moral question, the question probing the depths which this trial has forced us all to face—How could this happen?—that this question should retain all its weight, all its stark nakedness, all its horror." It would have been better "if we did not have the hangman stand between us and our great question, between us and the soul-searching account we have to settle with the world."[15]

So Eichmann's death was a false conclusion. Perhaps all conclusions are. But how does one end without concluding? Jean Amery, the wisest of survivors and memoirists, pointed us in the right, albeit a difficult, direction: "I had no clarity when I was writing this book, I do not have it today, and I hope that I never will," he wrote. Clarification "would amount to disposal, settlement of the case, which can then be placed in the files of history. My book is meant to aid in preventing precisely this."[16]

Bauman's window metaphor may be helpful, but it is also false. For a window implies clarity of vision. My studies of the Holocaust have produced, for me, anything but clarity. Perhaps a better metaphor is St. Paul's "through a glass darkly." Yet though Paul's language is beautiful, I, unlike Paul, do not expect a redemptive vision to follow. Even more, I am suspicious, even hostile, to any Holocaust conclusion that smacks of theodicy, even a secularized sociological theodicy.

So what can sociologists do? We cannot, by training and inclination, discover some new Holocaust fact; nor can we read, let alone interpret, some hitherto lost document. What we can do is think about what the Holocaust means for today's culture. Racism, state power, obedience to authority: these phenomena, to cite but a few, still afflict the body politic. Sociologists not only can study the Holocaust's mortal wound but also can keep it open and festering and, perhaps most importantly, not let the injustice, or any injustice, die.

John K. Roth

The Holocaust and Philosophy

AT THE BEGINNING OF *NIGHT,* THE CLASSIC MEMOIR THAT DETAILS HIS experiences as a man-child in Auschwitz, Elie Wiesel introduces one of his teachers. His name is Moshe, and the year is 1941. Although the Holocaust is under way, it has not yet touched Wiesel's hometown directly. One day the twelve-year-old Elie asks his teacher, "And why do you pray, Moshe?" The reply is: "I pray to the God within me that He will give me the strength to ask Him the right questions." Wiesel adds: "We talked like this nearly every evening."[1]

I am a philosopher, and I believe that philosophy, first and foremost, thrives on questions. Immanuel Kant was on the mark when he defined philosophy as the inquiry that pursues three questions in particular: *What can I know? What should I do? For what may I hope?* Those are some of the right questions for human beings to wonder about. Early in my philosophical training and career, I worked on them with little reference to the Holocaust. Then—it is now more than twenty-five years ago—I took a friend's suggestion and began to study the writings of Elie Wiesel. That brief description of his conversation with Moshe in 1941 stands out for me. As well as any, Moshe's few words sum up one reason why my philosophical work took decisively a Holocaust studies turn. More deeply, I wanted to be able to ask the right questions.

Philosophy always deals with questions, but Holocaust studies drove home to me that some of them are much more important than others. Specifically, I began to discover, questions do not give us the best possible insight when they are posed abstractly, without reference to real human experiences and their histories. The writings of Elie Wiesel showed me that. So have Richard Rubenstein's, another early influence on me, and Raul Hilberg's.

Filmmaker Claude Lanzmann's epic *Shoah* is a cinematic counterpart to Hilberg's monumental book *The Destruction of the European Jews,* and Hilberg plays an important part in Lanzmann's film. In a segment on the Warsaw ghetto, for example, he discusses the dilemmas faced by Adam Czerniaków, the man who headed the *Judenrat* (Jewish council) in that place. Czerniaków documented his role in the diary he kept until he took his own life on July 23, 1942, the day after the Germans began to liquidate the Warsaw ghetto by deporting its Jews to Treblinka. Hilberg knows the details of Czerniaków's life because he helped to translate and edit the diary, which survived the war. In another segment of Lanzmann's *Shoah,* Hilberg studies a different kind of document: *Fahrplananordnung* 587. This railroad timetable scheduled death traffic. Conservative estimates indicate that *Fahrplananordnung* 587, which outlines a few days in late September 1942, engineered the transport of some 10,000 Jews to Treblinka's gas chambers.

Raul Hilberg has spent his life detailing how such things happened. In his first appearance in the Lanzmann film, he observes, "In all of my work I have never begun by asking the big questions, because I was always afraid that I would come up with small answers; and I have preferred to address these things which are minutiae or details in order that I might then be able to put together in a gestalt a picture which, if not an explanation, is at least a description, a more full description, of what transpired."[2]

As a philosopher who keeps encountering the Holocaust, I keep in mind Hilberg's warning about "big questions." He does not deny that the Holocaust raises them—first and foremost the question *Why?* However, that a question can be asked does not mean that it can be answered well, if at all, particularly when it is one of the "big," fundamental, and sweeping ones that typically characterize philosophical and religious inquiries. So Hilberg concentrates on details instead. Those minutiae, however, are much more than minutiae. Their particularity speaks volumes and adds up to a terribly vast description. So full of life distorted and wasted, this accumulated detail makes the "big questions" less simple to raise but all the more important, too.

Put into perspective by work such as Hilberg's, the "big questions" become what Elie Wiesel's teacher, Moshe, called the "right questions," and thus they deservingly command respect. That respect enjoins our suspicion about "answers" that are small, inadequate for the facts they must encompass. That same respect also makes us aware that the big questions raised by the Holocaust nonetheless need to be kept alive. For the political scientist's details and the historian's minutiae, far from silencing the big questions, ought to intensify our wonder about them. Otherwise we repress feeling too much and deny ourselves the insight that can be deepened only by asking the "right questions."

As a philosopher who confronts the Holocaust, I keep a third statement in mind as a constant reminder about asking questions that are properly big and right: "The Holocaust demands interrogation and calls everything into question. Traditional ideas and acquired values, philosophical systems and social theories—all must be revised in the shadow of Birkenau."[3] Birkenau was the killing center at Auschwitz, and those words, like the first ones I quoted, are Elie Wiesel's. One of the important points his words make is this: whatever the traditional ideas and acquired values that existed, whatever the philosophical systems and social theories that human minds had devised, either they were inadequate to prevent Auschwitz or, worse, they helped to pave the way to that place.

There are a few of us philosophers, but not too many, who work on those particular problems. Philosophy and perhaps the world would be better off if there were more. But at the same time, when Holocaust scholars from the fields of history or literature, political science or sociology, ask the right questions, they move into the area that too many philosophers have ignored. How can they fail to do so, for Kant's big questions remain: *What can I know? What should I do? For what may I hope?* Fortunately, when these scholars who do not identify themselves primarily as philosophers get around to the big questions, they often do so with immense philosophical sensitivity and insight.

But what about philosophers and the discipline of philosophy in relation to Holocaust studies? I think philosophers and philosophy have avoided the Holocaust primarily because so much history is involved. To encounter the Holocaust philosophically, one must study what happened, to whom, where, when, and how. Reckoning with detail and particularity of that kind is not what philosophers are trained or naturally inclined to do. So it is likely that only a relatively few of us philosophers—maybe those who have grown impatient with the abstraction and distance from history that most contemporary philosophy reflects—will immerse ourselves in this field of study. Once there, however, we are unlikely to want to be anywhere else, for the work to do is so intense and important.

Think of the big questions that now and forever will need to be explored and which must be handled with great care if they are to be the right questions: How did the Holocaust happen? Who is responsible for it? How can we best remember this history? What can words say? What about God and religion after Auschwitz? What about human rights and morality in a post-Holocaust world? What can I know, what should I do, for what may I hope in the shadow of Birkenau?

Philosophers should ask the right questions. At least some of us should let our questioning be informed by the Holocaust in ways that heed Raul Hilberg's warnings about "big questions." We should next join scholars in other fields, using the insights that philosophy can bring, to revise traditional ideas and acquired values, philosophical systems and social theories. Then we might have a better picture, which, if not an explanation, would at least be a description, a fuller description, of what transpired and how its repetitions might be checked and even avoided.

Jeffrey M. Peck

The Holocaust and Literary Studies

ALTHOUGH I AM PRESENTING THE PERSPECTIVE OF A LITERARY CRITIC, I must admit from the outset that my approach to the Holocaust is shaped by a number of other disciplinary and intellectual influences. My research and my institutional affiliation are interdisciplinary. I was trained in German and comparative literature and then became increasingly engaged with ethnographic and anthropological questions of national identity and minority discourses. My recent work—a book and a video documentary on survivors of the Holocaust, in this case Jews who escaped, lived in exile, and returned to both Germanies after World War II—was done in collaboration with an anthropologist.[1] In this framework, I am most interested in the problems of narrative, especially the interview as a genre that raises central questions about subjectivity, voice, position, and representation. Thus my comments are an interdisciplinary mixture of literary and cultural perspectives, albeit always with a fundamental interpretive bent grounded in literature and literary analysis. Literature plays a singular role as the most self-conscious and explicit portrayal of subjective experience of a horror that renders its own representation problematic.[2]

From its philological roots, literary criticism as the practice of describing, analyzing, and interpreting written texts has a long tradition, at least in Germany, in hermeneutics. As a philosophical procedure whose intention, most simply formulated, is to make the strange familiar and the familiar strange, the application of hermeneutical thinking to the Holocaust may seem at best contradictory. On the one hand, how can an event so catastrophic and horrible, "strange" only in the broadest metaphoric sense, be made familiar? And on the other hand, how can the gruesome images so familiar to us today continue to resonate? Theodor Adorno's now famous dictum that poetry is impossible after Auschwitz was but a harbinger of the trials of representation to come. It is precisely this issue of translating, explaining, and interpreting—all definitions of the Greek word *hermeneuin,* from which "hermeneutics" evolved—that seems to be the task of the literary critic when confronting the problem of writing about the Holocaust. I can only hope to remind us of some of the obvious problems.

The notion of text has been broadened by hermeneutical philosophers like Paul Ricoeur and anthropologists like Clifford Geertz[3] to make a place for actions, behaviors, and practices in culture to be interpreted like a text, turning, so to speak, texts and their contexts inside out. Nevertheless, this only adds a complicating dimension to the dilemma of capturing in words or images an event like the Holocaust, which at its core is unrepresentable yet demands of its victims and those spared its immediate terror a rendering of these experiences. On the one hand, the limitations of writing and the imagination of the literary writer and, on the other hand, the interpretive facility of the literary critic are manifestly taxed by the increased demands and responsibilities of writing on the Holocaust. Thus, writing about the Holocaust becomes the most extreme and vexing example of what all literary and ethnographic work is about—rendering experience comprehensible in a form that "makes sense" or "gives meaning," in the German sense of *Sinndeutung.*

Literature is usually thought of as the imaginative realm where the so-called realistic may mingle freely with the mythological, the symbolic, the metaphoric, or the allegorical. Many might think, and it has been said, that it is only in literature—in the sphere of the subjective and even emotional—that the Holocaust experience can be grasped. And there is, of course, a wide range of literature and literary criticism on the Holocaust.[4] However, I am more inclined to think that it is experimentation in structuring experience in different narrative forms, such as interviews, memoirs, and diaries, rather than just in thematics, that gives literary narrative its special status and draws us nearer to rendering the strange familiar.

Poststructuralist criticism has emphasized literature as only one of the many discursive fields composing culture. Nevertheless, this penchant to privilege the discursive and to recognize the "literary" or rhetorical quality of all narratives, even in the social sciences, underscores the importance of the literary text. Still, the identification of the literary aspect of storytelling and its fictional basis, compared to the documentary with its supposed claim on truth, raises thorny questions. Where is the boundary between fiction and reality in Holocaust testimony? Cannot the exclusive focus on the discursive nature of experience ignore, especially in the case of the Holocaust, AIDS, or atomic bomb victims, the materiality of experience, concretely rendered in the body?[5] While words are one of the few means at our disposal to literally represent experience—of course there are photographs, sculptures, and other artistic forms—how far can these signifying systems take us?

Elie Wiesel's novel *Night,* Rolf Hochhuth's play *The Deputy,* and Paul Celan's poem "Death Fugue" are all renderings of actual Holocaust experiences in a form called literary. They consciously and conscientiously rearrange, alter, or intensify a moment or feeling to touch our emotions as well as our intellect. But even in cases where "real" events are fictionalized as another tool in the struggle to represent the unrepresentable, such authors do not "fictionalize" in a traditional sense. While they may create characters, times, and locations that are not "real," they never veer too far from the Holocaust itself, which keeps its firm grip on verisimilitude. As if to ward off the evil spirits of those who would deny the Holocaust's very existence with fallacious claims and spurious overtones, using notions like "fictions" and "interpretations" as arguments, Holocaust writers recognize the need to temper their imaginations, even when presenting alternative scenarios. Nonetheless, imagination and fantasy fuel the literary spirit that provides readers with both documentary and emotional experience.

Literature portrays experience in a form that both distances and draws in the reader while offering insight into the emotions provoked by the Holocaust. Providing situations that might have been, rather than actually were, literature gives the author opportunities to rethink and re-evaluate actual events and feelings in a form that may allow him or her to work out existential or ethical dilemmas removed from the "real," protected from actual pain and suffering. For the reader, literature offers new or alternative avenues of entry into Holocaust experience. Art Spiegelman's *Maus: A Survivor's Tale* is a singular example. Its cartoon characters do not mock or trivialize, but rather intensify a range of feelings by replaying events and relations between victims and perpetrators as a literal cat-and-mouse game.

Yet, with the existential and ethical limitations imposed on us by the magnitude of the horror and our responsibility as critics to "do it justice," we face the limitations of words on the one side and emotions on the other. The latter are often too personal or painful to be shared or too individualistic to make sense to someone on the outside. As scholars we are consistently confronted with the gripping and unique firsthand testimony that defies translation. Literature can filter and temper such pathos and trauma. But this particular narrative form cannot accomplish the task alone. No one literary genre or verbal or artistic rendering is adequate. However, literature provides the necessary critical tools of interpretation, analysis, evaluation, and self-reflection, which can be applied to other Holocaust representations. While literature and its criticism are a way in, a combination of other critical practices is perhaps the way out of the conundrum of representing the Holocaust, which centers so much on remembering, reconstructing, and recording. Literature, history, and even memoirs perform these duties. Important work on monuments and memory enhance the discussion of meaning and interpretation. James Young's work in *The Texture of Memory: Holocaust Memorials and Monuments* and Jane Kramer's essay on the proposed Berlin Holocaust memorial, entitled "The Politics of Memory," are good examples.[6] To address issues of memory from another angle, video testimony of a survivor, psychoanalytic-literary approaches to testimony,[7] and a play like Peter Weiss's *The Investigation* provide complementary points of view.

All Holocaust scholars share responsibilities not only to a subject matter but also to human beings who suffered or perished simply because they were Jewish, communist, "Gypsy," Jehovah's Witness, or gay. Those who study or teach the Holocaust are condemned to always fall short of completeness. Nevertheless, by gathering texts and reading them in dialogue with one another, one can mitigate the inevitable problem of "partial truths," as the anthropologist James Clifford calls the ethnographic project of rendering foreign cultures.[8] For is it not precisely the "foreignness" of the Holocaust that makes its translatability so tenuous and the event itself even impossible to render comprehensible? Historian David Lowenthal, in his book entitled *The Past Is a Foreign Country,* reminds those of us struggling to interpret the Holocaust that the task at hand has both temporal and spatial dimensions.[9] The difficulty of bridging both of these gaps is compounded by the inexplicability of human malice and suffering. These tasks burden all scholars, no matter what their disciplines. They confront us with enormous responsibility to recognize our own personal and historical position toward such sensitive material and the ways it shapes what can only be serious and well-intentioned gestures toward objectivity.

In fact, achieving "objectivity" is possible neither by proclaiming neutrality toward a subject that demands individual human involvement, nor by a single work. Instead, a critically reflective, interdisciplinary perspective that takes advantage of various potential renderings (films, novels, plays, memoirs, diaries, autobiographies, documentaries, photographs, sculptures, paintings) and various critical approaches can get us closer to grasping Holocaust experience. It is precisely this frustrating incompleteness and partiality that can provide the opportunity for setting off texts and approaches next to and against one other. What the philosopher or historian cannot answer may well be complemented by the literary author or critic. The elusiveness of a complete grasp should not deter us from including the various versions of this experience rendered in the allegories of the novel, the voice of oral testimony or interview, or the supposedly more objective illustrations of a documentary film recording, for example, the liberation of a camp. Precisely at these points of juxtaposition, one gains critical perspective on the inability to capture "truth." However, when "read" together, these versions enable the one who was not there to at least approximate experience and approach what T. S. Eliot called an "objective correlative."

Holding up a mirror to nature, to use the metaphor of realism, always reveals its cracks, the position of the viewer, and the angle of the mirror. While these limiting conditions have to be taken into consideration, they do not undermine the validity of the attempt. As scholars, aware of our disciplinary imperatives, expectations, and methodologies, we must reflect in our work and with our students on the way that our particular disciplinary vision shapes our understanding of Holocaust experience and how the confrontation of various disciplinary positionings, discourses, and methods can improve our chances of grasping the ungraspable and representing the unrepresentable.

Engendered by literature and literary study, the critical task of interpretation provoked by the Holocaust is essentially a pedagogical experience.[10] Teaching the Holocaust puts the teacher and students into a singular constellation of intellectual and emotional relationships. While learning the facts and figures about death camps and gas chambers, students are also confronted with ethical questions of guilt and responsibility. Questions of perpetrator and victim resonate beyond the Nazi period when these issues are understood as interpretations of power, authority, free will, and obligation. In fact, how one understands the events leading up to the Holocaust and the Holocaust itself constitutes for the student a lesson in personal involvement, often with existential dimensions. There is no one way to approach this very different kind of classroom experience. It requires both our openness and vigilance toward emotions, subjectivity, and personal engagement. Literature, I think, raises the challenge of facing the moral responsibility of understanding what this unique hermeneutical and human endeavor entails.

II. THE GERMAN CONTEXT

Michael Berkowitz

Beyond "the Crisis of German Ideology": Contextualizing German Culture, the Holocaust, and German Jewry

MY PURPOSE IN THIS ESSAY IS TO DELINEATE AN EXPANSION OF THE view of German culture beyond that which is sometimes employed in the teaching of the Holocaust.[1] I realize that many of those who offer courses on the Holocaust handle the subject in a thoughtful and historically sound manner. My thoughts here arise out of concerns that have been expressed by students in my own classes and by audience members during public lectures on European history, Jewish history, and the Holocaust. This paper, then, is an attempt to work through the problem, "How might one deal with the subject of German culture, in the context of a course or presentation on the Holocaust, to begin to do justice to its complexity?" I believe that if one takes a step back and asks, "What is the relationship of German culture to the Holocaust?" one will find that the answer is not as simple as it may appear at first glance.[2]

Here I will define "culture" as the received body of literature, the arts, attitudes toward learning and worldly experience, and perceptions of social relations in a national or communal context. A discussion of German culture is undoubtedly essential to explain the preconditioning and perpetration of the destruction of European Jewry by the Nazis during the Second World War. In addition, a broadly conceived examination of German culture can help students discern the contradictions and paradoxes inherent in the Holocaust as a historical phenomenon, as well as illuminate facets of European Jewish death and life—before and after Hitler—that do not always find a place in a crammed syllabus.

My main point is that German culture was not only a seedbed for Jew-hatred. It was an entity so diverse that it could only be protean in nature. German culture, particularly the traditions related to *Bildung,* Young Germany, and German liberalism, formed an important part of German-Jewish identity—not only for the so-called assimilationists and Reform Jews,[3] but for Zionists and even the Orthodox community. German culture, underscoring Schiller, Goethe, Kant, and Mann—but also Moses Mendelssohn, Heinrich Heine, Emile Ludwig, and Hannah Arendt—helps explain who the German Jews were, why they thought what they thought and did as they did. I therefore propose that a consideration of German culture in a course on the Holocaust should encompass not only the problem of why non-Jewish Germans hated Jews or were indifferent to their plight but also the reasons German Jews had deeply mixed feelings about their Germanness, and how German culture affected them even if they were oblivious to it.[4]

We also might reflect on the impact of German culture on the German Jews who evaded the reach of Nazi Germany and remade their lives in Palestine, the United States, Great Britain, Latin America, and elsewhere.[5] The task of history is to address and interpret changes over time; therefore, along with explaining how it was possible for the Holocaust to occur, detailing what happened, and exploring the fate of concentration camp survivors, we also may show how the Shoah affected the Jewish and non-Jewish world in various ways. Of course, the void in the Jewish and European worlds cannot be overstated. But the Holocaust left not just Jewish dead and survivors but also exiles who were influenced profoundly by the tragedy. Many of these exiles, I contend, may be best understood in light of the problem of German culture. As scholars such as Robert L. Koehl and Christopher Browning have admirably sought to put a human but unapologetic face on the Nazi perpetrators,[6] part of my motive here is to reconstruct the humanity of some of their victims, the German Jews. This would be inconceivable without the factor of German culture, however little resemblance it bears to the Germanness of their accusers and murderers.

The year 1999 marks the thirty-fifth anniversary of the publication of George L. Mosse's book *The Crisis of German Ideology.*[7] In this work Mosse traced the largely subterranean elements of German culture which surfaced in National Socialism. As Steven Aschheim,

Moshe Zimmerman, and others have noted, until the book appeared German intellectual historians tended to focus on the realm of "high" culture in attempts to locate the genealogy of the Third Reich.[8] Mosse's synthetic treatment of the reception of "high" culture and the infiltration of "low" culture into "respectable" circles, combined with the history of groups such as nationalist students and teachers, still provides a compelling interpretation of what made possible the rise of the Nazis, and particularly Nazi antisemitism.

George Mosse was careful to warn that the road to Nazism was not predetermined by the strains he uncovered in German culture; rather, he asserted, their eruption was due to an utterly unpredictable coincidence of simultaneous crises. It did not take long, however, before his argument was reduced to catchphrases such as "German Romanticism caused the Holocaust." Obviously, this is not what he said; nor did Mosse intend a demonization of German culture. But as the general public, such as the students we teach, before they enter our classes, absorbs a little about the Holocaust, many of them seem to see Germany and Germans as preprogrammed for genocide. This view is often intertwined with a reductionist notion of the "authoritarian personality" model. The limitations of time and space constrict many narratives in a way that does not genuinely reflect the more complicated outlooks of their authors. Indeed, in some of the more popular books and films about the Holocaust, German culture often assumes the singular role of a mounting arsenal for Nazi ideology.[9] This Manichean view of German culture also has been sustained by historiography influenced by Zionism, in which the entire European Diaspora is painted as a crucible of Jewish cultural strangulation and inevitable destruction.[10]

There are several problematic aspects to the too-obvious blueprint "from Luther to Hitler," which has been revitalized in the storm surrounding the publication of *Hitler's Willing Executioners* by Daniel Jonah Goldhagen.[11] That simplification robs German cultural history of its contradictions and layers of complexity, such as its Enlightenment tradition, which, it may be argued, was less hostile to Jews than the better-known French Enlightenment. If this distorted image is inauthentic for Germany in general, it also obscures the history of German Jews.

The aspect of German culture that I wish to focus on for the remainder of this paper is the relationship between German culture and the Jews. As problematic as the notion of a "German–Jewish dialogue" remains, it is critical to understand that, until their nationality was stripped from them, German Jews were Germans. Here I will not indulge questions such as whether or not *Bildung* was "good for the Jews."[12] More important is the lopsided picture of German culture that misinforms some students' views about German Jews, in which German Jewry's attachment to German culture becomes unduly enigmatic. When I was George Mosse's teaching assistant at the University of Wisconsin, a number of students expressed amazement that Professor Mosse did not have a visceral hatred for everything German. And at a lecture I gave recently for a synagogue group in Columbus, Ohio, a man told me that it was not until after I had talked about the experience of German Jews in Palestine that he began to understand why his German-Jewish cousin, who settled in Palestine in the late 1930s, could have returned voluntarily to Germany in the 1960s. Students repeatedly ask: How could Germany's Jews have felt comfortable in so evil a culture, enamored as it was with antisemitism? How could they have been so easily fooled? Why didn't they all leave much earlier? Why didn't Germany's Jews flee to Israel? Students typically misperceive the land of Israel as a more viable option for immigration than it actually was, and implicitly or explicitly condemn German Jews for not having the sense to choose the "Promised Land" over the "Fatherland."[13] I imagine I am not alone in having to respond to these types of student queries. To be sure, the spectacular emergence of the State of Israel was one of the most momentous outcomes of the Shoah, but it is often callously depicted as the positive or redemptive balance to the unprecedented mass murder.[14]

It is important to cast German Jewry from the perspective of its history *before* the Holocaust, rather than to rely on hindsight and blame the victims. Using a novel such as Lion Feuchtwanger's *The Oppermanns* helps to illuminate the Jewish internalization of German culture, and Jewish perceptions of the Nazi menace until 1933, when a number of responses still seemed feasible.[15] A particularly effective vehicle for exploring German Jewry's connection to German culture is the character of Gustav Oppermann, whose primary life's work is a biography of the non-Jew Gotthold Ephraim Lessing. The parable of the three rings in Lessing's drama *Nathan the Wise* is one of the most concise and vivid illustrations of the Enlightenment project, showing how the education of a harmonious society might be achieved through consideration of historical forces and the mutual respect of different religions.[16] Gustav Oppermann's devotion to the legacy of Lessing is part and parcel of his feeling of rootedness in German society. But although *The Oppermanns* is unmatched as an accessible, fictional portrait of German Jewry at the end of the Weimar Republic, it also has limitations. Some sense of the variety within the German-Jewish world is indicated by the presence of a lower-middle-class family, a recent male immigrant from Poland, and a young Zionist woman. But the novel nevertheless might feed into the myth of the hyperassimilation of German Jewry.

It is worth recalling that not all of Germany's Jews turned their backs on Judaism when beckoned by the promise of assimilation. As David Ellenson's analysis of Rabbi Esriel Hildesheimer and Mordechai Breuer's study *Modernity within Tradition* show, there was a significant minority of traditional Jews in Germany—whose sense of themselves also derived, to no small degree, from their embrace of German culture.[17] The work of Michael Brenner, *The Renaissance of Jewish Culture in Weimar Germany,* with its analysis of Jewish adult education and popular publishing, to cite but two examples, undermines the exaggerated view of nonobservant and non-Zionist German Jews as, on the whole, unfamiliar with and uninterested in the Jewish world.[18] Brenner convincingly argues that secular Jews' engagement with Jewish culture was vibrant and growing throughout the Weimar years. The works of scholars such as Jeffrey Grossman, Mark Gelber, and David Brenner, in the field of literary history, complement Michael Brenner's thesis with their interpretations of a secular but nevertheless distinctively Jewish cultural space that was being carved out since the late nineteenth century, in which German and Jewish culture were inextricably bound.[19]

My own work on the history of the Zionist movement in Germany (building on the studies of Stephen Poppel, Donald Niewyk, Derek Penslar, Hagit Lavsky, Glen Sharfman, and others) suggests that German Zionism was not as uncompromisingly Palestinocentric as it is sometimes represented. In addition to being strongly influenced by German nationalism, particularly in its youth and fraternity movements, Zionism in Germany more or less accommodated itself to the assumed persistence of Jewish life in Germany.[20] Its highly ideological youth contingent, the Blau Weiss, did indeed try to remake their lives in Palestine. But most never felt comfortable in the *Yishuv* (nationalist Jewish community in Palestine) and returned to Germany before Hitler took power. Surely the Blau Weissers' middle-class backgrounds made their integration difficult; but their palpable "Germanness" also precluded the existing Palestinian Jewish community's being able to accept them as Zionists first, as their coequals. Furthermore, as Steven Aschheim writes in his analysis of Nietzsche's reception, a number of German Jews, including Zionists of varying stripes, were deeply moved by the radical philosopher.[21]

A more nuanced treatment of German culture also might entail focusing more attention on the history of German-Jewish refugees who did resettle in Palestine in the middle to late 1930s. By then it was far less likely that they would attempt to return to a Germany that was becoming increasingly inhospitable. Tom Segev argues in *The Seventh Million* that the face of the *Yishuv* was noticeably altered by the arrival of the German-Jewish refugees. Their disproportionate impact on the political, economic, and educational arenas derived not only from the capital they possessed, their class background, and their detachment from the established community. Their very Germanness was grafted onto the *Yishuv,* Segev notes, despite the resistance, hostility, and occasional violence directed at the "Yekkes" (German Jews). Certainly their rough reception was exacerbated by the airs of superiority that many in the group affected. But their imprint on the *Yishuv,* which was far from dominant, was, at the very least, indelible.[22] It was the Yekkes who helped introduce the concept of binationalism into Zionist discourse, and it was mainly they who established the cultural institutions that Herzl regarded as vital to civilization, such as bookstores and cafés.

Palestine was not the only place whose cultural physiognomy was transformed by an influx of German-Jewish culture. Scholarly works now abound on the influence of German-Jewish refugee academics, artists, and intellectuals in the United States and elsewhere.[23] Not surprisingly, the Frankfurt school remains an attractive subject in studies of intellectual migration.[24] Both the Germanness and the Jewishness of these individuals deserves attention.[25] Recently the role of German-Jewish professors in traditionally black universities in the United States has been discussed.[26] With the relationship between history and memory relative to the Shoah receiving increasing attention, teachers of the Holocaust may be interested to discern, and share with their students, how the event has been recounted and analyzed. Is it possible to disconnect our learned perspectives from the interpretations developed by German-Jewish refugee scholars such as Gershom Scholem, Hannah Arendt, Fritz Stern, and George Mosse? To fully appreciate these critical minds, it is helpful to reground them in their German cultural contexts.

By no means do I wish to advocate an apologia for German culture. But the implication of German culture in the Holocaust should not be made at the expense of Germany's Jews, painted monochromatically as materialistic, myopic dupes. I suggest instead we revisit German culture's wider sweep, to provide a fuller picture of the ties between Jews, Germans, and modern history, and perhaps open up some different lines of questioning.

One of the main objectives for including this component in a Holocaust course is to break down national stereotypes and unitary views of national culture, which so often lead to simplification and error. Furthermore, discussing the relationship between Jewry and German culture poignantly illustrates the actual fragmentation of Jewry. German Jewry itself was perplexed by having to deal with the East European Jews who crossed into Germany, and feelings toward them were ambiguous.[27] Jewry existed, and to this day exists, as very different communities, separated by the forms of institutional attachment to Judaism, class, political preferences, and nationality. Although there is some grain of truth to the notion of Jewry being unified, unity is not the dominant force in Jewish life that antisemitic conspiracymongers and Jewish organizational fund-raisers would like their audiences to believe. From the perspective of modern history, it is critical for students to learn that Jewry is not one but many, and this is a reason why a concerted Jewish response to the Holocaust was so difficult to achieve, even in the confines of ghettos under siege.

Exploring the Jews' ties to German culture also highlights German Jewry's legitimate, not absurd, feeling of rootedness in German society. In Central and Western Europe, Jews were a part of their national communities. It is only in retrospect that we see how tenuous this hold was. To investigate the source of these sentiments, this sense of belonging, is essential in beginning to probe the depth of crisis among German Jews when they were accused of being un-German and anti-German, and their horror at becoming "stateless."

Although Hannah Arendt's discussion of the phenomenon of "statelessness" evinces a degree of revulsion perhaps unparalleled in political philosophy, she herself expounds primarily on the social and legal ramifications, not even the intellectual and spiritual violation.[28] Several historians have written that the mental duress of Jews in the ghettos and camps was related in part to their being accused of crimes and motives that they knew were grossly untrue. Another dimension of the cruelty accompanying systematic dehumanization and eventual murder was the stripping away of a sense of self that was tied to one's national culture.

It is important to dwell on a scene such as that which closes Marion Kaplan's study of the Jewish feminist movement in Germany. Kaplan quotes a letter in which Hannah Karminski describes her last visit with Cora Berliner (the former vice president of the Jüdischer Frauenbund) on the day of Berliner's deportation: "C. and our other friends took books along. They agreed on the selection. To my knowledge C. took *Faust I* and an anthology. When I went to visit them on the last day, shortly before their departure, they were sitting in the sun in the garden reading Goethe."[29] This cultural orientation was an ironic part of the tragedy of destruction, but it also was very much a part of Jewish history before the Second World War, and fundamental to the remnant that did survive the Shoah. German culture's centrality to the Shoah, to Jewish death, should not deter us from understanding its place in Jewish life.

Karl A. Schleunes

The Year 1933: Revolution or Continuity in German History

EARLY IN THE EVENING OF JANUARY 30, 1933, THE GERMAN RADIO NETwork began broadcasting live from Berlin to cover the day's momentous events. There was much to report. Shortly after noon that day President von Hindenburg had named Nazi party leader Adolf Hitler the new German chancellor. The celebrations had begun immediately as Hitler's jubilant followers poured into the streets. At seven o'clock, a huge torchlight procession began winding down the Wilhelmstrasse in front of the chancellery building. From the building's balcony, Hitler, and occasionally President Hindenburg himself, would wave to the cheering crowd below. To conclude their broadcast later that evening, reporters brought Nazi propaganda chief Joseph Goebbels to the microphone to give to the national audience his estimate of the day's importance. Goebbels, whose words were frequently drowned out by noises from the crowd in the street, told listeners of being "deeply moved to see how in this city, where we [the Nazis] began six years ago with only a handful of people—how in this city the entire population has risen up, how they are now marching down the streets: workers, burghers, farmers, students, and soldiers—all in one great *Volksgemeinschaft* in which no one asks who is a burgher or a proletarian, a Catholic or a Protestant; in which one asks only: who are you, where do you belong, and have you committed yourself to this nation?"[1] In his diary entry for that same day Goebbels concluded by observing: "The German Revolution has begun!"[2]

Was it in fact a revolution? The events of January 30, 1933, have been variously characterized as a *Machtergreifung* (seizure of power), a *Gleichschaltung* (political coordination), an *Umsturz* (overthrow), a revolution, and, of course, a counterrevolution. Each label represents an attempt to explain the essence of Adolf Hitler and National Socialism. How useful is it to focus upon a National Socialist *revolution?* As a label it seems innocuous enough. The Nazis themselves used it liberally to describe their own actions, and observers ever since have been inclined to accept their self-designation. Employed merely as a label, however, the term "revolution" has little heuristic value or analytical use. And when the term is elevated to the conceptual level, it meets resistance, usually because it seems to underestimate the importance of *continuities* in explaining the place of National Socialism in German history. The "Jewish question," after all, was not a Nazi invention and neither were antiliberalism, antisocialism, or antifeminism—all elements central to the Nazi worldview and to their subsequent policies.

Thomas Nipperdey once said, in reference to 1933 and the issue of continuity in German history, that the question becomes interesting only when its opposite, discontinuity, is taken into consideration. Only with constant reference to discontinuity, he suggested, could continuity be expected to yield analyses of scope and precision about Germany in 1933.[3] What Nipperdey says about continuity is, I suggest, equally true for revolution. If nothing else, the notion of revolution at least suggests significant breaks in political and social continuity.[4] In this paper I will focus upon the nature of these breaks, arguing that they fit comfortably into most classic definitions of revolution. We have no difficulty seeing the Nazi regime producing a sudden, violent change in the social location of power in Germany and radically transforming German processes of government, conception of social order, and notions of sovereignty, all of which converge to establish a recognizably new era in history.[5]

Not surprisingly, Joseph Goebbels, more than anyone else in the Nazi hierarchy, used the word "revolution" to describe Nazi activities. It was Goebbels who spoke of the need for "permanent revolution" until such time as the enemies of National Socialism had been eliminated. Hitler, too, regularly called his movement a "national revolution" or a "National Socialist revolution."[6] Years later he recalled how in 1933 he had considered marking "the Nazi new world order by adopting a new Nazi calendar."[7] That Goebbels announced in July 1933 that the revolution was now over did not stop his use of the term. A volume published under his aegis in 1934 commemorated the movement's heroic deeds of 1933 and labeled that year "*das Jahr I,*" Year One, of the new Nazi calendar. Goebbels continued to use "revolution" repeatedly, as did many others, down to the end in 1945. Alfred Rosenberg, for instance, at the founding of his Institute for Research into the Jewish Question in 1941, heralded what he called the Nazis' "biological world revolution."[8] Revolutionary talk does not by itself a revolution make, and the Nazis should not always be taken at their word. Yet to ignore Nazi rhetoric about revolution, as well as what Reinhart Kosellek has called the "chiliastic religious underlining" of so much of it, would be to overlook one of the largest hoards of evidence we have about National Socialism.[9]

Among historians, the revolutionary label is a common one. Alan Bullock in his magnificent biography of Hitler, the first edition of which appeared in 1952, includes a chapter on "Revolution after Power."[10] Karl Dietrich Bracher has a chapter on "Die 'nationale Revolution'" in the monumental work *Die nationalsozialistische Machtergreifung* that he published in 1960 together with Wolfgang Sauer and Gerhard Schulz.[11] Martin Broszat writes of a Nazi revolution in which the outbreak of war in 1939 marked a second stage.[12] Alfred Cobban discusses a "Nazi revolution of destruction."[13] More recently Gerhard Weinberg has spoken of a Nazi revolution committed to undoing the human rights revolution of 1789.[14]

The first scholar to look at National Socialism as a revolutionary phenomenon at the conceptual level was David Schoenbaum, in his 1966 book on *Hitler's Social Revolution.*[15] Since then a lively debate about the nature of that revolution, or whether it actually was one, has been a staple in analyses of National Socialism. Hermann Rauschning, however unreliable a source otherwise, witnessed the Nazi phenomenon firsthand and in 1939 called it, variously, a "revolution of nihilism," a "doctrineless revolution," and an instance of a "random revolutionary dynamic."[16] In 1983 Horst Möller argued in the affirmative and laid out a paradigm for defining a revolutionary movement. In the pages of the *Vierteljahrshefte für Zeitgeschichte* Möller asked whether the National Socialist *Machtergreifung* could be best understood as a "revolution or a counterrevolution." Using criteria defined by the sociologist Theodore Geiger in 1931, Möller concludes that the Nazi seizure of power was indeed a revolution in the same sense as the 1789 revolution in France, the European wave of revolutions in 1848, and the 1917 revolution in Russia.[17] Revolutionary movements, Geiger had postulated, emerged in political and social systems suffering from disintegration and ideological polarization in which nearly everything became politicized. Revolutions were long-term processes in which destructive and constructive forces played off against each other in a fierce dialectic. In Geiger's paradigm the *Umsturz* by which the revolutionary movement came to power was to be a "spectacular, event-filled phenomenon" and, most important, would be followed by the construction of a new, ideologically defined social and political system.[18]

Möller's argument notwithstanding, scholars have also raised objections to calling the Nazi regime revolutionary. How seriously, they ask, can Nazi rhetoric be taken? K. D. Bracher admonishes scholars to be wary of the self-consciously manipulative cast to Nazi rhetoric. Then there is the related question of how Nazi rhetoric corresponds to action. Can the Nazi leaders really be taken seriously as revolutionaries? Those with doubts usually trot out Robert Ley, the alcoholic leader of the Reich's Labor Front and its Strength through Joy agency, as exhibit A in the case against considering the Nazis serious revolutionaries.[19] Additional objections stem from the traditionally progressive connotations of the term "revolution." Revolutions, we have come to believe, should be concerned with the expansion of freedom for the individual in society, and no one has yet soberly proposed that such expansion was part of the Nazi intention. As a counter to this argument we need to remind ourselves that when sixteenth-century Renaissance historians first applied the term "revolution" to political events, it was to avoid what were for them the value-laden terms of "civil war" and "disorder."[20] They chose the term "revolution," moreover, because it bespoke the completion of a cycle in political affairs, just as for astronomers it bespoke the completion of a cycle in matters celestial. It is to the French revolutionary the Marquis de Condorcet that we owe our notion that a genuine revolution must be politically progressive. "The word *revolutionary,*" he wrote in 1793, "can be applied only to revolutions whose aim is freedom."[21] The twentieth century has proved him mistaken.

It violated no tradition, however, for the Nazis to designate as a revolution what they were doing in Germany during the 1930s and 40s. There is no intrinsic requirement that a revolution be progressive, however the term might be defined. Moreover, a German break with an exclusively progressive connotation of revolution certainly preceded the Nazis. To the best of my knowledge it was the very anti-Nazi Hugo von Hofmannsthal who, in his famous lecture at the University of Munich in 1927, coined the expression "conservative revolution," using it to describe his call for an antiliberal, antimodern transformation in the worlds of culture and politics.[22] The aim of such a revolution, he said, would be to heal "that spiritual condition of the isolated cosmopolitan German, who since the revolution of the late eighteenth century had been torn away from custom, from tradition, from the beliefs of his fathers, and given over to the limitless orgy of uprooted individualism."[23] The idea of conservative revolution, moreover, if not the expression itself, was much older, going back at least to the final decades of the previous century in Germany, the era Fritz Stern calls one of "cultural despair."[24] Nor was Hofmannsthal alone in calling for a conservative revolution. His contemporary, the Leipzig sociologist Hans Freyer, issued his own call in 1931 for a *Revolution from the Right,* one aimed against industrial society and intended to elevate the German *Volk* to a central role in a new political order.[25] By dismantling the revolution from the left, Freyer hoped to open the way for a revolution from the right.

An important objection to seeing the Nazis as revolutionaries centers on their failure (perhaps even their lack of intention) to bring about a fundamental change in property relationships. They did nothing at all to dismantle the capitalist mode of production; neither did they overthrow an older owning class and bring in a new one to replace it. These criteria are indeed substantial aspects of *some* revolutions, most notably the one in Russia in 1917. Yet, if they were essential to *every* revolution, we would certainly have to remove that label from the events of 1688 in England, in which no property changed hands. We might even run into trouble applying it to the events beginning in France in 1789. To be sure, Church property was seized in France, but whether 1789 was really a bourgeois revolution—whether one class replaced another in controlling the reins of power—is, according to recent historiography, doubtful.

What about the Nazism as a "counterrevolution"? Could it have been a revolution whose purpose was to undo a previous one, namely the 1917 Bolshevik revolution in Russia? Without the Bolshevik revolution, writes Ernst Nolte, "the world would have been spared the victory of parties of the Fascist type in Italy and Germany."[26] The Holocaust, moreover, Nolte sees primarily as a German reflex reaction to the Stalinist terror of the 1920s and 30s. Arno Mayer, for very different reasons, would agree with the first of Nolte's propositions. The essence of National Socialism, Mayer argues, lay in its self-proclaimed mission to destroy Bolshevism, the Holocaust being a reflex reaction to the realization that the mission had failed.[27]

That anti-Bolshevism was a basic element in the National Socialist worldview is beyond dispute. Nazi rhetoric abounded in its denunciation, and there is every reason to take those denunciations seriously as motivating factors in Nazi theory and practice. But was Nazism really impossible without the Revolution of 1917? Without communism, would there have been no National Socialism? Goebbels looked not to 1917 in Russia but to 1789 in France as the great historical catastrophe. The aim of the Nazi revolution, he once said, was to tear the year 1789 out of the pages of history. That was when history had gone wrong.[28] If we look at the juxtaposition of rhetoric and action, it is clear that it was the liberal, secular, modern, urban, parliamentary world the Nazis wanted to replace. They certainly had no intention of restoring or preserving much of anything from the pre-1789 world: not the churches, not the constitutions, not the monarchy, not the nobility, not the political parties, not the traditions of the *Länder*, not the values of the bourgeoisie. If there was to be any restoration at all, it was to be of something that had never existed, a mythical German past marked by a presumed purity of blood and culture, itself a utopian vision that had profoundly revolutionary implications.

What, then, was revolutionary about the Nazis? Between the February 28, 1933 Decree for the Protection of People and State, which suspended civil liberties, and the Law of August 2, 1934, which combined the offices of chancellor and president in the person of Hitler, the new regime managed to reverse a century and a quarter of constitutional development. The Enabling Act of March 23, 1933 gave Hitler powers of decree for four years, in effect the right to deviate from the constitution whenever he pleased. Hitler promised to use this power sparingly—which, in 1933, turned out to mean 218 times.[29] Already on March 9, 1933, the Reich had taken over the state government of Bavaria. In January 1934 all of the state governments were brought under control of the Reich, ending a thousand-year-long tradition of German federalism. In July 1933, the Nazis outlawed all political parties other than their own. The Nuremberg Laws of 1935 brought to an end the emancipation of Jews, a process begun more than a century earlier.

The revolution extended almost immediately into the realm of symbols. In Berlin the *Reichskanzlerplatz* was renamed for Adolf Hitler. Friedrich-Ebert-Strasse became Hermann-Goering-Strasse. Friedrichshain became Horst Wessel Stadt. Similar changes took place in every city and town of Germany during the next months. Any street, square, or district named to honor a Jew was renamed, most likely for Hitler or Goering, or for one of the Nazi martyrs such as Horst Wessel or Hanne Maikowski, the Berlin SA man supposedly shot down by communists during the celebrations on January 30, 1933.

More fundamentally, the Nazi seizure of power represented a complete inversion of political and social values. That which had been right suddenly became wrong; that which had been wrong became right. The energies unleashed by this inversion provided much of the drama during the early months of the Nazi era, helping to make of them a "spectacular, event-filled phenomenon." Enemies—communists, socialists, democrats, Jews—were terrorized; jails were filled; wildcat concentration camps were erected; judges and journalists were harassed, or murdered; neighbors settled scores with neighbors by denouncing them to the police; husbands denounced their wives and wives their husbands. In Berlin alone, during the first weeks of Nazi rule SA thugs set up fifty impromptu concentration camps, transforming the city into what Heinz Hohne has called a "terrorists' witches cauldron."[30]

These months were marked also by an intellectual revolution. University faculties were purged of political and racial undesirables. Books were burned, galleries cleared of degenerate art and concert halls of degenerate music. For some this was a time of great hope. Ernst Krieck saw his new position as rector at the University of Frankfurt as a platform from which to impose his theories about a racially informed pedagogy.[31] Eugen Fischer, the new rector at the University of Berlin, hailed the Nazi regime for its promise to take eugenics seriously.[32] Hans Freyer proposed to the Nazis that the "revolution from the right" begin with the requirement of a "political semester" for students entering the university. This semester was to awaken in them an appreciation for political greatness, develop their understanding of the dynamics underlying political events, and cultivate their understanding of Germany's political situation.[33] Meanwhile, Martin Heidegger, the new rector at Freiburg, in his *Introduction to Metaphysics,* was explaining how National Socialism, at its core, possessed an "inner truth and greatness."[34]

But was there a Nazi social revolution, that transformed social relations between classes or groups? Clearly, such a revolution had been part of the Nazi promise. Goebbels's first public utterance after the Nazis came to power on January 30, 1933, stressed how all Germans—workers, burghers, farmers, students, soldiers, Protestants and Catholics—would be gathered into one great community of blood, a *Volksgemeinschaft.* This *Volksgemeinschaft* represented the highest Nazi ideal. Within its confines would be squared the circle of social difference. Class and gender distinctions would not so much be overcome as rendered irrelevant. Differentiations of function between employees and employers, women and men, peasant farmers and big landowners were to be recognized and even celebrated—and transcended in the *Volksgemeinschaft* that defined them all. Equality was to be realized on a higher level by membership in the superior race. Simply to belong was a mark of superiority, of being biologically "chosen" for greatness. Material elevation for the lower classes was to be achieved through the ownership of a Volkswagen and the opportunities the Strength through Joy program provided to take a ski vacation in the mountains or a cruise on the Baltic. The new equality was symbolized in anyone's right to be addressed as a racial comrade, as a *Volksgenosse.*

That the first step toward realizing that ideal should be the destruction of the German labor movement, and the disbanding of its unions, suggests to some scholars that Nazi talk about the *Volksgemeinschaft* was nothing more than empty rhetoric. But was it? Once again it's time to trot out Robert Ley. Were his German Labor Front and its subsidiary Strength through Joy agency nothing more than fancy facades behind which Nazi leaders betrayed Germany's lower classes by, for example, extracting deposits for Volkswagens that would never be delivered? Anecdotal evidence to the contrary has been accumulating ever since Milton Mayer published his account in 1955 of a his year-long set of interviews with ten "little Nazis." "For the first time in my life," recalled one them, "I was really the peer of men who, in the Kaiser time and in the Weimar time, had always belonged to classes lower or higher than my own, men whom one had always looked down upon or up to, but never at."[35] Wolfhard Buchholz's 1976 Munich dissertation on the Strength through Joy movement supports Mayer's conclusions. Buchholz reports that by 1938 some 9 million Germans had in one way or another participated in a Strength through Joy cruise, tour, or holiday excursion.[36] That a disproportionate number of them were also minor party functionaries does not belie the program's widespread popularity or its effect in mobilizing support for the regime. The anecdotal evidence suggests that many people at the lower social levels did in fact feel themselves, often for the first time, the equals of people who had once been their supposed "betters."

The Nazi idea of *Volksgemeinschaft* not only identified who belonged in the new Germany, it also stipulated, by virtue of its racist antisemitism, who did not belong. As George Mosse has explained, the Nazis transformed the call for a "conservative revolution" in the 1920s into the call for an anti-Jewish one in the 1930s and 40s.[37] When Alfred Rosenberg proclaimed the "biological world revolution" in 1941, Nazi death camps were just beginning to carry out their "final solution to the Jewish problem" and thereby, in Nazi calculation, to destroy their revolution's bitterest enemy. At the same time, they were also in control of the "lesser races" in Eastern Europe, and SS planners were preparing the infamous Generalplan Ost to ensure those races' eternal subservience to the superior Aryans.[38] The Aryans themselves were being made even more superior by the eugenics measures the Nazis began adopting as early as 1933. Hereditary Health Courts in 1934 began forcing the sterilization of those suffering from hereditary diseases. The Nuremberg Laws in 1935 brought an end to the defiling effects of race mixing between German and Jews. Euthanasia measures begun in 1939 ensured that the mentally ill and physically deformed were removed from the collective Aryan body. Within several generations, Himmler promised, the German bloodstream would be repurified.[39] The ideal image of the new "Nazi man" and "Nazi woman" appeared in the statuary of sculptors such as Arno Breker and Josef Thorak.

The Nazi revolution, we know, was accomplished by a wholesale inversion of values. Within a very few years, it undid more than a century of constitutional development. Uneven as that development had been, the goals of the emancipatory movements emerging in the late eighteenth and early nineteenth centuries had finally achieved their goals, or so it seemed, in the Weimar constitution. Now Jews, women, workers—all German citizens, in fact—lost the rights anchored in that document torn to shreds by the Nazis following the Reichstag fire of February 27, 1933. In its place the Nazis vested arbitrary executive power in the hands of their Führer; they defined blood and race as the basis for citizenship, excluding all those outside their notion of the Aryan brotherhood; and finally, they designated another people, the Jews, to be the pariah race whose mere existence threatened that of the Aryan race. The twisted Nazi logic of racial purity reached its horrific culmination in the fires of Auschwitz.

Had the Nazis won the war and been able to carry their revolution to its ultimate conclusion, what would it have looked like? The geographical limits of their *Volksgemeinschaft* would have extended from the English Channel in the west to the Ural Mountains in the east. Millions of Slavs would have been deported to Siberia. Settled in their place would have been millions of Aryans from the Germanic countries of Europe. Within several generations one could have expected these representatives of the *Volk* to be completely "purified" of inferior blood. They would be living not only in a world without Jews but also, as Hitler had promised, in a world in which time would be measured by a calendar in which 1933 figured as Year One.

Peter Hayes

The Deutsche Bank and the Holocaust

UNTIL ONLY A FEW YEARS AGO, THE ROLE PLAYED BY THE—THEN AS now—premier German financial institution in the assault on the European Jews was impossible to depict in any detail. What little scholars knew about the conduct of the Deutsche Bank during the Nazi era had emerged in fragmentary and rather unreliable form immediately after 1945, then had largely been forgotten.[1] The only people or entities that appeared to be in a position to provide more information, namely the bank itself and its former executives, had chosen instead to offer only general, and generally self-serving, statements about their erstwhile actions, unsupported by credible written evidence.[2]

Then, in the early 1990s, a striking about-face occurred. Not only did the collapse of East Germany bring to light unsuspected and extensive caches of documentation from that state's archives, but also the bank, to which legal control over these papers reverted in 1990, resolved to place them at the disposal of an international team of professional historians and to let copies of the records remain in the public domain for the use of other researchers. These files from Potsdam, Dresden, and Leipzig—supplemented by others that have turned up in Prague, Vienna, and Amsterdam—now permit historians a remarkable glimpse into the extent of corporate complicity in the process we have come to call the Holocaust.[3] That the result is a depressing story is all the more reason to underline at the outset the promising and positive nature of the bank's recent openness. It bespeaks a degree of willingness to confront the past that is especially commendable because it is still infrequent among German private enterprises. If the Deutsche's history stands as a warning in many respects, the bank's current conduct is a welcome model in this one.

Well before Adolf Hitler became chancellor of Germany, the Deutsche Bank was already what it has remained ever since: the largest deposit-taking and credit-giving entity in the land. As one might expect of such an institution, it had also long taken pains to maintain good relations with the government of the day, within the context of a general preference for political figures who placed a premium on preserving stability and encouraging private enterprise. Thus, in the final, tumultuous years of the Weimar Republic, the bank's leading managers, gentile and Jewish alike, were consistent and financially generous backers of President Hindenburg and chancellors Brüning and von Papen.[4] Thus, too, they were predisposed to make their peace with and demonstrate their loyalty to the new masters of Germany after January 1933 and to adapt to the new business conditions being created. Nonetheless, if one compares the bank to its principal competitors, one can see why the firm never overcame the Nazis' mistrust and how difficult it is to encapsulate its relationship to the so-called Third Reich.

Alone among the major German banks, the Deutsche Bank emerged from the Depression shaken yet with its financial independence more or less intact. Since the bank's stock had not fallen into the hands of the government, the new regime could not virtually dictate the composition of its management, as in the case of the rapidly Nazified Dresdner Bank; neither did the Deutsche's chief executives have the same incentive to rush to join the Nazi party (NSDAP), as nearly all the members of the Commerzbank's managing board did by September 1933.[5] Moreover, because the Deutsche remained far more deeply engaged in international business than its competitors, its leaders retained a stronger interest in *not* being linked to the NSDAP. As a result, of the fifteen non-Jews who sat on the bank's managing board between 1933 and 1945, only three were party members, and each of them owed his election only to scuffles with the Nazis in 1936–38 and 1943–44. In the early years of the Third Reich, the firm could depend for political protection on a man it had dropped from the management in 1931–32 on business grounds, then hastily restored to prominence in 1933: Emil Georg von Stauss. Nominally a member of the People's party until it dissolved in that year, Stauss maintained such good ties to the NSDAP that he apparently never needed to join and could remain until his death in 1942 a member of the Reichstag as a "guest" of the Nazi delegation.[6]

The bank's middle management proved readier as time passed to affiliate with the NSDAP: by 1944, forty-four out of eighty-four branch managers were members. But the very evenness of the split among them, even at this late date, suggests that enthusiasm for the party fell far short of universal and that the bank neither encouraged nor discouraged joining, even implicitly. Moreover, among those who did not join, disaffection with the regime became great enough to prove literally fatal: two directors of branches of the bank were executed in late 1943, one for dismissing Nazism as "a mere fart" in German history, the other for calling Goebbels an "ape" and Hitler a "swindler."[7] On the other hand, the fervor with which bank officials applied Nazi racial policy to their responsibilities often increased as one went down in the hierarchy, since lower-level executives tended to be younger and less acquainted with any other operating context, as well as more desperate to draw attention to their ability to make money for the firm.

In one other important respect, the identification of the Deutsche Bank with the Nazi regime was strikingly and significantly limited, namely with regard to its economic policies in the early years of the Third Reich. Far from greeting road-building, re-armament, and autarky as wise and effective solutions to the Depression, the bank's leaders, especially its coming man during the 1930s, Karl Kimmich, repeatedly warned their fellow executives against the economic shortsightedness of these courses. From 1934 to 1938, in his monthly economic forecasts for a group of prominent industrialists from firms tied to the Deutsche, Kimmich consistently stressed the dangers of building up excess manufacturing capacity and becoming dependent on government orders and purely domestic demand. More specifically, he went so far as to doubt the net employment gains from Autobahn construction, to urge the resumption of disarmament negotiations in order to reduce the Reich's financial burdens, and to discourage firms from making the massive investments called for by the Four-Year Plan.[8] Such statements undermine the remarkably tenacious notion in the academic literature on Nazi Germany that many (perhaps most) men in big business embraced Nazi economics and accepted expansionism as the lowest common denominator between their interests and those of the regime.[9]

The very ambiguity of the Deutsche Bank's relationship to Nazi Germany is what makes the firm exceptionally interesting and important to the study of the Holocaust. For it turns out on close examination that the process known for brevity's sake as "aryanization"—that is, the separation of Jews from their jobs and their property, first in Germany, then in occupied Europe—came to be a form of this lowest common denominator between private and political desires. Moreover, the Deutsche Bank, regardless of its leaders' attitudes toward governmental policy, proved vital, almost indispensable, not only to carrying out aryanization, but also to minimizing its adverse effects on the German economy as a whole. The history of the Deutsche Bank's part in the Holocaust serves as an important reminder of the complexity of the persecution process, of the degree to which it depended on the "normal" functioning of "normal" institutions, penetrated much of German society, and, most chillingly, enlisted the cooperation of otherwise generally respectable people. Though at almost every step of the way the Deutsche merely followed the trend of events, in so doing the firm smoothed and accelerated that trend. The bank's behavior typifies that of the broad band of Germans who acted less out of racist conviction than practical self-interest, but whose deeds had no less vicious consequences for all that.

Nonetheless, if the Deutsche Bank acted out of self-interest, it is important also to recognize that the conditions dictating its interests were not of its own making. Through both direct and indirect pressures—that is, by both insisting on antisemitic actions and reducing the availability or attractiveness of alternatives to them—the Nazi party and state increasingly channeled the firm's behavior toward participation in persecution. That the bank proved manipulable in this manner is traceable, in part at least, to its commercial difficulties in the 1930s and 40s. In three key respects, the Deutsche spent the Nazi era trying unsuccessfully to recover from the Great Depression. By 1944, the value of the firm's nongovernmental assets was still about 25 percent less than in 1928; the Deutsche's total worth as a share of that shown on the balance sheets of all German banks—that is, its relative standing in the financial world—had fallen by more than 50 percent; and both of these declines testified to the force of a third one: the bank's annual earnings from brokering the sale of corporate stock issues stagnated throughout Hitler's rule at less than one-fourth of their former level.[10] All of these conditions were products of the Nazi economic policies Karl Kimmich spoke out against but could not change, namely, the soaking up of capital by government debt and the concentration of public and private expenditures on armaments and autarky. This was the context in which the officers of the bank became progressively more active in exploiting the possibilities of making money in one of the few ways open to them: from the dispossession of Jews.

The first test of the Deutsche Bank's character in the face of Nazi antisemitism developed within weeks of the Nazi takeover, and it hardly produced a profile in courage.[11] At issue were the seats of two observant Jews, Oskar Wassermann and Theodor Frank, and one man of Jewish descent, Georg von Solmssen, on the bank's six-person managing board and, to a lesser extent, the presence of several so-called non-Aryans on the supervisory board. During February and March of 1933, largely self-appointed Nazi employee representatives, often backed by howling stormtroopers, appeared in corporate offices, boardrooms, and stockholder meetings across Germany on an almost daily basis to demand the removal of companies' Jewish workers, directors, and even owners.[12] Panicking at the thought that Wassermann's prominence in the Zionist movement would lead to similar occurrences at the bank or its upcoming annual meeting at the end of May, a majority of the managing board, including Frank and perhaps Solmssen, apparently decided by early April that at least the unbaptized Jewish members had to go.

This readiness to bow to Nazi antisemitism no doubt owed something to intramural considerations: several directors probably still begrudged Wassermann his role in the general banking collapse of 1931, when his refusal to shore up the Danat Bank had, in the eyes of many, greatly aggravated the crisis; and some may have recalled with *Schadenfreude* that he had come out in favor of including the Nazis in the cabinet after the elections of 1930.[13] In the opinion of some of his colleagues, Wassermann perhaps was reaping what he had doubly helped to sow, and if he was dragging Frank down with him, then so be it.

But on April 6, when a delegation of the bank's executives called on Hjalmar Schacht, the new Nazi-appointed chairman of the national bank, to discuss the matter, they did not encounter the duress they had expected. Schacht told them there was no hurry; though Jews would have to resign promptly from all official bodies concerned with banking and all lobbying groups, their role in private businesses would be worked out in due time. His attitude probably reinforced the gathering disgust of Wassermann, and by now even Solmssen, at their colleagues' cravenness. On April 9, Solmssen wrote fellow director Franz Urbig to complain about "the complete lack of solidarity on the part of those who until now have worked shoulder to shoulder with Jewish colleagues . . . and the[ir] total silence in the face of the pain and shame to which all those innocents are subjected who are seeing their honor and livelihood destroyed overnight," adding that such conduct had convinced him "I, too, would be dropped, as soon as some outsider decisively insisted on my inclusion in the purge."[14] The next day, sure that his associates had betrayed him by meeting with Schacht behind his back, Wassermann moved to spite them by saying he planned to retire, but only as of the end of the year—that is, after the bank's annual meeting, over which he intended to preside. He stuck to this position over the next few weeks, as the embarrassed and unsteady board first tried to get him to stay on and then, following a tip that the party intended to begin forcing the issue after all, opted to head off trouble by peremptorily announcing his and Frank's departure before the stockholders' meeting.

The jettisoning of Wassermann and Frank was only the beginning of a year-long purge of Jews from leading positions in the Deutsche Bank. Contrary to usual practice, neither Frank, who emigrated to Switzerland, nor Wassermann, who died a year later, was named to the largely ornamental supervisory board. Solmssen was so relegated the following April, and he remained active in the Deutsche's affairs from his new residence in Zurich; but the bank chose henceforth to omit his name from its publications. Max Steinthal also lost his supervisory post, creating an opening that helped make room for two appointees with excellent Nazi credentials: Philipp Reemstma, a cigarette magnate closely tied to Hermann Göring, and Carl Eduard, the Duke of Saxe-Coburg-Gotha, a high-ranking officer in the SA. Meanwhile, the Jewish directors and senior staff at the branches in Breslau and Essen also were dismissed at the behest of the Nazis.[15] If all of this occasioned a certain unease among the remaining bank directors, it was hardly of a humanitarian sort. Their chief worry was about appearances. As Franz Urbig wrote to Hans Rummel in January 1934: "Times may someday change, and we must for the sake of the bank make sure that no one can ever offer the reproach that the highest administrative bodies contributed to the fact that the non-Aryans . . . had to leave the shop."[16]

Worry about appearances, and occasionally about old friends, fought a gradually losing battle with more material concerns as the Deutsche became ever more deeply implicated in the removal of Jews from other enterprises in the early years of Nazi rule. What generally drew the bank in was the presence of one of its chief executives as the chair or deputy chair of the supervisory board of a firm in which it held large blocs of stock or which allocated the bulk of its banking business to the Deutsche. Since the consent of the chair was required for major management changes and severance contracts, and that of the whole board for alterations in its own membership, attempts to dismiss Jews always led to the desks of these bank delegates. For about a year after Hitler's accession, they generally played a purely passive role. The bank withdrew even those Jews it had dismissed from its own boards from the boards of other firms only when they so requested, and it usually responded to Nazi threats against firms that retained Jews in prominent positions by advising them to resign but letting the matter drop if they declined to go. Only after April 1934, when the bank completed its internal adjustment to "the new political conditions" or "the requirements of the times," as the favorite euphemisms of the day went, did it also begin more aggressively executing Nazi demands. Because the Deutsche always preferred quiet exits, its representatives often did the best they could with regard to the dismissed Jews' pensions and severance terms, but played by the book nonetheless. In short, the bank's representatives paid more attention to their fiduciary than their human responsibilities.

The first case of involvement in extramural aryanization came to a head in April 1933, at the same time as the Frank/Wassermann crisis at the bank itself. It concerned the Deutsche Linoleum-Werke AG, one of the hundred largest German firms, where two members of the managing board (including one of the two general directors) and five members of the supervisory board were Jews.[17] Confronted with an entirely extralegal demand for their removal from the economics ministry of the state of Württemberg, then by the pleas of retailers who feared Nazi attacks on them for selling "Jewish" wares, and unnerved by the prevailing reign of terror, all the men in question quickly submitted their resignations and began negotiating their financial settlements. Completed by the fall, these generally provided for full payment for the unexpired portions of contracts or board terms, then retirement benefits for managers that came to between one-half and two-thirds of their last annual salaries. In the minutes of the meeting that recorded their departures, Director Boner of the Deutsche Bank, who chaired the supervisory board, prudently crossed out a passage expressing his "regret" at the "course of events," but let stand the remark that he had found accepting the resignations "extraordinarily difficult."

Essentially similar stories were played out in 1933 at the three preeminent construction firms in Germany, the Johannes Jesserich, Hochtief, and Philipp Holzmann corporations.[18] In each case, the leverage applied to obtain the removal of Jews was a threat by Nazi officials or organizations to exclude the firms from the awarding of municipal or governmental contracts. In the contexts of the ongoing Depression and the party rampage, no executive of these firms dared to try to rally the common front of refusal that would have left the regime with little or no choice of contractors, especially at the outset of the building season. Thus, whichever person or organization delivered the Nazi blackmail—at Jesserich it was the party trade union in the firm and the state-run clinics and children's homes that consumed the products of a chief subsidiary; at Hochtief it was the police, who arrested a member of the supervisory board; and at Holzmann it was no less a figure than Fritz Todt, the man in charge of Autobahn construction—the firms' non-Jewish managers immediately began entreating the Deutsche Bank executives atop the supervisory boards to comply.

This they did, soliciting the necessary resignation letters and arranging the associated settlements, though at varying paces and with varying degrees of flexibility. Bank Director Benz at Jesserich acceded to two departures from the managing board, but held out for almost four weeks before giving in to the removal of five Jews from the supervisory board, and then for five more months before accepting a Nazi politician as one of their replacements. Determined, as he wrote in July 1933, "to cover my own back," he made the two Jewish executives fight hard for every penny they then got from the firm, but he also interpreted several disputed points in their favors. At Hochtief, Sippell of the Deutsche Bank honored the request of one purged supervisory board member that the public announcement say nothing of conforming to political demands, and he left in peace the two "non-Aryan" representatives of Jewish banks, whom the Nazis had not included in their ultimatums. And in the Holzmann case, Director Blinzig actually managed first to stave off the party onslaught for three months through astute lobbying in Berlin, and then to supplement the settlements in gold marks for the dropped managers by assigning them rewarding consulting contracts abroad. Unfortunately, he soon tired of the task, especially as the Nazi party's Foreign Organization continued to hound the firm's former chief executive, Charles Rosenthal, demanding that Holzmann terminate his service as its representative in Colombia. By June 1934, Blinzig was privately complaining that the one remaining Jew on the supervisory body, Max Warburg, whom the Nazi party tolerated because of his international standing, would not retire voluntarily. Shortly thereafter, Blinzig worked to trim the sums being offered Rosenthal as a final settlement of the firm's contractual obligations, before finally relenting and accepting a deal that would have secured Rosenthal's financial future had he not died in New York a few years later, worn out by his ordeal at the age of only forty-eight.

The Nazi war of attrition also eroded the decency of Franz Urbig, the Deutsche Bank director who presided over the supervisory board of the Hutschenreuther Porcelain Corporation of Selb in Bavaria.[19] When the Nazi employees of the main factory began calling for the removal of seven members of that board in October 1933, Urbig at first behaved just like colleagues elsewhere and asked the Jews to resign for the good of the firm. However, he ran into the spirited resistance of Eugen Schweisheimer, the Jewish co-owner of a private bank in Munich, who condemned the request as incompatible with "my concepts of honor and equal rights." Urbig chose not to force the issue, fortified by a decree from the Reich's ministries of economics and the interior in December exempting commercial activities from all the racist regulations that had been imposed in other walks of life, and by the fact that the composition of the boards at the main rival enterprise left the Nazi party no real alternative for a supplier. There the matter rested until the Nazis resumed their offensive a year later. At first, Urbig instructed the firm to take refuge behind the decrees, but its position had been weakened in the interim by the completion of the purge at Rosenthal Porcelain. The Nazi county leader now had the wit to refocus his pressure directly on the Deutsche, making the issue a test of its power and political loyalty. This had the desired effect. Late in November 1934, the banker carried out a reorganization that deprived all but one of the Jews of their seats. Reproached once more by Schweisheimer, he defended himself in pragmatic terms no doubt echoed by many gentile business executives at the time:

> No one aspires to do unpleasant things. One tackles them, when one has to or when one wants to avoid the charge of having been blind to events in the wider world. . . . My experiences and observations in diverse professional positions have shown me that one cannot see the matter before us as one wishes to, but only as it—despite all ministerial pronouncements—in reality is.

There is no need to review more such cases in detail. The stories at the Hirsch Kupfer- und Messing-Werke, the Hermann and Leonard Tietz department store chains, Orenstein & Koppel, and Daimler-Benz in 1933–34 were not appreciably different.[20] Minor and short-lived instances of greater courage surface occasionally in the documents; the Deutsche Bank's representatives wrote glowing letters of recommendation for the people they had abandoned; and in May 1937, when Erich and Egon Loewe were driven from the firm that bore their family name, Karl Kimmich tried to organize at least a farewell breakfast, as he put it, "in order that their departure not proceed so unkindly."[21] But such gestures hardly alter the general picture. Neither does the fact that the bank provided cover until July 1937 for the baptized Georg Wertheim, so that he could remain active in his famous department store, by voting the stock that he transferred to his Aryan wife and using Emil Georg von Stauss to obtain the party's consent to these arrangements.[22]

One may be able to explain why, but the hard fact remains: the Deutsche Bank stood by almost no one when push came to shove. Indeed, it was increasingly prepared to do the shoving itself. In April 1936, Director Schmid of the Waldhof Fibers Corporation told Dr. Sippell of the Deutsche Bank, his supervisory board chair, that his high regard for another bank representative on that body, Dr. Fuld of the Mannheim branch, made it impossible for him to ask Fuld to step down. Schmid insisted, therefore, that if this became necessary in the coming year, the bank would have to take the initiative. "But of course" ("Selbstverständlich") was Sippell's reply.[23]

Until 1937, the Deutsche Bank's role in the other side of aryanization, the transfer of Jewish-owned firms and shares, resembled that in the personnel cases but occurred less often. The bank moved not so much in order to make money as to protect existing investments and interests. In only a few instances, such as at Daimler-Benz and the Ludwig Loewe AG, had the purges directly benefited the bank, in that the departure of Jews from other financial houses led to the transfer of business to the Deutsche.[24] Similarly, the bank's first, episodic involvements in property transfers were undertaken out of defensive considerations. In the most notable case, that of the Kaufhof department store chain, the Deutsche appears to have purchased about half of the 30 percent holding that the Leonard Tietz family had virtually to liquidate between 1933 and 1935, since Nazi attacks on the firm so damaged sales that the only hope of recovering the substantial loans the bank had made the company during the Depression seemed to be to accelerate the divestiture. Kaufhof's business remained so soft in the 1930s that the stock could not be resold at a gain.[25]

Of course, as time passed, the Nazi regime looked increasingly entrenched in power, and both sellers and buyers began to draw conclusions from this situation. The bank began to exploit some opportunities. It thus became in the third quarter of 1935 the intermediate owner of 100 percent and 60 percent, respectively, in two Berlin electrical firms that a Siemens subsidiary intended to buy: Dr. Cassirer & Co. and the Aronwerke, the former on very advantageous terms to the sellers, the latter on less favorable ones. The surviving records do not disclose the size of the bank's commission on these transactions; that they involved between 10 and 12 million marks suggests a fee of 50,000 to 120,000 marks. The chief and documentable gains, however, were of longer-term sorts: Siemens's satisfaction and the banking business of the acquired firms, which had been in the hands of competitors.[26] More precise information is available concerning the returns on the assistance rendered the Kronprinz AG in taking a pipe plant owned by Alexander Coppel in 1936. Here the bank's immediate proceeds came to 50,400 Reichsmarks.[27] Despite such examples, however, the Deutsche's participation in such deals remained infrequent. It duplicated neither the Dresdner Bank's willingness to work hand-in-glove with the Gestapo to induce readiness to sell or accept harsh terms, nor the Dresdner's creation of a special office, sometime in 1936–37, to specialize in brokering the takeovers of Jewish property.[28]

Compared to the Dresdner, the Deutsche Bank always pursued a more moderate course, but the gap closed measurably in 1937–38, as government policy took a radical turn. For years, the Nazis had mostly contented themselves with harassing the Jewish owners of major firms into retiring from their boards, and otherwise had relied on the increasing unbearability of life in Germany to induce Jews to sell out. As a result, while 60 percent of the small businesses in Jewish hands as of 1933 had been taken over by Aryans or liquidated by the end of 1937, only about 30 percent of the large ones had undergone similar fates.[29] Impatient Nazi activists had long talked of founding a state-backed enterprise to buy the remaining businesses up at a fraction of their worth and resell them over time at a profit, an idea which Karl Goetz of the Dresdner Bank broached to Kimmich in the summer of 1937. But Kimmich rejected it as likely to damage his firm's international connections and as smacking too much, in any case, of government intervention in free enterprise.[30] Then, in November 1937, Hitler decided to force the pace and appointed the like-minded Göring as acting economics minister. Göring promptly promulgated a series of decrees formally defining and establishing punishments for "Jewish influence" over firms.[31] These set off a virtual free-for-all, as sellers scrambled to make a deal before their bargaining positions completely collapsed, and buyers plunged in lest rivals come away with more of the spoils.

In what followed, the response of the big banks was pivotal. They now competed intensely with each other and with empire-building private banks, such as Merck Finck and Richard Lenz, to collect brokerage commissions that came to 1–2 percent of the purchase prices, to loan the necessary capital, to speculate on blocs of shares, to hold on to the regular business of client firms that were changing hands or secure that of new owners, and even to make their own advantageous acquisitions.[32] Here, as in other commercial sectors, the gold rush was intensified by the presence of state-controlled firms, such as the Reichs-Kreditgesellschaft and the regional banks, which stood ready to gobble up anything worthwhile that private firms neglected.[33] The possible immediate rewards of success were exemplified by the 800,000 marks that the Berliner Handels-Gesellschaft and the Deutsche Bank divided for executing Mannesmann's takeover of the Hahnschen Werke in April 1938.[34] As an illustration of the proximate stakes, consider the transformation of the Norddeutsche Trikotwerke of Berlin and the Sigmund Göritz AG of Chemnitz into the Venus-Werke. The Deutsche Bank not only acquired some of the stock at 98 percent of par and later resold it at 148–52 percent, reaping some 92,000 marks in this fashion, but also meanwhile pocketed an immediate fourfold increase in receipts from the new firm's business (from under 3,000 marks in the second half of 1938 to over 12,000 in the first half of 1939).[35]

In pursuit of such returns, the Deutsche began in January 1938 soliciting lists of "aryanizable" firms from its branches, then collating and distributing the results.[36] Although the headquarters urged regional offices to handle their inquiries and intelligence with great discretion, it also stressed, "It is very important that the new business possibilities arising in connection with the changeover of non-Aryan firms be exploited and that care be taken not to lose old ties as a result of the, according to our observations, extremely active competition in this field."[37]

Thus impelled, by July 1938 the Deutsche Bank had collected data on some 700 target firms and played the role of intermediary or financier in approximately 260 aryanizations; by November, the figure was 330, and the number of major ones in that calendar year alone probably came to about 75, including such substantial firms as Roth-Händle (tobacco), Bachmann & Ladewig (textiles), and Adler & Oppenheimer (leather).[38] How instrumental the bank was nationally in the drive to aryanize the most significant Jewish-owned enterprises can be gauged from the extant data on takeovers in and around Frankfurt. In 300 cases surveyed, the Deutsche provided 33 percent of the loans needed for all purchases (2 million marks out of 6 million) and 12 percent of the credits extended for operating costs (.6 million marks out of 5 million)—that is, substantially less than the Dresdner Bank in both respects, but no trivial sums.[39] Moreover, the Deutsche Bank's own takeovers of two celebrated Jewish private banks, Hirschland in Essen and Mendelssohn in Berlin, further bolstered its balance sheets.[40]

Though reliable aggregate figures apparently may never exist, it is safe to say that the Deutsche grossed millions of marks from aryanization, but also that it netted far less. This is one reason the bank's chief executives were never enthusiastic about the whole process. For every old debt they saved from default and every mark they earned (or kept their competitors from earning), they also lost large funds through the state's liquidation of Jews' deposits. For instance, the state probably eventually siphoned off nearly all of the 35 million marks that had been in non-Aryan accounts at the Frankfurt branch as of November 1938, via emigration taxes and currency conversion at extortionist rates, the postpogrom levy on the Jewish population, and the general confiscations from 1941 on.[41] Indeed, the biggest profiteer from aryanization was indubitably the Nazi state. It eventually raked off 60–80 percent of the prices paid for large-scale property transfers within the Reich and a total of at least some 3 billion of the 7.1 billion marks in wealth that native and stateless Jews possessed according to the compulsory declarations of April 1938, not to mention substantial but indeterminate sums in increased proceeds from taxes on stock market transactions throughout 1938–39.[42]

But less significant for both contemporaries and historians than what the bank made is what it did. Without its participation, aryanization would have proceeded far less smoothly and at a higher cost in economic disruption to the Reich. The regime would have found it virtually impossible to freeze the bank accounts of Jews and deprive them of disposition over their assets, as it did in the summer of 1938, had the Deutsche not been ready, however grudgingly, to enforce the relevant decrees.[43] The bank's own takeovers of Hirschland and Mendelssohn, the former over the energetic opposition of Gauleiter Terboven in Essen, succeeded precisely because foreign creditors were willing to accept the Deutsche as the Jewish firms' successor and thus not renounce the delicate Standstill Agreements governing Germany's international debts.[44] In addition, the funds of Jewish emigré customers that the bank absorbed by acquiring Mendelssohn soon came in handy as a means of refinancing the banks in the Sudetenland and Czechoslovakia that fell to the Deutsche.[45]

Meanwhile, it, like all other major banks, collected the financial instruments with which Jews partly paid the enormous assessment on them after the pogrom of November 1938, and transformed these into cash for the Reich. By allowing its major corporate clients a right of first refusal on any of their own shares in these deposits, and by itself buying packets in certain enterprises, the Deutsche helped ensure that aryanization did not destabilize the stock markets.[46] Finally, though the bank repeatedly claimed that competent, financially qualified buyers for Jewish firms were in short supply, its labors to identify those who were available no doubt reduced the number of jobs and the volume of output that were lost as a result of takeovers.

All in all, then, the Deutsche Bank contributed significantly to ensuring that the only economic losers from aryanization were the Jews, and the chief economic winner the Nazi state. How much difference this made in the horrors that followed is indicated by the fact that funds collected from Jews in the critical budget year 1938–39 provided over 5 percent of the Reich's tax revenues, at a time when intensified spending on preparations for war was running up against declining sales of government bonds. To cite only one concrete consequence of this windfall, the Finance Ministry now withdrew its objection to further government subsidies for the construction of synthetic fuel factories.[47]

Once the expansionism aided by the bank's services began subduing other countries from 1938 on, the Deutsche's role in the pillaging of Jews proved, paradoxically, both less essential to the Nazi regime and more profitable in specific cases to the bank. On the one hand, the Reich developed more comprehensive and politically directed administrative means of conducting the dispossession itself. Intent on restricting the gains of large, private German firms and expanding that of state-controlled ones such as the Hermann Göring Werke; on strengthening or winning the support of ethnic Germans, collaborators, and indigenous firms in the conquered lands; on rationalizing production by liquidating as many Jewish-owned enterprises as feasible; and, usually, on favoring the Dresdner Bank—intent on all that, the Third Reich narrowed the possibilities for gain open to the Deutsche. On the other hand, when it was willing to let the bank participate significantly, the regime often permitted it to reap larger returns abroad than at home, either because the monies involved had been themselves plundered from foreign owners or because an even larger proportion of a property's sales price went automatically to the Reich than had been the case earlier within Germany.[48]

This general pattern was set in Austria following the Anschluss, then refined in the subsequent occupations. The Deutsche Bank's aspirations to take over the state-dominated Creditanstalt Bankverein in Vienna were checked long enough to permit the Reich to serve as both seller and buyer of most of that institution's Aryan industrial assets and to preside over its acquisitions and resales of non-Aryan shareholdings. Not until December 1938, when this process was well along, did the Reich allow the Deutsche to acquire a 25 percent stake in the Creditanstalt, along with managerial leadership; not until 1942 did the bank succeed in gaining majority control. Largely shut out of the Austrian aryanization process until then, the Deutsche thus still gained commissions on the Creditanstalt's sales of Jewish-owned stock, worth 1.5 million Reichsmarks through mid-1938 and probably at least as much thereafter.[49]

It is not yet possible to estimate what the Deutsche Bank earned in other occupied nations where the state applied similar procedures for disposing of Jewish property. In Poland, where all Jewish firms were confiscated by the Main Trusteeship Office East in April 1940, one Deutsche Bank branch listed the assets it was administering for that organization some eight months later. The tally included fifteen properties worth 100,000 to 500,000 marks and five more worth from one-half to one million.[50] There is no reason to assume that this branch was any less active in brokering such sales for the Reich than, say, the Commerzbank's vigorous unit in Lodz, whose records have survived.[51] In the Low Countries, the occupation authorities made clear that virtually the only takeovers in which the Deutsche might participate would be of firms held by enemy nationals or Jews.[52] Accordingly, the bank's affiliate, Albert de Bary & Co. of Amsterdam, busily set about trying to match sellers with the Reich-appointed trustees.[53] As it did so, the Deutsche devoted itself to aryanizing and reselling the shares that two Jewish-owned Dutch firms still held in the former Adler & Oppenheimer, now Norddeutsche Lederwerke, of Berlin; by the time it finished, the bank had turned a profit of 2.75 million marks or 35.2 percent on its efforts.[54]

If historians ever succeed in expanding appreciably on this

sketchy information, the resulting picture of the Deutsche Bank's motives, actions, and earnings may correspond to that provided by its role in the occupied regions for which the extant documentation is most complete, namely the Sudetenland and the Protectorate of Bohemia and Moravia. Here the way in which competitive considerations drew the bank into complicity in persecution, and the depth of that complicity, emerge starkly from the written record.[55] At the center of the story is the Böhmische Union Bank (BUB), one of the four or five principal financial institutions that served the German-speaking population of Czechoslovakia between the wars. With stock capital of about 12.5 million marks, it was worth about 250 million on its balance sheets before Germany annexed the Sudetenland, about 160 million thereafter. Since five of the six members of its managing board and many of its assets were classifiable as "Jewish" under Nazi definitions, the BUB was predestined for aryanization. So, however, was another, financially sounder bank with a similar clientele, the Böhmische Escompte Bank, on which the Deutsche's ambitions initially focused. But the Nazi economic apparatus allotted that enterprise to the Dresdner Bank instead and issued a general prohibition on the founding of branches of German banks in either the Sudetenland or the protectorate. The Deutsche thus faced the choice of either taking over and refinancing the BUB or abandoning a new and potentially profitable portion of the Greater German Reich to its rivals. To make this consolation prize more acceptable, the Reich agreed to cover at least some of the Deutsche's potential losses, notably those attendant on the expulsion or despoiling of Jews, with direct subsidies and tax breaks.[56] It also sweetened the deal by simply assigning the Deutsche 80,000 pounds sterling from the reserves of the Czech National Bank, which were then sold to Jews seeking to emigrate at an exchange rate that brought the German firm 15.8 million marks. With the bulk of this money, the Deutsche bought and refinanced the Deutsche Industrie- und Agrarbank, another Czech firm with mostly German-speaking clients, then fused it with the BUB in hopes of strengthening its prospects.[57] Having thus built a toehold in the protectorate, the Deutsche Bank officers who took over leadership of the BUB proceeded with the internal purge of the firm. By January 1940, they had reduced the number of Jewish employees from 460 (in 1939) to 41; in May, the rest were all given notice.[58]

From 1940 to 1944, the BUB became probably the most aggressively aryanizing subunit of the Deutsche Bank, primarily because, as one of its directors wrote as late as July 1943, its clients were confined to German firms in the protectorate, and "the expansion of German business depends entirely on the aryanization of formerly Jewish enterprises."[59] Accordingly, the BUB and the Deutsche head office in Berlin quickly devised a system for exchanging lists of Czech firms to be sold off and German ones interested in buying up such enterprises.[60] To manage the flow of such business, the BUB formed its own aryanization bureau under Director Pohle from the Deutsche Bank, and this bureau rapidly became the clearing agency for several lucrative transactions.[61] One of these was a deal with the SS, by which the Deutsche sold its claims of over 600,000 marks against the Bohemia Ceramics Works for some 750,000 marks, half paid by the German Finance Ministry and half by the Bankhaus Petschek & Co., a Jewish-owned firm that was being liquidated.[62] A second exchange involved conveying the Metallwalzwerke to Mannesmann at a profit of some 200,000 marks.[63] In still a third instance, the sale of the Kupferwerke Böhmen, in which the BUB owned 38 percent of the stock and acted as broker for about half as many Jewish-owned shares, the BUB earned an interest rate of 5 percent on its outlays, plus the usual commissions, even after being forced by the Reich to accept a different buyer and a lower price than it wanted.[64] Such minor disappointments were more than offset by the proceeds on perhaps the most profitable of the BUB's services: the buying up and reselling, at a commission of about 300,000 marks, of Jewish-owned shares in the Berg- u. Hüttenwerke AG Prag.[65] In all of these cases, the Jewish stockholdings had been acquired—by either the bank or the regime—at depressed prices or by seizure, a fact of which the BUB and Deutsche officials were fully cognizant.

All in all, one cannot yet say how much the Böhmische Union Bank earned on such sales; on the retailing of miscellaneous shares in East European firms that the Nazi state acquired from Jews in Western Europe and the former Czechoslovakia and handed over to the bank; and on purchases of Jewish-owned stock in allied states such as Hungary from 1940 to 1945.[66] What is clear, however, is that the Deutsche's subsidiary became inextricably bound up in the process of plunder during these years—indeed largely dependent on it as a source of income. By 1944, in fact, a large portion of the BUB's assets consisted of the most blatant manifestations of that process, namely the so-called emigration and resettlement accounts of dispossessed Jews (some 25 million marks at midyear, when their worth peaked) and the funds held in the name of the Theresienstadt concentration camp, which came to at least 30 million marks in October of that year.[67] Small wonder, then, that the Deutsche Bank went out of its way to conceal its association with the BUB throughout the war years.[68]

Between the initial and the final years of Hitler's rule, the dispossession and disappearance of first the German and then the European Jews went from being a matter of awkwardness and, on occasion, discomfort for the leaders of the Deutsche Bank to being a matter of course. Throughout, their conduct was governed above all by a pragmatic concern with their own and their enterprise's interests within the context of what they were all too ready to treat as given political conditions. Although few of the bank's executives can have remained entirely immune to the pervasive racism that animated Nazi policy, what emerges most strikingly from the written record of their motives and actions is not their ideological but their *professional* susceptibility to implication in the process of persecution and murder that was the Holocaust. If one reflects on the relevance of these bankers' behavior to human conduct in other times and places, that form of seductability emerges as the most deeply alarming part of this tale.

III. M • E • M • O • R • Y A • N • D M • E • M • O • R • I • A • L • I • Z • A • T • I • O • N

Henry L. Mason

Accommodations and Other Flawed Reactions: Issues for *Verwerking* in the Netherlands

THE MOST GENOCIDAL CENTURY IN HUMAN HISTORY MUST BE COMprehended in all of its unthinkability if there is to be a chance for us to avoid similar or even worse occurrences in the future. This understanding must be more than a scholarly endeavor. The various national societies under whose auspices the unthinkable was perpetrated or tolerated must, as national societies, become aware of the acts that took place within them. The nations' populations and elites must come to terms, must cope, with that past. In this essay, I look at the harsh experiences of the Dutch during World War II—the kinds of experiences requiring coping, or as the Dutch call it, *verwerking*.[1]

The wartime fate of the Netherlands was profoundly tragic and disturbing. Its large Jewish population was almost totally wiped out in the gas chambers of Auschwitz and Sobibor, destroyed more completely than any other nation's Jewish population except for those of Poland and the Baltic states. Its highly regarded civil service contributed significantly to making the German occupation regime a model of efficiency, requiring a minimum of German manpower. The German war economy probably benefited more from production by enterprises and workers in Holland than in any other occupied country. More Dutch volunteers joined the Waffen-SS and the quasi-military labor units of the Organisation Todt than from any other occupied nation, at least proportionately. The "gathering" and concentrating for deportation of the Jews took place more smoothly in the Netherlands than elsewhere in the German realm because of the willingness of Dutch police personnel to participate in these tasks—and because of the efficiency and obedience of the Amsterdam *Joodsche Raad* (Jewish council), instituted by the Germans but staffed entirely by the Jewish elite. In addition to all this, and uniquely among the Western nations experiencing World War II, the Netherlands further had to cope with Japan's occupation of the Dutch East Indies and, after the Japanese surrender, the Dutch attempts to regain control there. Some 140,000 Dutch men, women, and children spent years in Japanese internment camps, again far more people than from any other European nation. The Dutch campaigns against the Indonesian nationalists, after VJ Day, were conducted as tough "police actions" to defeat supposed collaborators of the Japanese whose aspirations were seen as no more honorable than those of the Dutch Nazis.

The *verwerking*, the working through, of the Dutch experience in the war and its aftermath has only since the late 1980s been recognized as an urgent national task. The conventional view depicted the occupation scene as populated by "good" and "wrong" (*fout*) actors: a majority participating in or at least admiring the resistance, and a small minority of collaborationists. With this kind of image, *verwerking* of World War II was generally seen as unnecessary. Nevertheless, deep down there was a current of feeling that *verwerking* was needed, that behavior during the occupation had not just been a battle between good and bad guys. The suspicion developed in the 1980s that the occupation was at best a period of "uncertain and unsafe twilight," a time of anarchy with few certainties.[2] Of course, everyone knew about the heroic February strike of 1941 in Amsterdam, the first and only general strike in a city occupied by the Germans, called partly to protest German measures against the Jews (before their deportation had begun). Also, some 25,000 Jews in the Netherlands did find shelter among their "Aryan" fellow citizens, and perhaps 18,000 of these managed to remain undetected. Still, it was difficult to ignore the many disasters and humiliations of the occupation, particularly the Jewish fate. Some kind of accommodation to the circumstances of occupation had been the only choice open to the Dutch individual; and many individual attempts at accommodation had had horrible consequences.[3]

Topics relating to the wartime experience have not penetrated extensively into the curriculum of Dutch universities. There has been some coverage. For example, Professor Hans Blom gave a special seminar on comparative Jewish victimization at the University of Amsterdam in the mid-eighties. Professor Ido Abram, also of the University of Amsterdam, has been scheduling annually a seminar titled "Education after Auschwitz," with some attention to *verwerking.* No regular lecture course on the occupation appears to be available at any Dutch university, however. As for the high school level, one expert stated in 1991 that Dutch schools did not really teach about World War II. The (then) director of the State Institute for War Documentation, Harry Paape, admitted in 1985 that the elementary and high schools were a constant worry for the institute: no adequate textbooks on the war period had been produced.[4]

Nonetheless, extensive coverage of the Dutch experience did begin to reach a large public in the sixties. Louis de Jong, the long-term first director of the State Institute for War Documentation, wrote a multivolume history of the Netherlands in the period of the Second World War, published between 1969 and 1991. More than 2 million copies of volumes from this series have been sold. In the early sixties, de Jong also produced a television series on this topic, which was viewed by a large audience. In 1965 Jacques Presser published a widely read two-volume book on the annihilation of the Jews in the Netherlands. Other important monographs depicted the role of the Dutch railroads (Adolf J. C. Rüter, 1960), the February strike (Ben A. Sijes, already in 1954), and the forced-labor system (also Sijes, 1966).

These fascinating studies were unique among the countries formerly occupied by the Nazis with respect to their completeness and their popular reception. Yet, as Blom and others have emphasized, publications such as de Jong's and Presser's failed to provoke true *verwerking,* since they were still largely narrative in form and still reflected the spirit of the "good versus wrong" formulations. Only in the late eighties and early nineties would a third generation of researchers and readers ask the kind of analytical questions that could lead to real *verwerking.*[5]

PROBLEMS OF ACCOMMODATION

The "Tolerant" Civil Service

During the disastrous years from 1940 to 1945, governmental functions in the Netherlands were carried out mostly by the regular civil servants. It was basic German policy to preserve the prewar bureaucratic structures and personnel, intervening only sporadically—except in matters pertaining to the Jews, where intervention was constant and penetrating.[6] The queen and the ministers had fled to London just before the Dutch surrender. Therefore, the traditionally nonpolitical permanent heads of the ministries, the secretaries-general, assumed ultimate governmental responsibilities. Unfortunately, neither the secretaries-general nor the other civil service and judicial leaders were prepared for the nightmarish political burdens that the milieu of a Nazi occupation would impose.

The greatest disasters, of course, concerned the fate of the Jews. In successive steps, the Dutch civil service virtually abandoned first its Jewish colleagues and then the Jews in general. In October 1940, all qualifying civil servants and other government employees (including, for example, teachers and streetcar and train workers) had to complete a statement attesting to their non-Jewishness. Jews would be eliminated from all government employment.[7] This so-called Aryan Declaration was signed by 98 percent of civil servants.

At about the same time, the advisor of the secretaries-general for questions of international law, Jean Pierre François, opined that dismissing higher Jewish civil servants and judges would be "understandable" and not "contrary to law" (*onrechtmatig*)—if one took into account the "pathological" hatred of the Germans for the Jews. The elimination of Jewish civil servants would have to be "tolerated," he stated. One might call it a "temporary" measure undertaken to maintain the public order.[8] Professor François's toleration turned out to be important in legitimizing the ever-expanding spectrum of measures against all Jews in the Netherlands, not just civil servants. Gradually they were eliminated from all occupations and employment in general.

A crucial threshold on the path toward the ultimate anti-Jewish measure imposed on Netherlands territory, the deportation to the "East," was crossed by the secretary-general of the interior, Kazel J. Frederiks. In November 1941, he was asked by the German SS chief, Hanns A. Rauter, how he would react if the Germans decided to deport some 14,000 German Jewish refugees who had been granted asylum in the Netherlands (and had already been stripped of their German citizenship by the Nazis before the war). Frederiks informed

Rauter that, as a Dutch official in an occupied country, he would not react at all to such measures by Germans against "their own Jews."

Soon after this episode, the Germans took the next step, this time the deportation of the Dutch Jews—"Frederiks' Jews." Again the secretaries-general did not react, although they had at one time expressed their intention to resign if this were to happen.[9] The secretaries-general claimed they had to remain in their posts "to preserve Dutch interests," since their resignations would be followed by an immediate takeover of all ministries by the Dutch Nazi leader Anton Mussert and his cohorts. Yet it was certainly no secret, even at the time, that Germany would not have allowed a Dutch Nazi takeover, for reasons of legitimacy and efficiency, and distrust of Mussert.

The most powerful secretary-general was Hans Max Hirschfeld, of the crucial Department of Trade, Industry, and Shipping as well as the Department of Agriculture and Fisheries. In announcing he was staying on, Hirschfeld specifically declared that he was accepting the facts of the occupation as imposed by the German presence—and "therefore" any sabotage directed at the Germans would also be against Dutch interests! Since three of Hirschfeld's grandparents had been Jewish, he apparently had been elevated to the rank of "honorary Aryan" by the Germans, an extremely rare largesse on their part. That Hirschfeld stayed in office during the entire occupation demonstrates again how crucial the occupiers considered continuity and legitimacy in their domination of Dutch governmental processes. (Hirschfeld also held important government posts in the Netherlands after the war.)[10]

The Netherlands Supreme Court (*Hoge Raad*) also submitted readily to the realities of the occupation. It accepted the dismissal of its Jewish presiding judge, Lodewijk Visser. The remaining judges argued that if they had resigned in protest, their example might have been followed by numerous lower judges and prosecutors. Such potential chaos in the justice system could not be risked, even in the context of a Nazi occupation.[11]

The Dutch bureaucracy, from top to bottom, strove for accommodation to the occupation: things were to remain as "normal" as possible. (Most officials, after all, continued to receive their regular instructions from their regular superiors. Only a handful had direct contact with Germans: the secretaries-general, the provincial heads, and some mayors and judicial officials.) But the police, at all levels, were an exception to this low-key pattern. While "toleration" may fairly describe the accommodation reached by the civil service, that term hardly suffices to characterize the zealous behavior of the various police organizations in the Netherlands.

The Eager Police

The police proved to be the most eagerly accommodating sector of Dutch society, participating extensively and often decisively in the actions, however odious, demanded by the occupier. Police worked with and for the Germans in searching for people in hiding, for example for downed Allied pilots attempting to avoid capture. Most significantly, they searched for Jews, arrested them, and put them on transports to German concentration or "transit" camps. Typically, in their weekly reports in 1941 on various categories of crime, the Amsterdam police listed thieves, pickpockets, disturbers of the peace, black marketeers, and "persons who refused to register as Jews."[12]

Dutch police units worked in close cooperation with the German police, military police, and SS organizations. Some became virtual dependencies of the German security police, especially in Amsterdam, where 80 percent of Dutch Jews lived. From the very beginning, Dutch police units played prominent roles in the various *Judenaktionen*. In smaller towns and in the country the local police was usually on its own as it carried out the German order to collect the local Jewish families for further shipment. In Amsterdam the newly appointed chief of police (Sybren Tulp, a former officer in the Dutch colonial army) created a special bureau for Jewish affairs in June 1942, as the deportations began. He staffed this bureau, which was soon to become notorious for its brutality against Jews, with policemen who had pro-Nazi records. But despite the creation of a specialized Jewish affairs office, some 90 percent of the Amsterdam police in general seem to have participated in actions against Jews. It was said that police cells always seemed available for Jewish detainees, even when no space was on hand for "regular" criminals. The all-important transit camp at Westerbork, from which more than 100,000 Dutch Jews were shipped to the gas chambers, was guarded by an elite police corps, the Royal Marechaussée.[13]

Willy Lages, the head of the German police in Amsterdam, claimed after the war that without the aid of the Dutch police only 10 percent of the Jews in the Netherlands would have been caught. That figure sounds self-servingly exaggerated, to say the least; but it is undoubtedly true that without the local police providing the eyes and ears attuned to local conditions, the "alien" and grossly understaffed Germans would have run into all kinds of extra problems. According to Arthur Seyss-Inquart, the German boss in the Netherlands, and others, Dutch police became less eager, somewhat less cooperative, by mid-1943—as the news about a possible German defeat had spread. By then, however, most Dutch Jews had already reached at least the transit camp.[14]

Working for the German War Economy

By the fall of 1940, a few months after the invasion of the country, German military authorities had signed armaments contracts worth 740 million guilders with Dutch firms. Soon more than a hundred Dutch companies, with some 55,000 workers, were working full time for the German navy. Fokker Corporation, the famous Dutch aircraft builder, had orders from the Luftwaffe. By 1943, close to one-half of the goods produced in the Netherlands went to the German war economy, including, for example, parts for the V2 missile.[15]

The *Aanwijzingen* (directions) distributed by the Dutch government to higher civil servants back in 1936 had been intended to provide the nation with a guide to behavior in case of enemy occupation. In them, production for the military needs of the occupier was specifically prohibited. Nevertheless, when occupation came, Dutch officials decided not to object to such orders. Secretary-General Hirschfeld argued that production of all types for Germany was necessary in order to maintain the industrial base and social structure of the occupied country—the same kind of reasoning he applied in his opposition to anti-German violence. Refusing any German orders would result in the dismantling and removal to Germany of Dutch industrial plants, he feared, as well as the deportation of their workers.

Dutch workers were not discouraged from accepting jobs in Germany or elsewhere in the German realm. To the contrary, Dutch authorities ruled that workers who declined work in Germany would not qualify for unemployment benefits in the Netherlands. In February 1941, Dutch officials even supported a German decree that threatened detention in a forced-labor camp for any Dutch worker who refused work in Germany. At least 30,000 Dutch workers accepted positions in France in the Organisation Todt, whose main task was the building of an Atlantic wall to stave off the Allied invasion.[16]

The Germans greatly preferred to keep the Dutch industrial complex intact, for all kinds of logistical reasons in addition to their usual concerns for stability and normalcy. And this worked to their advantage. Later, when Allied strategic bombing became a major problem, they were to discover that Allied bombers targeted industrial sites in the occupied Western European nations far less often than ones in the Reich.

The Hapless Joodsche Raad

Both Presser and de Jong (both happened to be Jewish), in their histories produced at the State Institute for War Documentation in the sixties and seventies, are quite critical of the role of the *Joodsche Raad,* the Jewish Council of Amsterdam. This was, de facto, the only organ that represented all the Jews in the Netherlands until their deportation. One of the historians' criticisms concerned the *Joodsche Raad*'s composition. Although 85 percent of the Jews in Amsterdam could be identified as lower or lower-middle class, all the board members of the council (around twenty-one men) came from the Jewish elite. (A butcher was finally appointed to represent the others.) The two leaders and key activists of the council, Abraham Asscher (owner of a large diamond firm) and David Cohen (a professor of ancient history), had served Jewish causes and philanthropies all their lives, and had been honored leaders of the Jewish community. They certainly could not be called cowards. Both could have escaped from the occupied Netherlands but refused to leave their posts. But what they were unable to do was to provide meaningful leadership under the unthinkably hard conditions imposed on the Jews from the very start of the occupation. And what is much worse, as a Jewish honor board (*Ereraad*) concluded in 1947, they ultimately served as accomplices of the Germans in the deportation process.[17]

Asscher once proudly commented to Cohen that they would be

the mayors of Jewish Amsterdam. In his first official speech he emphasized how the *Joodsche Raad* would provide an appropriate setting in which Jews could work and live in an "orderly" manner. Almost no prominent Jew seemed to disagree. The association of rabbis accepted membership. Even the former chief justice of the Supreme Court, Lodewijk Visser, who had organized a Jewish group of his own that refused all contacts with the Germans, sent a representative. Only a well-known professor, Herman Frijda, refused membership: he predicted that the council would become a tool of the Germans.[18]

The Germans had decided to set up the *Joodsche Raad* after the surprising turmoil of the February strike and earlier incidents. The council was to insulate the Jewish population from any contact with Dutch officials and other non-Jewish leaders and groups. It had to publish a weekly, the *Joodsche Weekblad,* where henceforth all German decrees and other rules pertaining to Jews had to be printed: these were no longer to be covered in the regular Dutch press. The *Joodsche Weekblad* was to reflect normalcy; it urged its readers to behave in a calm and law-abiding manner.

Segregation of the Jewish population was a primary function of the *Joodsche Raad.* Typically, when one of the German leaders discovered that former chief justice Lodewijk Visser had had the "brutality" to contact one of the secretaries-general "directly," the council was instructed to warn Visser that for the next such attempt at "direct" contact with a non-Jewish authority, he would be punished with detention in a concentration camp. David Cohen duly notified Visser of this threat. Only through the council could any Dutch Jew, high or low, contact any Dutch agency or official.[19]

The council's most critical functions related to the deportation process. Already in May 1941, on the occasion of an alleged Jewish attack on German personnel, the Germans demanded from the *Joodsche Raad* the names and addresses of 250 "German-Jewish Zionists" who, in reprisal, would be sent to a concentration camp. After some hesitation, Asscher and Cohen agreed to provide such a list. The 250 men named on the list were picked up and shipped to Mauthausen, perhaps the deadliest of the concentration camps. None survived. In May 1943, the *Joodsche Raad* was told by the Germans to reduce its then large staff by 7,500 people, who would be put on the deportation list (from which they had up to now been excused as council staff). Its leaders picked 7,500 names. Those individuals were duly deported.

In general, however, the council did not provide names for deportation purposes: the 250 and 7,500 were the exception. But while the Germans ordinarily decided, from their own lists, which Jews were to be put on a transport, the *Joodsche Raad* did, in fact, make the crucial *"blijf"* ("stay behind") decision. Those on its staff, or otherwise certified as indispensable by the council, were initially immune from deportation, for the moment. Of course, its staff and the "indispensables" were gradually reduced in number as the Germans ran out of other Jews to transport. At the very end, Cohen and Asscher were also deported. They survived. The Germans' list of all Jewish names and addresses had been given to them in 1941 by secretaries from the *Joodsche Raad,* who, using council typewriters, had copied the relevant Jewish data from the Dutch population registers.[20]

After the war a "Jewish honor board" (*Joodse Ereraad*) was set up by the remainder of the Jewish community as a private tribunal to judge the wartime behavior of the *Joodsche Raad* and other Jewish officials. In its opinion of December 17, 1947, the honor board did not find objectionable (*laakbaar*) per se the establishment of a Jewish council on orders of the Germans—but the board found it very objectionable that the members of the *Joodsche Raad* had not resigned en masse when the deportations began: "even a blind man" should have seen how fatal the deportations would be.

On November 6, 1947, while the *Joodse Ereraad* was still deliberating, the public prosecutor of the special court for collaborators in Amsterdam unexpectedly ordered the arrest of the *Joodsche Raad*'s two former leaders, Abraham Asscher and David Cohen. The prosecutor charged that without the collaboration of the *Joodsche Raad,* far fewer Jews would have been deported from the Netherlands. Asscher and Cohen were detained only briefly, but not until July 1951 did the minister of justice formally drop the case, "for reasons of the general interest." Public opinion seemed to agree with letting the case go: if Asscher and Cohen were to be prosecuted, much of Dutch officialdom would have to be prosecuted also, from assorted civil servants and police officers to streetcar and train personnel.[21]

The leaders of the *Joodsche Raad* had hoped they might be able to contribute to the "orderliness" of Jewish lives even during a German occupation; the alternative would be "chaos." Obviously, what really happened at the end of the deportation line was indescribably worse than chaos. Although the postwar honor board seemed to assume that Asscher and Cohen knew about Auschwitz, other knowledgeable observers disagreed. Asscher and Cohen stated after the war that they had known about the mass killings by the *Einsatzgruppen* in Poland and Russia, but that they could not have imagined that Dutch Jews, too, would be killed. They had attempted to send a staff observer along with a train to Auschwitz, but the Germans had naturally refused. (Cohen's mother, three brothers, and sister were gassed at Auschwitz and Sobibor.)[22]

All the groups we have examined attempted some kind of accommodation that they hoped would enhance survival: the tolerant bureaucracy, the eager police, those working for the German war economy, and even the *Joodsche Raad.* Blom, writing half a century later, posits that some of these attempts at accommodation might be considered more favorably today if the Dutch had gotten a lucky break, some more helpful circumstance, at the time[23]—such as did occur in Belgium, Denmark, Norway, and France, where the percentage of Jews victimized was much lower, and the occupation in general somewhat less disastrous. In the Netherlands, unfortunately, there was no "moderate" German military authority battling SS fanatics; no body of local officials familiar with occupations from World War I; no one-year delay in the gathering of the Jews or early liberation before the gas chambers closed down; and no narrow waterway or mountain range leading to neutral territory. The Dutch, therefore, have had to come to terms with, have had to *verwerken,* a particularly flawed set of attempts at accommodation with a particularly ruthless occupier.

ASIAN TRAUMAS

Unlike any other Nazi-occupied country, Holland also had to cope with the occupation by the Japanese of its vast colonial empire overseas, the Dutch East Indies. This occupation had been preceded by the quick, humiliating defeat of the Dutch colonial army.

After their victories of 1941 and early 1942, the Japanese forced 120,000 Western civilians into harsh internment camps; 100,000 of these civilians were Dutch. In addition, 41,000 Dutch military personnel were held as prisoners of war under conditions that blatantly violated the Geneva convention, which the Japanese had not signed. The gruesome camp experiences, followed by a late and difficult return to the Netherlands, made the fate of the internees (35,000 of them children) part of the Dutch problem of *verwerking* in the aftermath of the war.

Even after the Japanese surrender in August 1945, the Dutch did not regain effective control over the colonies, partly because of a large-scale revolt by Indonesian nationalists. Although the Netherlands' military efforts against the nationalists in the period from 1945 to 1949—the so-called police actions—were not altogether unsuccessful from the Dutch point of view, they had to grant the colonies independence in response to international pressure.

The element of "race" inevitably added itself to these Dutch traumas in Asia. The colonial masters had been defeated and then interned by a non-Western power, by fellow Asians of the 70 million "natives" in the colony. The Japanese went out of their way to play the racial card, emphasizing in diverse ways the humiliation of the European master as they claimed to bring freedom and dignity to the Indonesians.[24]

The racial context had traditionally been cloaked in the Dutch East Indies, partly perhaps because of the large number of socially accepted "Indos"—children from the not infrequent marriages between Dutch colonials and Indonesian women, presumably from noble families. Yet there was a deep gap, also socially, between the colonial establishment (including the "Indos") and the "native" masses.[25] Before the war, the Dutch had sternly suppressed nationalist movements; their leaders often faced long-term arrest. One of these leaders, Sukarno, led the large revolt immediately after the Japanese surrender, before any Dutch or Allied troops could move in. The Dutch government and the public underestimated the nationalist fervor and chose to view Sukarno and his fellow nationalists as Japanese quislings. Not surprisingly, the ensuing police actions against them produced their share of "My-Lais," duly recalled—or repressed—when the *verwerking* of decolonization had to be attempted.[26]

Some observers think that even as late as 1985, taboos relating to decolonization, the Japanese camps, and the colonial experience as a whole had not been adequately dealt with by the Dutch.[27] In any case, Asian traumas added to the problems of *verwerking* resulting from the German occupation.

THE ABANDONMENT OF THE RETURNEES

Even an author who can hardly be said to unduly emphasize problems of *verwerking,* Ed van Thijn, was astounded at the evidence of *onverwerkt verleden* ("uncoped-with past") he saw among Dutch citizens returning from the catastrophes of World War II. The Jewish survivors were the most obvious group of these returnee-victims. Others entering or reentering the country, according to van Thijn, were the more than 100,000 ex-internees of the Japanese, the tens of thousands of members of the Moluccan minority fleeing the newly independent Indonesia, and, paradoxically perhaps, the 125,000 Dutch troops back from the police actions in the former colonies. Evidently, liberation and the task of rebuilding the nation did not leave space—real or symbolic—for those whose very reappearance kept in the spotlight tales of previous disasters and failures.[28]

Only in 1990 did the publication of a book by Dienke Hondius adequately reveal how miserable (*schrijnend*) the treatment of Jewish survivors had been when they finally managed to return to the Netherlands. There were no welcoming committees, not even displays of gladness or warmth at the reception centers, if such centers were available at all. One frontier guard officer informed a group of returnees that he was no friend of the Jews. The survivors' stories were mostly disbelieved, and soon the Jewish returnees sunk into silence and frustration. Tales of Dutch Jews' suffering, and particularly of the 100,000 who did not return, were treated as spoiling the merrymaking of the liberation period. Worse, they provoked feelings of bystander guilt. "Whining" Jewish survivors were told they were not the only ones who had suffered under the Nazis. When finally, months after the liberation, the real facts of the Jewish fate in the East became more widely known, traces of sympathy combined with feelings of guilt still tended to add up to an attitude of embarrassed silence toward the survivor. Even then, there was no real effort to make these returnees—dehumanized and stripped of their "Dutchness" as they had been by the Nazis—feel whole again, as equal and worthy fellow citizens. In contrast, resistance fighters were greeted with much enthusiasm on their return from German camps—and unlike the Jews, they were likely to still have intact their families and their homes.[29]

Although the more than 100,000 Dutch returnees from Japanese camps had not faced extermination, 13,000 of the civilians and 8,500 of the military had died there as a result of horrible conditions. These returnees, too, encountered a lack of appreciation for their suffering. Nobody seemed interested in listening to the "old colonials'" tales. Moreover, a bizarre set of legalistic interpretations issued by the government deprived most of them of appropriate financial compensation for the years spent in Japanese camps. Again, no provisions were made for their reentry into Dutch society.[30] Van Thijn also notes the unappreciative reception given the thousands of Moluccan refugees who refused to recognize the new Indonesian rulers. Although the Moluccan men had served loyally in the old Dutch colonial army, they received no special treatment on arriving in the Netherlands, nor consideration for their own traditions. Another poor reception, according to van Thijn, was that of the 125,000 soldiers returning home after the "police actions" against the Indonesian nationalists—similar perhaps to the initial reactions in the United States toward the soldiers returning from Vietnam later in the century.[31]

The returnees were abandoned by the nation. What they needed was recognition of their worth as individuals, as fully qualified participants in the national community after the years of dehumanization in German and Japanese settings. Of course, material aid was also needed, and providing that involved real sacrifices under the conditions of great scarcity in the postliberation period, especially in housing. The material aid given was modest, but perhaps less so than the symbolic assistance. The returning victims did not fit in—partly, one might posit, because of the bystanders' improper *verwerking* of their own guilt as it related to the returnees' fates.

PROCESSES OF *VERWERKING*

In a world dominated by the nation-state system, the individual and collective *verwerking* of events can be crucial for a national society. The society needs to account for its own passive bystanding or worse as genocidal acts were perpetrated on its soil. *Verwerking* is not only important for the internal relations of the national society; it is also needed to help the nation avoid further such occurrences. The efforts of a later generation to understand accommodation to an occupier, for example, may make it possible to do better in a comparable situation in the future.

Processes of *verwerking* are complex and often obscure. Consensus on the effectiveness of an effort is difficult to achieve. Some, such as Blom, argue that only in the late 1980s did the Dutch really begin to face *verwerking* of the Nazi period as an essential task. Others criticize what they term the current preoccupation with the failure: given the huge number of Dutch books on World War II, asks van Thijn, are we really to believe that *verwerking* has only recently begun? Anyhow, he queries, what really is *verwerking:* a container concept, an unsorted shoebox, collective madness, collective failure, or some sort of spiritual flood emergency affecting the entire nation? Who is to engage in the tasks of *verwerking:* historians, politicians (possibly through a parliamentary inquiry), criminologists (perhaps by creating a special tribunal), the media (producing "definitive" documentaries), church leaders, the queen (visiting Auschwitz and Indonesia)?[32]

Another Dutch author, Friso Wielenga, wrote in 1993 about German attempts at *verwerking,* both Germany's handling of the Nazi past and its more recent dealing with the East German "Stasi" past. In his opinion, *verwerking* has to be a continuing process of dealing with the past, a process that is never completed, and its form and content will reflect the changing times. It must be based on a nationwide debate, stimulated by the political and intellectual elites. These elites must give direction to the processes of *verwerking,* and they must also see to the education of the younger generations, making sure they are taught to face the past properly. Wielenga thinks that German efforts at *verwerking* of the Nazi past have been quite successful: the disasters of the Nazi period have indeed burned themselves into the German identity, collectively and individually, and regardless of any particular German's approval or disapproval.[33]

The abandonment of the various Dutch returnees revealed severe flaws in Dutch society, notably its inability to recognize the needs of the returnees to affirm their worth as individuals and restore their ties to the national community and its recent history. Such a recognition would have required a prior *verwerking* of issues relating to the occupation and decolonization.

"Education after Auschwitz" must provide insights into the motivations and mechanisms that made human beings part of the Holocaust. Accommodation was the crucial Dutch response to the occupation. Its quality depended ultimately on the circumstances, judgments, and reactions of each individual and each group. It is the nature of the adjusting or accommodating, individually and collectively, to a hypothetical future extreme situation akin to the Nazi occupation that lends urgency to the study of *verwerking*.[34]

Debórah Dwork

Custody and Care of Jewish Children in the Postwar Netherlands: Ethnic Identity and Cultural Hegemony

GERRY MOK WAS THREE YEARS OLD WHEN THE GERMANS INVADED THE Netherlands. He was nearly five when a friend of his great-aunt's took him from his home in Amsterdam to hide at her house in Hoorn in February 1942. His parents were to come a day or two later. "I loved swimming and so did my mother, and since I figured she might forget to take her swimming suit I packed [it] in my bag. I went into hiding, and I was taken from my family, separated from them, and in the moment that I was separated—the most important thing that happened in my life—I was thinking of the problem of getting a bathing suit for my mother because I wanted my mother to go swimming with me."[1]

She never came. His parents were deported and killed in Auschwitz. The house in Hoorn where Gerry was hidden also was raided, but he was saved by a Catholic family across the street with many, many children who swooped him up into a game of hide-and-seek. He was put in a cupboard.

Gerry subsequently was moved about fifteen times, but the original family with whom he hid, his "foster parents," kept in contact with him wherever he went. "After liberation they came to fetch me from my last address and took me home." Gerry then lived with that foster family, and he went to school, and he waited for his parents to return. "I expected them to come back, reasonable or not, and even notwithstanding the fact that people told me that probably my parents were dead. . . . I expected my parents to come back. I expected everybody to come back. And no one came."[2]

*

It was Gerry Mok's historical fate to be one of the 2,041 Jewish children hidden in the Netherlands who were orphans, united with neither mother nor father, when the war ended. The prewar Jewish community had numbered about 140,000. Between 25,000 and 29,000 survived, of whom some 4,000 to 6,000 were children. Of these youngsters, 3,512 were registered as *oorlogspleegkinderen,* or war foster children; eventually 1,471 were reunited with one or both parents, and 2,041 were not.[3] In the Netherlands, the question that arose, at least in theory, about all 3,512 *oorlogspleegkinderen,* and certainly about the 2,041 children who, like Gerry Mok, were orphans, was: to whom did they now belong?

This problem had begun to plague resisters dedicated to the rescue of Jewish children long before the war ended. "In the summer of 1944 we were involved with formulating a proposal for a law" to deal with the guardianship of Jewish children after the war, Piet Meerburg recalled. An Amsterdam university law student who had organized a network that saved between 300 and 350 children, Meerburg had "felt a responsibility for the children." After all, it was "we [who] had taken the children from their parents," he explained. And what would, or should, happen after the war was "a difficult question. If the parents come back, there is no question."[4] (In fact, in at least a few instances parents were denied rights to their children.)[5] "It may be very hard on the foster parents sometimes, but there is no question. But what do we say if there is an aunt who was coming back who has never seen the child, and she is all alone while the child is completely happy and assimilated in his family? Would he go and live with that aunt who has no child, who has no [emotional] relation with that child? That's why we made the Commissie voor Oorlogspleegkinderen [Commission for War Foster Children], which could decide every single case—based on certain principles, of course."[6]

It was precisely because Piet Meerburg and his co-workers had been so deeply involved with and committed to saving the children during the war that "we felt absolutely that we had the obligation to protect the children" after the war.[7] He was not alone. Many of those engaged in child rescue work worried about the children whose parents would not return. During the summer of 1944, however, a number of child rescue workers were picked up, or deported, or busy, and although it is not known for certain it is probable that five people discussed the first draft of a special guardianship bill to be sent to the Dutch government-in-exile in London. Two, Annie de Waard and Ger Kempe, were members of the university student group the Utrecht Children's Committee. Another, Sandor Baracs, a converted Hungarian Jew, belonged to a Calvinist resistance organization called Trouw (Faith, Loyalty). The fourth, Lau Mazirel, had contact with all the networks; and the fifth was Piet Meerburg.[8]

The perspective these people brought to the task they had set themselves, their vision of who was to have custody of the children and how that care was to be transferred legally, reflected the principles that had guided their underground work—and those differed from person to person. Child rescue work in the Netherlands was not like other forms of resistance: it was not supported financially by the government-in-exile, it had little to do with patriotism, and it was not an activity undertaken by organized (albeit underground) political parties. To the contrary, saving Jewish children was a spontaneous response by, for the most part, university-aged young people who did this work because it was there to be done.[9]

Piet Meerburg was, and has remained, an ardent humanist and an atheist, and for him the impetus to act came out of these convictions. He had no sense of duty to God, no feeling of membership in organized religion or a political party. His thinking was framed by rational humanist principles, and he was impelled to act by what he saw happening to human beings around him.

> One day [early in 1942] I was sitting at the students' club and I was studying with a friend, a Jewish boy. We were sitting together in the club and he was called to the telephone. He came back, and he said to me, "I have to go home, there's something wrong with my family—the Germans." I said to be careful. I never saw him again. . . . Well, if you experience something like that you say, "Why am I studying?" . . . Then (that was about mid '42) things got really bad. You live within the city, you see what happens, you see the razzias [manhunts]. You see the Jewish people picked up, the whole blocks of houses. . . . At that time I said, "I stop my studies." There was only one thing: that you resist these absolutely inhuman and impossible actions of the Germans.[10]

Meerburg went to Friesland to find families who were willing to hide Jews. He was successful and, with local contacts, set up small bases of operation. The other center of activity of the Amsterdam Students' Group, as the network came to be called, was in the south, in the province of North Limburg. With identified homes to which Jewish children could be sent, the group now had to make contact with those who needed to be hidden.

Wholesale deportation of Dutch Jews had begun in the summer of 1942. Marched or driven to a central deportation point—first the Central Office for Jewish Emigration and from mid-October to a theater, the Hollandsche Schouwburg—the arrested Jews were interned prior to their removal from Amsterdam. The adults were kept in the theater; children under age twelve were sent across the street to a day care center, or crèche, which was taken over as an annex to the Schouwburg.

The Jewish director of the day care center, Henriette Rodriquez-Pimentel, and the young Jewish women who assisted her were determined to smuggle the children out of the crèche and pass them on to others who would take them to safe addresses. As the young women who worked in the crèche were not under arrest, they were free to go in and out of the building and, in their backpacks, they carried out infants with pacifiers or bottles in their mouths, praying that the babies would not start to cry. Articles commonly used in the center and therefore not likely to arouse suspicion served the same purpose: potato sacks, food crates, suitcases. Older children had to be smuggled out in other ways. Accompanied by one or two of the staff, toddlers and older children were allowed to go on walks and, at a previously specified point, some were whisked away by an underground worker.[11]

Finally, Pimentel obtained the cooperation of a neighboring institution. At one side of the crèche was a small teachers' training college, the Hervormde Kweekschool. Seen from the street the two buildings were not connected, as there was an alley between them. Contrary to appearances, however, their back gardens adjoined. According to the then-director of the day care center, "The head of the school, Professor van Hulst, saw in the garden that there were a lot of Jewish children and, well, he was good (we call it 'good' or 'not good') so he tried to help. . . . We could bring the children from the garden of the crèche to the garden of the *kweekschool,* and the students and other 'illegal' people came to the *kweekschool* and took them out [by the two side streets], the Plantage Parklaan and the Plantage Kerklaan."[12] As the entrances to the college were not guarded, the controls could be avoided completely.

The training college continued to function as an educational institution and, as before the war, an external examiner participated in the teachers' final examinations. In July 1943, the external examiner was Gesina van der Molen. The founder of the underground group Trouw, van der Molen was already very much involved in resistance activities. She worked on two illegal newspapers, *Vrij Nederland* and her own paper, also called *Trouw,* whose target audience was, like she, Orthodox Calvinist. According to an interview she later gave to the historian Joel Fishman, when van der Molen saw Jewish children in the garden adjoining that of the teachers' college, she exclaimed, "I understand why God led me here. I see my task."[13] By the summer of 1943, few Jewish children were left in Amsterdam to help or hide, so there was not much scope for Gesina van der Molen's considerable energies in that line. A year later, however, the question of the postwar custody and care of the orphans loomed large, and she could, and did, participate actively in formulating those plans. Indeed, it was she who emerged as the central figure, and it was her ideology that prevailed.

Gesina van der Molen was not one of the original five child rescue resisters who worked on the postwar guardianship bill. But as more and more people were arrested or deported, and as those who remained were divided on central issues and too busy with the hundreds of children under their care to meet regularly, and since there were no adult leaders of the Jewish community to participate in these discussions, Gesina van der Molen—strong-willed, severely Calvinist, and a lawyer—took control. The draft of the Law Pertaining to Measures to Be Taken in the Case of War Foster Children bore her signature and her stamp. Passed clandestinely from the still-occupied north of the Netherlands to Eindhoven in the newly liberated south, the bill was sent by courier to the Dutch government-in-exile in London.[14]

It is important to note that this proposal, which with changes was passed into law, was not written by any government official, elected or appointed, nor was it reviewed by Jewish leaders in the liberated south. As the document itself stated explicitly, van der Molen felt that the rescuers' work could not end until the children's future had been ascertained. Her first recommendation was to establish a Guardian Commission for War Foster Children (called OPK) with a central office and a government budget, "to continue and bring to a close the work done during the Occupation, through underground means, for the social welfare of children threatened by the enemy."[15] The system she devised granted to the commission guardianship of all war foster children "whose parents or guardians have not registered [at the OPK office] within one month of publication of this law." In a radical departure from the prewar norm, whereby orphan and foster children fell under the jurisdiction of their religious community officials or the civil child welfare bureaucracy, the commission was to be composed of members of the child rescue groups.[16] Van der Molen believed that the resisters—and not any Jewish community authority or civil child welfare bureaucracy—knew what was best for the children, because it was they who knew intimately the conditions under which the youngsters had lived for the past three years and who had risked their lives for the children.

Lau Mazirel, one of the original five child rescue workers who discussed the bill, advocated an even more socially radical position. Mazirel held that not even the parents themselves were so competent to act in the children's best interests as the resisters were. Surviving parents, she maintained, had no right to children who had adapted successfully to their foster homes. Others on the committee opposed Mazirel, including Ger Kempe, but he, like many child rescue workers, was arrested in the summer of 1944.[17] The committee effectively dwindled to one, Gesina van der Molen, who adopted much of Mazirel's language to effect a political agenda that had little in common with that of the younger woman. "At their request, parents whose children are under the guardianship of the Guardian Commission OPK, will have their parental authority returned to them by the judge when they are physically, spiritually, and socially capable of exercising that authority over their children."[18]

Gesina van der Molen was also eager to erase the differentiation between Jewish and Christian Dutch citizens. No special social or financial assistance was to be made available to "our hidden Jewish compatriots," as that "would generate the impression among Jewish

---

*OPK stands for *oorlogspleegkinderen.*

and non-Jewish Dutchmen that the dual fate the enemy created was accepted also in the liberated Netherlands." Refusing to continue to distinguish between Jews and non-Jews as the Germans had done, van der Molen eschewed divisions of any sort; the goal, she said, was "to come to a true melting together."[19]

By refusing to distinguish, van der Molen also refused to differentiate. Treating all Dutch citizens equally, the bill ignored the special assaults their Jewish compatriots had endured and, consequently, their particular needs. The Calvinist arrogance of the elect that Gesina van der Molen brought to this proposed legislation (reasoning that it was the underground which most clearly had seen the Germans for what they were, and therefore it was the underground workers who most clearly could see what would be best for the Jewish orphans) was matched by the willful blindness of the humanists (who reckoned: we saved Jewish children because they were children, not because they were Jews, and therefore the help to which Jewish children were entitled after the war should be precisely that available to all children).

The Netherlands was liberated on May 8, 1945, and a shorter, modified form of the draft bill was promulgated as an official decision by the acting secretary-general of the Department of Justice. Although this version would become law in August, in May it was merely a decision that, as it transpired, was immediately overturned by the interim military government. A few days after liberation, however, an unofficial OPK commission held a meeting to establish policy guidelines for the reunification of children with their biological families: to prevent disturbing or shocking changes, to maintain a stable environment for the child, in short for the child's own good, close relatives were not to be given the current address of the children they sought to find; parents' requests had to be judged individually on a case-by-case basis. On May 14, OPK opened its doors in Amsterdam at Herengracht 410. Van der Molen, who by this point had taken charge completely, understood that this move was not legal, but she and the commission proceeded as if it were.[20]

In the south, by contrast, the NV (Naamloze Venootschap, or No Name Organization) child rescue network, which had had 252 children under its care, had been delighted to reunite biological families. And in the north, the military governor of Friesland, Aninga, found it ridiculous that family members of the formerly hidden children were kept at bay. Finally and most importantly, a newly reconstituted Jewish communal authority based in Eindhoven in the south, the Jewish Coordinating Committee (JCC), established its own Jewish guardianship association called Ezrath Ha-Jeled, To Help the Child.[21]

Ezrath Ha-Jeled's conception of helping the child was radically different from OPK's vision of the best interest of the child. Supported financially by the American Jewish philanthropic organization the Joint Distribution Committee, and morally and in practical matters by Jewish soldiers from Palestine, the Jewish Brigade, a group of displaced, disillusioned, and disaffected survivors in the south began to implement their project for rehabilitation and restoration.[22] The members of the Jewish Coordinating Committee spanned a spectrum of ideologies ranging from Orthodox to Zionist, and they advocated very different programs for the future. The Orthodox supported the reconstitution of Jewish life in the Netherlands, while the Zionists saw little future for themselves or their coreligionists in their country of origin. On one issue, however, they were united: Jewish children who had survived in hiding and Jewish children who returned from the East were part of the Jewish community. Without the children there was no future for Dutch Jewry, either in the Netherlands or in Palestine. The recovery of the children was so important to them, so central an issue, that people who would not have dreamed of speaking to each other, either before the war or after, were eager to work together to achieve that goal.

Clearly, the positions of the Jewish Coordinating Committee and OPK were in direct contradiction, and little compromise was possible. The JCC wanted Jewish orphans to be returned to the authority of Jewish communal bodies, as would have been the case before the war, when Protestants looked after Protestants, Catholics after Catholics, and Jews after Jews. OPK insisted that the children remain where they were: they might or might not be returned to their parents, they certainly should not be given to other family members, and on no condition were they to be turned over to the authority of the Jewish community. Both parties were convinced that the program they advocated was in the best interest of the child. In fact, of course, whether or not the programs they advocated were in the best interest of each individual child, they certainly served the best interests of their own ideologies.

Despite the attempts of the JCC to enlist the sympathy of the government, the May 8 decision became law by royal decree on August 13, 1945. Framed by the perspective of the child rescue workers, the law did not recognize either the needs or the sensibilities of the Jewish community. OPK was to gain guardianship of those children whose parents did not inform the commission within one month that they were prepared to accept their parental responsibilities.[23] Furthermore, the state attorney had the power to entrust to OPK those children whose parents or guardians were not fit, and OPK itself could petition for such a decision.[24] In other words, Jewish community authorities were cut out entirely, as were family members who had not previously been designated legal guardians, and biological parents could be found unfit to raise their own children. As presumably any living parents who would not have reclaimed their children by the deadline were survivors of slave labor and death camps in the east, this meant that the task they faced upon their return to the Netherlands was particularly arduous. They were instructed to submit a claim for their children which would be decided by the court. They did not, however, have to pay court costs or notary public fees for processing the paperwork.

Gesina van der Molen had anticipated this eventuality, and had addressed it explicitly in the "Explanation" and "Guardian Commission for War Foster Children" sections of the proposal. "Parents who have not registered within a month most likely will be those who were deported from the Netherlands. In general, they will not immediately be able to exercise their parental rights in a manner that is desirable for the child. Therefore, their parental authority will not be restored until they are shown to be competent. It will be bitter enough for them to understand this, and therefore it is necessary not to phrase this explicitly in the law."[25] She went on to say that "the commission will help parents who return from abroad to regain their parental rights. But it will have to be kept in mind that parents who have faced the trials of concentration camps most likely will be alienated from the protected atmosphere in the foster families in which their children grew during that time; in many cases a short transition period will be necessary to allow [the parents] to reaccustom themselves to the Dutch lifestyle, which since ancient times has maintained certain minimum standards of physical and spiritual hygiene."[26]

Many of the explicit and implicit concepts in the bill were not new. The child protection legislation of 1901 had required magistrates to appoint a temporary guardian for any child whose parents' whereabouts were unknown, and the whereabouts of deported parents of Jewish children hidden during the war certainly were unknown. Thus, the appointment of a temporary guardian (in this case, OPK) for the war foster children was in accordance with well-established precedent. The 1901 legislation, however, had provided for the automatic return of a child to his or her parents upon the latters' physical presentation and request; only after that did child welfare organizations have the right to petition for guardianship on the grounds of neglect. The principle that children had to be returned to their parents, that the parents' wish could not be denied, was the subject of heated debate during the first decade of the twentieth century, and the law was modified in 1909. Badly worded and ill-phrased, the legislation of 1909 sought a compromise between the interest of the child and the rights of the parents. It provided for the return of an abandoned child to the parents upon the approval of the magistrate, who was no longer obliged to return a child upon the parents' physical presentation. If the magistrate feared that the parents would neglect the child, it was his right to conduct a hearing (which included the parents, guardian, guardian council, and relatives) to assess the situation. If he found just cause to anticipate neglect, the magistrate could refuse to return a child to the authority of the parents. Thus, the principle of denying parental authority was also well established by precedent in 1944.[27]

The proposed war foster child guardianship bill differed from its legal antecedents in that, ignoring the magistrates entirely, it assigned power and authority to one central body. The magistrates operated on a local level; they were part of and they represented the interests of the local community. OPK, by contrast, was envisioned as a national commission, reflecting a national agenda. By cutting out the magistrates, the authors of the proposed bill effectively silenced the parents' relatives and neighbors. Furthermore, while the 1909 formula for denying parental authority rested on an "only if" clause (parental wishes could be ignored only if, upon conclusion of an inquiry, there was just cause to fear neglect), the 1944 bill introduced an "only when" clause: parental authority would be reinstated only when the parents demonstrated (to whom?) competency.

Whether or not the authors of the bill sincerely assumed parental neglect, they used the neglect clause to carry out their objectives.

The explanatory text of the bill was not included in the royal decree of August 13. As Gesina van der Molen had suggested, a suitably broad and vague clause was introduced instead, but it too carried an "only when" formula: the guardianship of OPK was to be terminated only when it was no longer in the interest of the child. And of course, the court could decide that the committee should *not* relinquish its guardianship to the returning parents.[28] The Jewish Coordinating Committee got the message. The focus of the battle which erupted, however, was not on the rights of the parents or other surviving family members to guardianship of the child. The bitter four-year dispute centered around the claims of the Jewish community versus those of OPK and the gentile foster parents.

The OPK commission—the official guardian agency of Jewish children who had survived the war by hiding with gentile foster families—was appointed by the minister of justice: Gesina van der Molen was the chair, and Sandor Baracs, another member of Trouw, was the director. As on minors' protection boards (which were not guardianship agencies but child welfare advocacy bodies attached to a specific court), all confessions were represented. Of the commission's twenty-five members, ten were Jews by birth; a number were assimilationist in ideology and one was baptized.[29] The child rescue organizations, whose work this commission had been set up to bring to a close, were represented only by members of Trouw. Not one participant of the NV, the Utrecht's Children Committee, or the Amsterdam Students' Group—in short, not one of the three groups who had saved the vast majority, indeed nearly all, of those children who had been hidden through the help of an underground network—was appointed.

The first meeting of the OPK commission was held immediately after the law went into operation, and it was a disaster. A Catholic priest upset nearly all the other committee members when he asserted categorically that all children who had been baptized into the Church were now and forever Catholics, and that they needed to be turned over to the authority of the Church.[30]

A few days later, the leftist newspaper *De Groene Amsterdammer* ran a surprising article on "Jewish Youth" that articulated the position of the Jewish community. The author, Caroline Eitje, pleaded for the return of the orphans to the community. Sympathetic to the foster parents, she acknowledged freely that many of them loved the Jewish children they had raised. But, she pointed out, the children had been "entrusted to them, and what is entrusted must be returned." Eitje believed that Jews—as Jews and as Dutch citizens—had a future in the Netherlands. "The existence of a clearly defined, separate Jewish community is an acceptable and unavoidable reality; it is pure fiction that a Jewish sense of community is incompatible with being a true Dutchman." The problem, she argued, was straightforward: "What community can, with impunity, give away its younger generation, those who embody the future; it would be an enormous disaster for that small remnant of Dutch Jews, which consists mainly of older men and women. They are undoubtedly driven by the desire to repair what was destroyed by the German occupation. But the first condition for that goal is to have a younger generation to continue their work." She concluded, "Without hope for a future there is no sense in beginning a reconstruction which cannot be completed. That is the reason why the Jewish community must demand its younger sons and daughters, and why it cannot make any concession on this point. Gratitude for the foster parents and educators cannot stop it from defending its position on this matter to the very end."[31]

This was too much for a humanist such as Piet Meerburg. "I didn't see, and I still don't see, that the Jewish community had a right to the children," he later asserted. "The family, yes. The family, and to what extent the family, that is the question. [But if there was no family] then the foster parents had a right. These foster parents risked their lives to save these children, [and] I don't think that the Jewish community has in itself a right to the children." To be a Jew simply had no weight for him. "For us, it didn't make any difference if [the child] was Jewish or not Jewish. That had nothing to do with it. If it had been Chinese children we would have done the same." To the contrary: to give weight to Jewish identity, to accede to the principle that a community—the Jewish community—has a right to its children is, he believed, "a very dangerous point of view. I can understand very well that the Jewish community, which has such terrible losses, wants to compensate, wants to grow, wants to build. But I think that, in principle, I am too liberal for that. The only thing that matters is the welfare of the child itself, not the Jewish community. And I don't give a damn about that. (May I say that?) And I think it's not right because it is dangerous. Then it becomes a racial question. I hate that. I can understand that the Jewish community wants to fulfill all the losses, but oh my God, I think we shouldn't do things like that." Piet Meerburg had no stomach for the quarrels and divisions. "I'm happy that I didn't have to be present at those fights because that was not—I won't say my interest—but I didn't want to be confronted with that. I think that's a not so nice side of it. Maybe I'm a coward not to face that, [but] in that battle, I didn't want to be involved. I quit."[32]

Gesina van der Molen, by contrast, did not consider quitting for a moment. In an interview published in *Trouw* on June 13, 1945, she presented her position to the general public. "Our commission . . . considers the issue a Dutch affair, which must be solved in a national—Dutch—manner." Her plan, therefore, was to act in accordance with what the parents would have wanted. "The wish of the parents comes first. This always will be respected. But often this is not known and then we have to act according to probabilities." In other words, "if it can be shown that it is very likely that the parents would have wanted an Orthodox or Zionist education, then the children will be taken to a Jewish family which is both willing and able to treat the child and raise the child completely as its own. If such a family cannot be found, then we will have to place the child in a Jewish institution. It is different with children about whose parents' wishes nothing is known, or of whom it reasonably may be assumed that the parents would not have wanted a Jewish education. If . . . the foster parents would like to keep the child, and are capable of raising it in a way which befits both its talents and its social class, and if, moreover, the child has grown into that family, then we do not want to cut those ties. In this we differ from, for example, the Zionists, who absolutely want to bring the children back into a Jewish environment."[33]

The weakness of van der Molen's plan, however reasonable it may have appeared, was that the placement of the child depended on someone's (whose?) interpretation (how?) of the wishes of the parents. For van der Molen these questions were not problems. In an article on "Theft of JEWISH CHILDREN?" in *Trouw* a year later, she continued to insist on the central role of the underground child rescue workers, to rail against the Jewish community's demands for the children, and to assess the wishes of the parents on the basis of a phantom scale of Jewish identity. "In most cases the children were entrusted by the *parents* to resistance workers, and in other cases [the resistance workers], on their own, spirited them away from the Germans. Does the Jewish community really have the right to demand the children now?" Indeed, she wondered, were these children so Jewish after all? "Do these Jewish children really belong to the Jewish community alone? Even if the parents did not have one single tie to Judaism? Even when they felt more Dutch than Jewish? Even when they showed that they were attracted to Christianity?"[34]

Van der Molen's scale measured Christian preconceptions and prejudices, not Jewish identity. It reflected what Calvinists thought Jews should do to be good Jews, not how Jews saw themselves. Earnest and well-meaning but perfectly ridiculous investigations were conducted to determine parents' degree of Jewish observance, and therefore their degree of Jewish identity, and therefore their presumed child-rearing practices and education plans for their children. Despite the efforts of the Jewish minority on the OPK commission to educate the gentile majority about the meaning and importance of culture as well as customs, the non-Jews remained woefully ignorant and wonderfully oblivious. Basing their assessments and analyses of the prewar behavior of the parents on documentary evidence and the testimonies of friends and relations, the majority argued, for instance, that the parents were not really Jewish because they had not kept a kosher home, or because they had worked on Saturdays.[35] Perhaps they married in synagogue only to satisfy their own parents; maybe they belonged to the community merely out of habit.[36] In case after case, the commission denied a "positive Jewish environment" in the home of a child's parents, and recommended that the child remain with the foster parents.

The judges invariably accepted its opinions, and indeed sometimes went further. In one instance reported in the *Nieuw Israelitisch Weekblad,* a judge ruled that, even though the father had attended synagogue regularly and the parents had kept a kosher home, they obviously did not have a Jewish way of life because their little girl had eaten non-kosher cookies in the home of a non-Jewish neighbor.[37] In another case, the judge ignored the testimony of three women, survivors of Auschwitz, who attested to the wishes of little

Hannie Morpurgo's mother. Before her death, she had asked them to make sure her daughter received a Jewish education. The judge found, however, that the woman had been incapable of thinking logically.[38]

Van der Molen spoke the postwar liberal rhetoric of Dutch citizenship and Dutch identity—all Dutch citizens should be simply and solely Dutch—but she supported a deeply conservative political goal of assimilation, and a Calvinist religious agenda of saving souls. She operated on the *a priori* assumption that dual loyalties were impossible, and that the best thing that could happen to a Jew would be to become a Christian. The majority of the OPK members shared her views.[39] The Jewish Coordinating Committee and the Jews on the commission understood this only too well but, a fragile and traumatized minority, grateful to the committee's resistance members, and lacking the political base (none of the Catholic, Calvinist, or humanist liberal parties offered support) or resources to mount a concerted campaign, they could do little. Frustrated, they walked out.

The leadership of OPK evidently felt that the Jews were a greater menace off the commission than on it, and nine days later (on July 26, 1946) the director, Sandor Baracs, sent a circular to all foster parents with Jewish children in their care to remind them that OPK was "the only organization with official authority over war foster children." By law, the foster parents were "obliged to give information only to [OPK] and its representatives [and] to follow only the instructions which have been given by or in the name of the commission. It is therefore in no way necessary—and in many cases even highly undesirable—that you give information about your foster child to other organizations or individual persons." "I tell you this," he warned the foster parents, "because I know that, on a large scale, individuals and also representatives of Jewish organizations visit foster parents of Jewish war foster children. . . . Confusion and uneasiness on the part of both child and foster parents are the unhappy result." Writing in time for the school summer vacation, Baracs emphasized the legal obligations of the foster parents. "You are not allowed to give your foster child to any other person, except with written authorization by this office. This also applies to vacations, and so forth."[40]

Outraged by both the content and tone of the circular, Reine

Friedman van der Heide, director of the social division of Ezrath Ha-Jeled, wrote a pamphlet on *The Jewish War Foster Child* to explain the minority position. Published in November 1946 and widely distributed and circulated, *Het Joodse Oorlogspleegkind* clarified the issues at stake: the infringement on the traditional autonomy of religious communities in the Netherlands, and the sheer impertinence of the majority's arrogation of authority on the question of Jewish identity. No community before the war had suffered such treatment, and only the Jewish community had to bear it now. "In the Netherlands of 1939 just as in the Netherlands of 1945 it would be inconceivable that a commission with a majority of non-Catholics would determine . . . the significance of sacraments such as baptism, confession, marriage, and so forth. But . . . it is [now] acceptable for a group with a non-Jewish majority to decide what significance can be attached to membership in one of the Jewish religious congregations, a synagogue wedding, yes, even circumcision."[41]

The Jewish community newspaper, the *Nieuw Israelitisch Weekblad,* published a call to arms that same month. Now was the time for the survivors to act. "The Jewish community must demand its rights in a clear voice. . . . What is going on here has to do with the rights of Jews. We demand that only Jews be considered experts on the Jewish upbringing of Jewish children. And that the Jewish clergy have the final word in the evaluation of Jewish religious practices for Jews." No circular such as that of July 26 must ever be sent out again, the author, Awraham de Jong declared, and no non-Jewish committee may meddle in specifically Jewish affairs.[42]

A year and a half after the liberation of the Netherlands, the government at long last considered the wishes of its Jewish citizens on this issue. A three-person committee, chaired by the well-known and very assimilated Jewish jurist E. M. Meijers, was appointed by the Minister of Justice to mediate between the two factions. To everyone's surprise, the Meijers committee supported the Jewish minority. OPK was ordered to cooperate with Ezrath Ha-Jeled. Furthermore, any parent who was a member of the Jewish community in 1940 was to be considered a Jew, and therefore to have wanted his or her child to be raised as a Jew. The Jewish ex-members of OPK withdrew their resignations.[43]

Court battles continued to be waged about the detrimental psychological effects of removing a child from a foster home, and about the Jewish identity of parents. But the minority now had clearer guidelines to which to refer, and a more secure legal foundation for its position. That foundation was so secure, in fact, that it changed Gerry Mok's life irrevocably.

"[My foster parents] were asked whether they would mind if, for a Jewish holiday, I would be in Jewish surroundings, to which they said, 'Oh no, of course not, fine, he is a Jewish child,' and so on. So I went to several parties. One day, I went to a Hanukkah party, and they [my foster parents] came to fetch me, but it turned out it was an Aliya Bet group [an organization that organized illegal emigration to Palestine], and they came to fetch me but they did not get me." In short, as Gerry Mok himself put it, "So I became a legal affair and a court affair, and in the end I was put into the Jewish orphanage. . . . The court took the decision that I should go to that orphanage and stay there until I was twenty-one, which I did."[44]

We have heard about the Protestant, liberal humanist, Jewish, and Catholic positions on the subject of the *oorlogspleegkinderen,* but we have heard very little from the children themselves. The adults published their views at the time, and their quarrels and battles are part of the political history of the Netherlands. The children, however, did not record themselves in print; they were not public figures. Indeed, in this story they can be seen merely as property: to whom did they belong?

If this were the only history to be told, if this were the only way to think about history and to write history, then the controversy over the war foster children in the Netherlands would be of limited interest. It would be just another, perhaps a bit startling, version of our paradigm that "society" consists of productive or participatory members, and the only place of children in that scheme is as future participants, the citizens of tomorrow. Thus, the usual theme of history written ostensibly about children has been child-rearing practices and education, how adults develop the next generation of adults. In such histories young people are the pawns, not the players, and while these histories tell us a lot about the adults who shaped the children's lives, they tell us very little about the experiences of the young people themselves.

Seen from this perspective, the history of the *oorlogspleegkinderen* tells us a great deal about how adults use children to further their own projects, whatever they may be. It lays bare the divisions within Dutch society (which, as it happens, also applied in other countries in Europe after the war). And it can help us to sharpen our critical and analytical assessments of current programs and policies: perhaps, knowing this history as we do, we may ask different questions of and about our own projects.

The history of the very public fight over the war foster children will not tell us anything about the young people themselves, however. It is they, and only they, who can tell us what it meant to have been in hiding; to have waited—if they were old enough to remember—for their parents; to have been disappointed, as Gerry Mok was, or to have been reunited with that memory-in-the-flesh. What relationship did children have with their foster families during the war? How did children whose parents did not return cope with that loss? And how did children whose parents did return negotiate the transition from one family life to another?

Much of the discussion about the war foster children was, and still is, rooted in the myth that Jewish children had become an integral part of their foster family—that, as Joseph Goldstein, Anna Freud, and Albert Solnit put it in *Beyond the Best Interest of the Child,* they "had grown intimately into the families of their foster parents."[45] While many children had developed close relationships, they did not necessarily feel utterly at home there, and many other children did not have warm ties at all. It is important to remember that children were sent to people who were willing to take them and who were trusted not to betray them; considerations of "a happy family" or "a stable home" were superfluous. The mortal danger posed by the Germans and their allies had prompted the gentile hosts to offer shelter, just as it had forced the children to seek refuge. These were neither love matches nor true adoptions; Nazism, altruism (mostly), greed (sometimes), and need brought them together.

Very young children, newborn to the first or second year of life, who were in hiding but living visibly passing as gentiles, may have fit in seamlessly with their new families. But even three-year-olds, even if they could live openly with people who loved them, felt the burden to adapt—which means, of course, that they were not "at home." Max Arian was one of the children looked after by the NV group. When he was not yet three years old, he was taken from Amsterdam to a temporary address in the south of the Netherlands. "I think I learned a lot there that has to do with the whole building of my character," he recalled. "I learned to be silent, not to sit in the window, be sweet and be a nice little child." Shortly thereafter Max moved to the Micheels family, where he was very much loved. Even there, however, he molded himself into a boy who would be little trouble or bother, and would therefore be allowed to remain. "I think I acted. I don't know. After the war I found out that I liked many things that were crazy. [For example] I'm the only person I know who likes a little skin in his milk. Nobody ever likes it. I reconstructed it. Perhaps at that time already I got used to wanting the milk with the skin." To like what his foster brother and sister detested was a way of fitting into an empty space in the family. "Also, my foster mother would tell me that I liked so much home-fried potatoes. Now here in Holland, it's kind of a left-over [food]. You first cook the potatoes and then the next day you fry them. I still love them. It's very nice to eat. She was ashamed when the neighbors would come and I would be eating fried potatoes and they would eat bread because it would look like she would give me something worse. But I still liked it! And I still like it. So that's an adaptation you do being hidden."[46] By transfiguring his own desires, Max Arian transformed himself from the stranger, the outsider, the little Jewish boy, into a child his foster family not only could but would treasure and cherish.

This sort of obvious and insidious pressure to adjust, adapt, and conform was not healthy for either the foster parents or the children. Inevitably, it occasionally led to the psychological and sexual abuse of the children. Ineluctably, for young children it was an obstacle to building up an integrated sense of self. And inexorably, in the case of older children, it caused a certain disintegration of their former identity. Children in hiding but living visibly, like Max Arian, and children in hiding and hidden (those living a totally concealed existence) were in a complicated and fragile situation. They were vulnerable and they had no rights. They had no choice but to adapt to the customs and manners of the family that hid them. They recognized that their hosts risked a great deal on their behalf. They felt they ought to be grateful, and tried to please. The assertion of their own likes, dislikes, desires, former habits and customs was out of the question. As Gerry Mok explained, "I always had the feeling that I was not behaving as if I were myself, but as if I were somebody else. I took my new identity and tried to live in that new identity."[47]

Max Arian and Gerry Mok lived with families who were fond of them. Other children did not. Another man who was then a hidden boy, Max Gosschalk, remarked, "When the war was over, I didn't want to see any of [the people who had hidden me] again because somehow no one ever understood what they were doing."

> I came from a safe home. [In hiding] I had to understand so many things which I could not understand. You had left all your safety, all your security. You had to grow up in a week; it's not possible. But you felt so insecure. If you took something with you it was always fear; fear of being caught, fear of being tortured, fear of betraying other people. Those are three of the worst. You never got any love from anyone. As a young person, I've been in the houses of wonderful people. And I never could trust them because today I was there—how long? One week, two weeks, nobody ever said anything. Then suddenly, something new. Never a chance of getting attached to someone.
>
> If I had been in the position of the people who hid me, I would do it differently or I would not do it. They were hiding not a Jew but a human being, a child at that time, [and that they did not] recognize. You never were welcomed; you were tolerated.[48]

It was not easy to be in hiding, whether openly passing as a gentile or hidden from the world. The children were hard-pressed: safe for the moment, but also trapped by gratitude and self-abnegation. They lived with people whom they felt obliged to please and toward whom they were beholden because they, the gentile adults, allowed the children to live, because they risked their lives also, because they too lived outside the law. Not only did this unnatural situation preclude a healthy relationship between hider and hidden, it also reinforced the prevailing ethos that to be a Jew was despicable and dangerous. What kind of pride or dignity, self-esteem or self-respect was possible when one was forced to feel grateful for what should have been one's right? Children in hiding were denied a normal childhood, and they were robbed of all that would have ensued from such a youth: education, development of abilities, models for familial relationships, a normal socialization process. Instead they suffered deprivation and a persistent psychological dilemma between the (usually silent) assertion of their right to live and a (too often manifest) gratitude toward those who protected them.[49]

For Jewish children old enough to remember, the memory alone of family life was a source of strength and solace. Children who were separated from their parents when they went into hiding remembered them as they were at the time of parting. Throughout the war they preserved the hope or dream that some day the family would be reunited. In a vague, inchoate way, they expected that when the war ended they would resume their former life, and the old structures and certainties would be restored. They never were, of course.

Maurits Cohen was eight years old when he went into hiding; his older brothers who also hid were ten and eleven. Neither older brother survived. One was picked up by the Germans when he bicycled into a nearby village. The other was hiding with a different family and attended the local school; he had been told to say that he was an evacuee from Rotterdam.* One day, German soldiers, tipped off to this scheme, entered his classroom and asked which children came from Rotterdam. The little boy said he did, and he was caught. Maurits Cohen was not told of these tragedies at the time. "I learned of everything after the war," he explained. "During the war, I was a child and I was engaged with everyday living. The very impact of the consequences of the war I experienced after the war ended. My war began in 1945, and not in 1940. When I learned that my father and mother would not come back, and my brothers, then the war started."[50] Long after liberation, Maurits, like many other children who had been hidden, still hoped his parents would return.

> For years after the war I maintained that hope. . . . When you are with your parents, you identify with your parents, you are one, you form a whole, you feel at home. To feel at home, I think, is the most important feeling for a human being; feeling kept, feeling secure, feeling at home. . . . But when you are in hiding, you know it is temporary, these people are looking after you. As long

*Bombed extravagantly by the Germans during the first days of their campaign against the Netherlands, Rotterdam was reduced to ruins. Municipal records and church registers had gone up in flames. With no proof to the contrary, Jews could claim they were Christians from Rotterdam.

> as you try to hold on to the thought that it is temporary, you don't have to get involved with these people too much—but yet it is difficult because you want to have a father or a mother, or at least something that looks like it. So as a child I was looking forward to the time that everything is together again, everything is safe again. And that doesn't mean that everything is without Germans again, but that everything is with your father and mother again.[51]

The children discovered after the war that their dreams had been fantasies, their hopes, illusions. Very few nuclear families were reunited in their entirety, and no extended family escaped without losses. Maurits Cohen went to live with an aunt who "after everything she had experienced, having lost everything, her family, was not able to give me motherly love." She could not "replace my mother," and her husband "could not replace my father—not even for a part." Many things had happened to Maurits Cohen during the war. "A man was shot before my very eyes and I had to flee in the middle of the night, I, a young child, it was most traumatic, with Germans running after me." Nevertheless, and he was very clear about this, "the impact is not half as great as realizing that I didn't have a mother and I didn't have a father. All the time, I had to say yes to [to acknowledge] that fact. Everything else is less important. Coping with the consequences of the war, right after the war and nowadays, what's happening with my own self, being a Jew in the middle of a non-Jewish environment, [took and] takes over."[52]

Gerry Mok, Maurits Cohen, indeed thousands of Jewish orphans had to accept and assimilate the loss of their parents after the war. Fewer children were united with one or both parents, but for no one did the past return as it had been, and the adjustment was not easy for anyone. Betty Knoop and her twin brother were four years old when they were sent into hiding, and their younger sister was one. The three children went to different families, and although they were geographically close to each other, they did not see each other once during the war. The couple with whom Betty lived was very poor; they had a tiny house with no electricity or running water. "They were already married fifteen years, they had no children, and I was received there as their child," she remembered. "I never knew I was not their child; I thought I was. They never, never, never talked to me about my parents, and I forgot in those years that I had a brother and sister."[53] She called her foster parents "Mother" and "Father," and forgot about the past. Betty's biological father was killed, but her mother returned and looked for her children.

> It was very shocking when, after the war, my mother came to see me there, and they told me, "This is your mother." What is this? I didn't want to believe it. Only because the resemblance between my mother and myself was so great, I had to believe it. If not, I would have had many more problems. It would have taken years—because I didn't want to believe it. Also later, when I was reunited with my brother and my sister, I was convinced they were my brother and sister only because of the resemblance. Especially when I was taken away from that family, and my mother took me again—[both] the resemblance and the taking away—it was like I was torn apart. This was a very bad period emotionally.[54]

The situation did not improve quickly. "Finally we came back, the three of us, the children, and then the problems started for my mother. She was a widow without any money. Actually she had two [eight-year-old] children who were not too happy to be with her again. We always said we had a much better life there [with our foster families]." In short, she concluded, "We were very difficult children. Whatever my mother did, we said we weren't happy. We said we wanted to go back."[55]

Gerry Mok, Max Arian, Maurits Cohen, and Betty Knoop had very different experiences after the war: Gerry was sent to a Jewish orphanage, Max was returned to his mother and grandmother, Maurits to an aunt who had converted and her Calvinist husband, and Betty to her mother. But there are commonalities, and a certain pattern emerges from their oral histories. First and obviously, they all had difficulties. What is less obvious, but equally true, is that the decisions, and the moves, and the feelings and adjustments immediately after the war were only temporary. The *oorlogspleegkinderen* legislation that was passed, and the battles that were fought, reflected the paradigms of legal thinking: the need, in law, to simplify issues, to create clarity. In the case of these children, that clarity may have been more destructive than constructive. The structure of either/or choices—either the foster parents or the biological parents, either the foster parents or the extended family, either the foster parents or the Jewish community—failed to accommodate the childrens' own real needs. The social apparatus itself (the law, the social workers' investigations, the court proceedings) was not flexible or supple enough to meet the needs of someone so rapidly evolving as a child.

Gerry Mok was attracted to the Jewish community and attached to his foster family. He sensed the duality then and, as he grew older, understood it better. The Aliya Bet group that kidnapped him in 1947 urged him to emigrate to Palestine; his foster parents did not want him to leave them or the country. "'If he wants to go to Israel later, fine, but we want him to be educated,' [they said,] which I think is a reasonable approach. The other approach was also reasonable. That's the trouble. There were two contradictory reasonings. The Jews in this country were convinced at the time that there was no place for Jews in this society. Although it turned out not to be true, it was true nevertheless because it was the Dutch police who took us from our home. It was the Dutch who waved us good-bye. It was the Dutch that confiscated our property."[56]

The legal case began when Gerry was ten years old, and he was torn:

> I did not want to go to Israel. I was very curious to see Israel, but I didn't believe my parents wouldn't come back. And I still didn't believe it; it was 1948 but there was no reason why I couldn't wait and expect them to come. So I didn't want to go to Israel and not be here to be met. Each day I read in the paper that some miracle had happened and that somebody turned up after all those years anyway. So there was no way I wanted to go to Israel.
>
> Apart from that, Jews told me that you couldn't live with non-Jews. I had lived with non-Jews for five years at the time, and I knew for myself that that wasn't true. That's the other side of the story. . . .
>
> So I had this mixed feeling of, on one hand, nice that finally people spoke my own language, used my own words, could understand my own jokes—which was really important. . . . So, I didn't want to go, but on the other hand, I was very much attracted by the whole thing of Judaism and Jewish atmosphere. So I didn't know what I wanted. All I knew was that I wanted to stay with them, but on the other hand I didn't want to stay with that family because I knew also that it was not home, it was a different social atmosphere, a different social background.[57]

In the end, Gerry knew he was "a stranger in the house. I knew I belonged somewhere else, and the somewhere else didn't exist any more."[58]

Max Arian, by contrast, was not faced with an either/or decision at the time or later, and he negotiated the transition with greater ease. In August 1944, his foster parents received a letter from Mrs. Arian, and they began to prepare the by then four-and-a-half-year-old boy for her return. "Of course I said, 'I want to stay with you, I don't want to go with this mother I don't remember anymore.' And they said, 'We won't give you to just anybody!' So I think I hoped I could stay with them, because I was very, very happy there." Max called his foster parents "Uncle" and "Aunt," and in retrospect he has come to believe that this "made it very clear that they weren't my parents," and this knowledge helped him allow someone else that place.[59] One day, his mother came by car; "the car stopped and a lady got out. That's what I remember, and the rest is the story of my foster father. He said he looked out the window and he saw my mother getting out of the car and she just picked me out of that crowd of little children [playing in the street]. My mother asked him later on, 'Why did you give me Max so easily?' . . . And my foster father said, 'When you picked out Max from all those children, of course we knew you were the mother of Max. It couldn't be otherwise.'"[60]

Max left with his mother, but she promised they would return as soon as possible to stay for a few days, and she kept her word. While they were visiting with the Micheels family, they heard that a transport of people returning from the East would arrive, and the whole group went to the station. Max's grandmother was on that train. She was very thin and extremely frail. "My foster parents said that they wanted us to stay, and also my grandmother. . . . They cared for my grandmother very well; they gave her very good food, and she could rest."[61]

When Max's grandmother had regained her strength, she and her daughter and grandson returned to Amsterdam. It was not easy for Max. He felt, he said, as if there were a glass wall around him, and he himself was "distracted, dreamlike, closed into myself, having dialogues with myself." Both his mother and grandmother had been widowed by the Judeocide, and "small as I was, I had to take an emotional responsibility for my mother and my grandmother." Little by little, the situation improved for the women and for Max. They took up the wholesale fruit business which had been Max's grandfather's trade, and "although it was very difficult, because this whole business is a very male thing, my mother made a living. We had a small house, I lived with my mother and my grandmother, it was a peculiar situation. And of course, I longed very much to go back to Limburg. And they let me."[62]

The Catholic foster family in Limburg and the Jewish biological family were linked through Max, and the ties were never cut.

> My mother would go, she would stay by herself with my foster family. Or she would go with me. Whenever it was possible, she would go. I was very young when they sent me alone on the train. I think I was eight years old. So as a very young boy, they would send me, and in my memory I was there on Easter and on Christmas, always on Christmas. I think every Christmas I was there. And some of the summer holidays too, when I was young. I did that even when I was a university student, for fifteen years. Only when I was married did it change. And always I was very happy there. I would play in the street, as a child, or I would go bicycling. It was very, very free.[63]

Far from an either/or proposition, Max Arian had two families, one Catholic, one Jewish; one in the country, and one in the city. As he grew older, he realized that his mother's ideas about his future and his place in society were different from his foster parents'. She took it for granted, for instance, that he would go to university; they did not understand it. He also came to recognize that his own ideas, his own interests, were closer to those of his mother and other surviving relatives than to his foster parents'. But his relationship with them "always stayed very, very close and very good."[64] He was a member of that family. He went to their weddings and to their funerals; he belonged.

Betty Knoop did not visit her foster parents after the war. She resolved the conflict of "being torn apart," of both being separated from her foster family and of quite clearly resembling her mother, by becoming a social worker. "Although I would not advise it to anybody now, I chose the profession of social worker only because of what I had learned in my early childhood. I could not choose any other profession." She transmuted what she had seen and experienced—"reunion, separation, the influence of the father, of the mother, bad marriage, alcoholism"—into understanding and empathy for her clients.[65] And her mother did not give up or give in. No matter how difficult her children were, she persevered. "It was not so easy for her, but I had a fantastic mother. She lives near to our neighborhood now. I think she spoiled us more than is normal because we had no father, and she gave us whatever was possible to give. Nothing was refused. And I really had a wonderful childhood with her."[66]

Maurits Cohen's integration of his multifaceted past clearly illuminates the underlying issue of identity. During the war, he had been hidden by Christian people and, during those periods when he was "passing," he himself was at least externally a Christian. After the war, he went to live with his converted aunt and her Christian husband. "So I got, next to my Jewish identity, a Christian identity." This was extremely important when he chose a career. "In those days, I thought the best way to show that I am alive, contrary to the whole family which isn't, was to become a person who is able to help other people. And I thought that would be the ministry." Maurits did not see himself as solely Christian; this was not an either/or proposition. "During that time, my Jewish identity was present but small. It was vital but not grown up. So after ten, twelve, thirteen years of the ministry, which were rather successful years, I think, I felt there was a shortage in my life, that I do not fulfill my own needs of being a Jew with other Jewish people."[67]

Realizing that he was both a Christian and a Jew, he understood that he could not ignore either strand of his youth, nor could he allow one to overwhelm the other. "There came a day when my Jewish identity became so suppressed by this other world that I decided to leave the Christian world and to go back into the Jewish world," Maurits explained.[68] "It was a homecoming. The first evening I was in synagogue, a woman sat three benches in front of me, and she had a big blue number on her arm, and I thought, 'I belong to you and you belong to me.'"[69]

Max Arian became a well-known and highly respected editor and journalist for the left-wing weekly *De Groene Amsterdammer.* Married, a father, and then a grandfather, he maintained the Christian–Jewish duality of his youth in his social vision of respect and tolerance. Gerry Mok also became a journalist, and the political editor of the conservative weekly *Elsevier.* He too married, and he had a daughter. Clear and combative, he translated the either/or choices of his past into a profoundly political vision of contemporary life. Betty Knoop (married, with children) became a social worker who, as we have seen, metamorphosed her experiences into empathy with and understanding of others. And Maurits Cohen (married and divorced, with children and grandchildren) transformed the apparently irreconcilable opposition of either a Jewish or a Christian identity into a constructive duality.

The history of children such as Gerry Mok, Max Arian, Betty Knoop, and Maurits Cohen provides us with a new and different perspective on the postwar controversy over Jewish children in the Netherlands. Through them we can see with startling clarity that the *oorlogspleegkinderen* controversy was over the children but not about them, and in the end it is they who were the battlefield. There were two issues at stake for the adults. The first was the ever-unresolved problem of balancing the collective against the individual good. (What was best for "the Jewish community" was best for the Jewish child. What was best for "the new Netherlands" was best for the foster children.) The second was the equally persistent problem of the hegemony of the dominant culture. Indeed, the children were called "war foster children" and not "war orphans"; they were seen from the perspective of the gentiles who took them in, not from their own situation of loss and devastation.

Analysis of the history of the children does more than foreground the issue of adults' interests, however. From the half-century postwar history of now-adult children such as Mok, Arian, Knoop, and Cohen, two distinct patterns emerge. First, when it comes to children, every plan, every program, and every solution is marked for obsolescence. The needs of a four-year-old are different from what the needs will be when that child is fourteen. Understanding this problem from the children's perspective gets to the heart of the question of identity: are they who they think they are, or who society thinks they are? While adults may have a more fixed identity, and a single, definitive solution may work for them, children are, by virtue of their age alone, growing and evolving. The second pattern that has emerged is that, one way or another, each child has integrated the prewar and wartime experiences with his or her postwar life. It turned out to be impossible to create a caesura in 1945 between the "then" and the "now." Both eras were part of the children, and inevitably, maybe inexorably, both found expression in their adult lives. If we adults do not accept the complexity of a child's history, we reduce and diminish that child, and we participate in a denial of the past; in the case of postwar Jewish children, we deny the pervasive effects of the Shoah, and we pretend to the child that the multifaceted life she lived did not occur.

Harold Marcuse

Dachau: The Political Aesthetics of Holocaust Memorials

COMMEMORATING HISTORICAL EVENTS IS NOT A SIMPLE ENDEAVOR, ESpecially when an event as complex as "the Holocaust" is the object of commemoration.[1] For analytical purposes we can distinguish between two basic types of actualizing past events in the present. First, at the individual level, there is the act of *remembering,* the recalling to mind of actual experiences or acquired information. And second, on the group level, there is the social process of gathering together lived and learned experiences and sharing them with other members of a collectivity, a process we can denote *recollection. Commemoration* is thus part of the second category: it is the ritual and usually public recollection of past events. *Collective memory* (or *historical consciousness*) can denote the knowledge about the past that is shared by members of a group.[2] Collective memories develop when individual memories of lived experiences are shared within groups. This process is mediated by the public dissemination of historical information through films, novels, scholarly works, formal instruction, commemorative ceremonies, and the like. If a group considers these collective images of the past to be an important part of its public identity, it will seek to represent them in the public sphere. Here, at the intersection of private interest and public politics, is where the political aesthetics of monuments and memorials come into play.

To write about the political aesthetics of holocaust memorials is to examine which groups have selected which aspects of the past to represent, and how each group represented those aspects it chose, and why. Dachau, a former Nazi concentration camp located on the outskirts of a town about six miles from the center of Munich, is an ideal site for the exploration of these questions. For more than fifty years it has been subject to the competing and conflicting recollective agendas of the local populace, of regional (Bavarian), national (German), and international politicians, and of survivors' organizations from nearly a dozen countries. Associated with the Dachau concentration camp today are more than a dozen memorial sculptures and buildings; several more were planned but never constructed, or existed only temporarily (see appendix).[3] The conceptions behind these memorials are worth studying. Additionally, the appearance of the memorial site as a whole reveals a great deal about the political aesthetics of holocaust commemoration.

Visitors today enter the former Dachau prisoners' compound through a gap in the southeast corner of the camp wall, roughly opposite the historical entry gate with its inscription "Arbeit macht frei" ("Work liberates") (fig. 1). They file past a large billboard with a plan of the memorial site around to the front of the former service building. The service building once housed the camp kitchen, showers, and a storeroom for the prisoners' civilian clothing but now contains a library, archive, museum, and discussion rooms. At the corner of this building the view opens across the expanse of the former roll-call square to the entry gate in the distance. On the right are two reconstructed barracks; on the left, in the courtyard enclosed on three sides by the museum/service building, stands the large international memorial: a broad bronze sculpture of emaciated bodies interwoven to form a barbed wire fence.

Most visits begin with a walk through the museum, which occupies the long central tract of the former service building. Visitors exit behind the international memorial (fig. 17), then proceed down the central camp street, bordered left and right by poplar saplings and low cement curbs outlining the former barrack foundations. A lone billboard stands to one side, displaying an aerial view of the street teeming with prisoners in the late 1930s. Straight ahead, 800 yards down the axial street, rises the cylindrical form of a Catholic memorial chapel, flanked by the low outlines of Protestant and Jewish memorial buildings (figs. 20–22). The crematorium lies out of sight off to the left at the end of the camp street, in a separate enclosure beyond the compound wall. After traversing a bridge and passing a Russian Orthodox chapel outside the wall on the left, visitors enter the parklike area around the crematorium. Just beyond the wall an inscription on a stone proclaims: "Remember how we died here." A bit further stands a small statue of a concentration camp inmate on a high pedestal. Ahead to the right stretches the "new" part of the crematorium, built in 1942, with its disinfection chambers, undressing room, gas chamber, morgue, furnaces, and towering rectangular chimney. Hidden behind bushes and trees on the left is the simple hut of the "old," two-oven crematorium built in 1940. Paths through the nicely landscaped park lead past benches and trilingually inscribed stones marking various historical sites: "Execution Range," "Blood Ditch," "Ash Grave." A small marker with a star of David is among them.

When visitors leave this park again, they sometimes visit the religious memorial buildings at the back of the camp; but after several hours in the museum and about a mile of walking, most people opt to go directly to the memorial site exit, crossing the gravel-strewn expanse of the former camp. Visitors who do not choose to tour the museum at the beginning of their visit often start by walking through the one reconstructed barrack that is furnished with bunks recreating interiors from three different periods of the historical camp. If you are one of these visitors, you are more likely to explore the religious memorials after visiting the crematorium. You may even find your way behind the Catholic chapel to a gate cut through one of the watchtowers. It leads into the courtyard of a cloister of Carmelite nuns, where several relics from the concentration camp are displayed, including a monstrance fashioned by inmates, and a Madonna that adorned the chapel in the German priests' barrack.

With time permitting, a very few people, usually repeat visitors or individuals with a personal connection to the site, will drive the mile or so to the Leiten cemetery and the Hebertshausen shooting range, two camp-related memorials indicated on a map at the entrance to the Dachau camp memorial site itself. The road there passes the unmarked greenhouses and research buildings of the former camp plantation, a large agricultural complex that is now used as public housing and by the town's park department.

At the Leiten a steep hill climbs past carved stone stations of the Cross and a small chapel modeled after the Roman Pantheon to a gently forested cemetery. In a clearing within a low stone wall stands a tall cross emblazoned with bronze reliefs of the apostles. A low stone star of David, several individual plaques, and a poetically inscribed monolith are nestled in the greenery along the paths. On the

Figure 1. Aerial view of the Dachau concentration camp memorial site around 1970, after the dedication of the international memorial. The entrance to the memorial site is at the bottom right: the three religious memorials and the convent outside the northern wall of the camp are visible at the top. (Dachau Archive)

Figure 2. Aerial view of the former Dachau concentration camp in 1956, when it was a residential settlement for around two thousand people. Note the factories on the former roll-call square and the camp-era buildings at the north end of the camp (top). The crowded barracks contrast markedly with the clean memorial site created a decade later. (Dachau Archive)

Figure 3. Aerial view of the Buchenwald memorial site near Weimar, 1954–57. This memorial is located at a mass grave site some distance from the concentration camp. (Volker Frank, 1970)

Figure 4. Camp kitchen, shower, and storage building behind the roll-call square, 1946. The cross in the foreground was erected by liberated Polish inmates. Note the Nazi-era inscription on the roof: "There is only one path to freedom. Its milestones are obedience, industriousness, honesty, orderliness, cleanliness, sobriety, truthfulness, self-sacrifice, and love of the Fatherland." (Dachau Archive)

Figure 5. Karl Knappe's proposed *Temple of Liberation* for Leiten grave site, November 1945. This monumental building was to be thirty-five meters wide, and the disk atop the thirty-five-meter-tall pylon was to be covered with gold mosaic tiles. (Landratsamt, Dachau)

Figure 6. Sketch of *Temple of Liberation,* rear view. The semicircular rear wall of the memorial resembled German national monuments erected since the late nineteenth century. (*Süddeutsche Zeitung,* October 26, 1945)

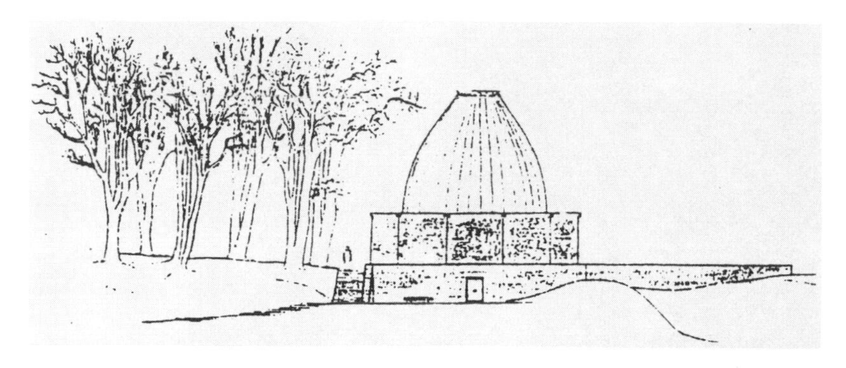

Figure 7. Third-place entry in the 1950 Leiten competition, by Roth and Hiller. A simplified version of this design, without the arching cupola, was later constructed. (*Baumeister,* January 1951, p. 23)

Figure 8. The 10.5-meter-tall memorial hall actually erected on Leiten hill in 1951–52. (Dachau Memorial Site)

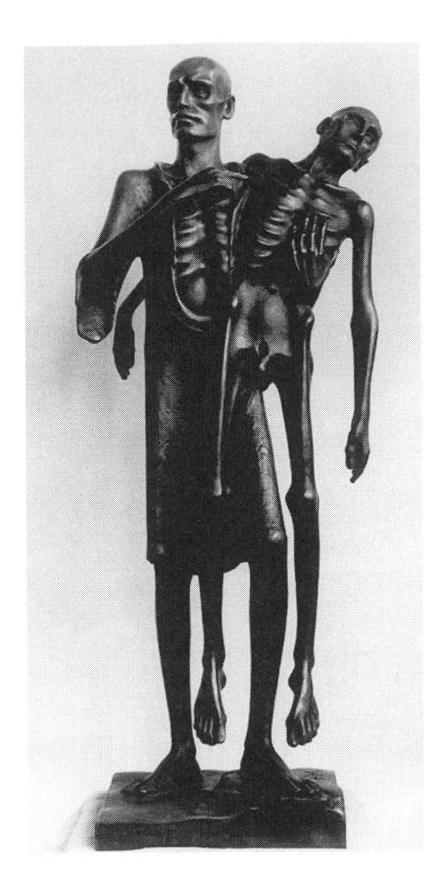

Figure 9. Prisoner *pietà* by Fritz Koelle, 1946. This was the first design selected in 1948 by State Commissioner Auerbach for a memorial at the crematorium. (Dachau Archive)

Figure 10. Statue of an "unknown concentration camp inmate" (1.4 meters), by Fritz Koelle, dedicated April 1950. (Author)

Figure 11. World War I memorial in Rot on the Rot. (Photograph by the author)

Figure 12. Poster of Dachau Information Office, 1946. The text reads: "Their sacrifice, our guilt. Make it good again!" (*Concentration Camp Dachau: Album,* around 1946)

Figure 13. Visitors viewing mannequins in the first crematorium exhibition, 1945–49. (Dachau Archive)

Figure 14. Second exhibition in the crematorium, 1950–53. This exhibition tried to strike a less vivid, more objective tone. Note the whipping horse in front of the window. (Preuss, *Remember That,* p. 53)

Figure 15. Third exhibition in the crematorium, 1960–64, in its provisional state in 1960. Note how the whipping horse is displayed. (Dachau Archive)

Figure 16. Third exhibition in the crematorium, 1960–64, after the 1961 renovation. Note the sign "Brausebad" (showers) with the erroneous explanation that the gas chamber was never functional. (Dachau Archive)

Figure 17. View through the international memorial (dedicated 1968) down the camp street to the Catholic chapel. The emaciated, twisted limbs entwined like barbed wire symbolize the suffering of the inmates. (Author)

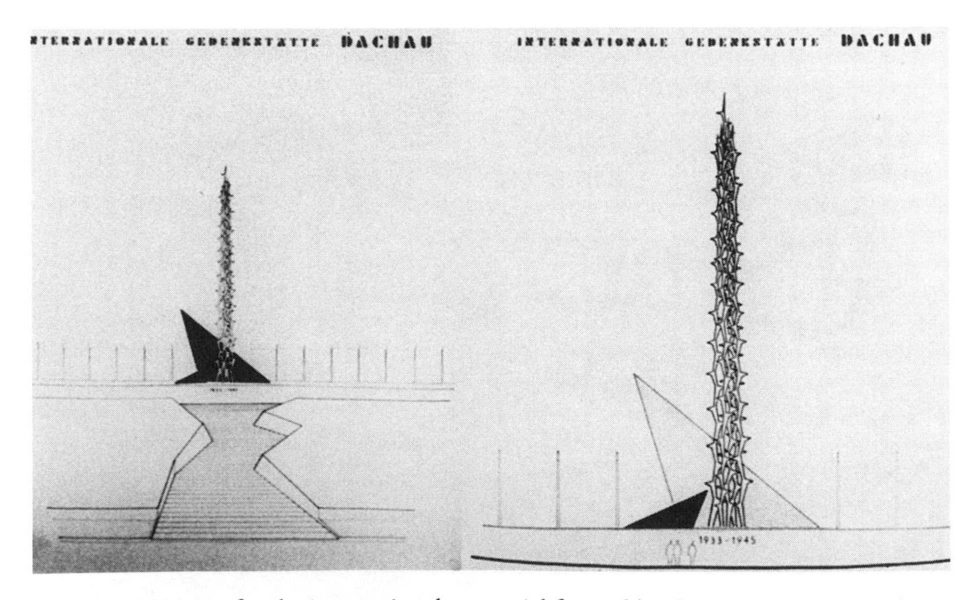

Figure 18. Design for the international memorial favored by German survivors, 1959. The rising and towering forms (thirty-five meters tall) represent the resistance of the camp inmates. (Dachau Archive)

Figure 19. Chain sculpture with triangle badges at the base of the international memorial. (Photograph by the author)

Figure 20. Catholic Chapel of the Mortal Agony of Christ, by Josef Wiedemann, 1960. The bell tower was added in 1961. (Author)

Figure 21. Jewish memorial building in Dachau, by Hermann Guttmann, built 1964–67. (Author)

Figure 22. Protestant Church of Reconciliation, by Helmut Striffler, built 1964–67. (Author)

back side of the hill, outside the cemetery wall, a dark, eight-sided hall looms among the high trees (fig. 8). If the heavy bronze doors are open, visitors find a bronze basin resembling a baptismal font, bronze torch-holders in the corners, and painted coats-of-arms adorning the interior. From this enigmatic building, near a boarded-up wooden concession stand, another path leads back down to the parking lot.

At Hebertshausen, a short way down the road to the east, a short gravel drive leads past a small explanatory sign to a massive concrete billboard whose German inscription reads: "Thousands of PRISONERS OF WAR were MURDERED here by the SS." Curious visitors may wander back through the high grass and nettles to the bullet-pocked garagelike shooting range backdrops, into which Soviet prisoners of war were herded before being gunned down. From Hebertshausen it is several miles back past the Leiten Hill and through the town of 30,000 inhabitants to the public cemetery, where several thousand more concentration camp inmates are buried and a few more commemorative markers stand. In Dachau town itself, only a small, weathered plaque on a bank opposite the city hall and a small square named "Square of Resistance" (*Widerstandplatz*) recall events associated with the concentration camp.

When examining holocaust memorials such as those in Dachau, it is important to realize that, among different groups and at different points in time, there have been radically different conceptions of the underlying event to be recollected. A survey of memorials in Dachau yields a typology of eight different "holocausts" that have been recollected over the years by as many groups. Each of the eight recollections is fairly specific, focusing on selected aspects of a complex phenomenon, and each one is highly dependent on the shared experiences, beliefs, and characteristics that bind together the recollecting group (i.e. its identity).[4]

The most tenacious recollected image in West Germany since 1945 has been of what I call the *"clean" concentration camps,* that is, the image of the concentration camps as educational work camps, which Nazi propaganda disseminated in the official media of the day.[5] Never very close to the historical reality of the camps, this image was recollected by a "quiet majority" of the West German populace primarily during the 1950s and 1960s; it has figured in the literature of "Holocaust deniers" since its emergence in the 1950s.[6] Although this "clean" image was never publicly accepted by scholars or mainstream politicians, it has, as I will show, been realized in Dachau and several other West German memorial sites conceived in the 1950s and 1960s.

Other recollected images correspond to different phases in the Nazi-era history of the camps. Historically, the first of these commemorated aspects was the system of punitive *political prison camps* set up by the Nazi government in 1933 to neutralize and liquidate real or perceived opponents.[7] Not surprisingly, this "holocaust" is recollected by survivors from that period, primarily by members of the past and present German Communist parties, but also by some conservatives, Social Democrats, and Jews.

In a third type of recollection, the camps are conceived of as *extermination centers* and factories of annihilation as they were experienced especially by Jews.[8] This conception of the Nazi camps is most tangible in the memoir literature by survivors of camps such as Auschwitz-Birkenau, Treblinka or Sobibor, although of course there were no survivors of the "quintessential" experience: gassing immediately upon arrival at the extermination center. A fourth image derives from the experience of foreign prisoners after 1943: *huge, barbaric slave labor complexes.*[9] Since this experience was eclipsed by the dissolution of the camp system at the end of the war, and because this memory group has never wielded much political power, this idea of the camp has rarely been publicly recollected. A fifth image of the concentration camps has figured prominently in the recollective activities of Britain and the United States, whose publics first learned about the camps primarily at liberation: the chaotic and pestilent *"death camps"* that emerged during the final phase of the war in 1945.[10]

Other groups, similar to the political prisoners who were specifically targeted during the first phase of the camps, have positioned the Nazi concentration camps within their own system of understanding. Religious Catholics, for example, especially those who were themselves imprisoned by the Nazis, tend to envision the camps as *part of a divine plan.*[11] Many Protestants, on the other hand, have viewed the holocaust as *a burden for which atonement is due.*[12]

Finally, we can distinguish an eighth recollected image of the Nazi camps that one might call *historical:* a multifaceted reality encompassing several of the images described above. This historicized view (to use a phrase whose utility was hotly debated in the mid-1980s) is, not surprisingly, held by interested members of younger generations who have no immediate personal connection to the camps or their survivors.[13]

The plethora of memorials representing these different holocausts at Dachau can be analyzed best if we subdivide the postwar decades into five periods: first, the first months after liberation in 1945; second, the years from 1946 to 1955, when a process of forgetting and then eradicating historical aspects of the Dachau camp took place; third, the years from the mid-1950s to the late 1960s, when political and religious groups established memorials enshrining the holocausts of their collective memories; fourth, a transitional decade during the 1970s; and fifth, the years since 1980, which have witnessed the gradual modification of the memorial site to present a more complex, historicized view of the holocaust.

The first memorials proposed for Dachau illustrate an important feature of all successful memorials: they draw on older, inherited symbolic and stylistic languages. In order to function in the recollective process, a memorial must make its message understood by its viewers. Therefore, most early holocaust memorials did not present aspects of the camps, which had never before been symbolically represented. Instead, they used traditional religious symbolism or a heroic monumental style. They referred not to any of the individual holocausts listed above but rather to the cessation of an unspecified historical calamity. They did not invoke a past that was still all too present in the minds of contemporaries but directed attention toward the future. Let us return to liberation day, at the end of April 1945, to examine the historical context of their origins.

When Allied soldiers entered Dachau, more than 2,000 corpses in various states of decomposition were strewn throughout the camp. To alleviate the sanitary crisis, they added these corpses to mass graves on a nearby hill that had been used by the SS since November 1944, when a lack of fuel curtailed the operation of the crematorium. Shortly after this first postwar burial, in which the corpses were transported through the town in open farm wagons, the U.S. military ordered local officials to construct a memorial at the gravesite. The first design considered by the town elders consisted of two columns, one crowned by a cross, the other topped by a star of David.[14]

In June 1945 this design was proposed for the camp roll-call square and endorsed by the Archbishop of Munich, one of the few uncompromised figures of regional public life. The newly instated Dachau town leaders, representing a cross-section of the political spectrum (two Communists, two Social Democrats, two Bavarian Catholic party members, and two nonaligned) found it suitable as well, but it was abandoned only weeks later when it was discovered that its designer had been a member of the Nazi party. In July the town council decided to solicit alternative designs.

Although the two columns were never erected in that form, this first proposal had a long afterlife in the memorial history of Dachau. A large wooden cross erected shortly after liberation by Polish survivors did adorn the roll-call square for a year or more in 1945–46 (fig. 4).[15] And in 1949 a wooden cross and a star of David were erected at the mass grave on the Leiten Hill,[16] to be replaced in 1956 by the more permanent versions in bronze and stone that still stand today.[17] In 1960 they appeared in yet another project, when a suffragan bishop who had been imprisoned in the concentration camp, and who had just spearheaded the construction of a Catholic chapel at the end of the central camp street, suggested that such crowned columns flank his chapel to represent what he referred to as the "other two major world religions," Judaism and Protestantism.[18] The popularity of these ahistorical memorials reveals a continuing desire not to recollect any holocaust but instead to use the historical location to affirm a bond with the recollective community in the present.

Once most of the survivors of Dachau had been repatriated in the summer of 1945, the camp was used by the U.S. army as an internment center for German army officers and Nazi party officials. Commemorative markers in the camp were not accessible to the public, so by default the Leiten gravesite became the focal point of commemorative activity.

The next proposal for a Dachau memorial, unveiled on November 9, 1945, at an internationally broadcast commemorative ceremony in the castle of Dachau township, abandoned religious symbolism and drew upon a different memorial tradition: large structures in prominent natural settings, such as the national monuments of the nineteenth century and the Bismarck towers of the early twentieth.[19] This proposal, which I will refer to as a *Temple of Liberation,* was envisioned by Karl Knappe, a Munich artist who had sculpted war memorials during the Weimar and Nazi periods (such as the prone figure of a uniformed soldier in Munich's tomblike World War I memorial) (figs. 5 and 6).

The base of this rectangular building atop the Leiten Hill was to be 35 meters wide and 20 meters high, containing cavernous rooms with memorial plaques, paintings, and frescoes. A steep exterior staircase led to the roof, which offered a panoramic view of the former concentration camp in the foreground and the peaks of the Alps in the distance. From this base rose a 15-meter pylon consisting of an obelisk crowned by a large sunlike gold mosaic disk, which would have been visible from afar. The temple's "rugged mass" was to have, as the artist phrased it, an "elemental naturalness." His idea was

> to point to the gravity of the events only in the lower rooms, and then to guide the visitors of this memorial site up onto the walls, which were to be built out of the ruins of Munich. Visitors would have climbed onto these walls and found . . . a "liberating" view of the Alps. I think it would have been sufficient to allude to the horrors in the large lower rooms, and not eternally block the road to freedom and salvation with remembrance.[20]

The candid formulation of Knappe's concluding sentence concisely expresses the predominant antirecollective sentiments of the broader German populace at the end of the war, which was composed to a substantial extent of former followers and supporters of the National Socialist regime. However, in occupied Germany that silent majority was not in a position to express approval or dissent. Several progressive German architects publicly criticized the design, linking it to nationalistic and militaristic monuments of Germany's past. This prompted U.S. military and Bavarian authorities to withdraw their support for the project shortly after the November 1945 ceremony, and it was never built.[21]

This unrealized project is not the only example of a German holocaust monument drawing on this monumental tradition, however. At Buchenwald near Weimar, in what was communist East Germany, an expansive memorial site near the camp was designed in the mid-1950s and dedicated in September 1958 (fig. 3).[22] Its centerpiece is a 50-meter stone bell tower erected on the foundations of a Bismarck tower torn down to make room for it.[23] The ensemble features a massive entry gate, a series of large narrative bas-reliefs, huge pylons with flame basins, and funnel-shaped, concrete-lined circular graves, as well as a monumental sculptural group with figures almost twice life size. In contrast to the Leiten temple project, which would have been limited to unspecified allusions to camp life in the interior rooms, the narrative reliefs and sculptural group in Buchenwald are unequivocal representations of the "political" holocaust in the concentration camps of the early 1930s. Throughout the history of East Germany, that was the holocaust whose recollection was supported by the state apparatus.

In the years after 1945, two developments facilitated the break with older commemorative traditions in West Germany. On the one hand, Cold War politics and pressing problems in day-to-day life enabled many Germans to forget the hideous images of the concentration camps that had been forced into their consciousness at war's end. This led to a dearth of official commemorative activities relating to the holocaust during the late 1940s and early 1950s. On the other hand, after commemorative activities began to revive in the mid-1950s, artists and memorial makers found new forms and symbols that did more than mark the concentration camp sites as symbolic cemeteries. From 1945 to the early 1960s a whole iconography of the Nazi camps gradually evolved, including barbed wire, triangle badges, smokestacks, emaciated or skeletized bodies, coffins, chains, flames, walls, ramps, fences, railroad tracks, and cattle cars.[24] Two international artistic competitions also helped to break with the established tradition: the competition to design a memorial for the "Unknown Political Prisoner" in 1953, and that for a memorial for Auschwitz-Birkenau in 1956.[25]

One early example of this new language is a plaque erected by the Association of the Persecutees of the Nazi Regime (*Vereinigung der Verfolgten des Naziregimes,* VVN), an organization of German survivors, on a bank in downtown Dachau in 1947. Dachau camp inmates and oppositional townsmen had attempted to wrest power from the town's Nazi leadership shortly before Allied troops arrived. The revolt was unsuccessful, however, and the corpses of insurgents were displayed as a public warning in front of a bank opposite city hall. The 1947 plaque, which simply names the victims and the event, depicts a row of triangle badges, which had been used in the concentration camps to designate categories of prisoners according to the reason for their imprisonment. This badge of shame, which was unmistakably linked to the Nazi camps, was now used as a badge of honor.

The first figurative memorial proposed for Dachau, a smaller-than-life statue of a concentration camp inmate holding a naked and emaciated comrade with his left arm, shows how the traditional sculptural motif was adapted to present an old message with icons of these new events (fig. 9). Fritz Koelle, a well-known proletarian sculptor of the 1920s working in an expressionistic style, took the centuries-old motif of the *pietà* (the Virgin Mary with her dead son)—which represents mourning, sacrifice for the greater good, and a close bond between the two figures—and applied to it symbols of the camps: emaciation, a shorn head, pyjamalike uniform, and a sallow face with sunken eyes.[26] Koelle gave the pair an unsettling twist in that the clothed figure's right hand is raised and pointing at the emaciated comrade in an accusatory gesture.

The *pietà* motif is common in memorial sculpture and has been adapted to other situations as well: a World War I soldiers' monument in the German town of Rot on the Rot shows a statue of Jesus as the man of sorrows supporting a fully uniformed German soldier (fig. 11); in a poster printed by the Dachau survivors information office in 1946, a German civilian supports a clothed prisoner in striped garb (fig. 12); and Nathan Rapoport's bronze statue "The Liberator," dedicated in 1985 in New Jersey's Liberty Park, depicts a U.S. soldier carrying a withered concentration camp inmate.[27] In each case, the commissioners wanted to represent a bond between the two symbolic figures: the sacrifice of Jesus and that of the fallen German soldiers of World War I; German civilians and the sacrifice of concentration camp inmates; American GIs and liberated concentration camp prisoners.

The Dachau *pietà* was initially selected in 1948 for a memorial to be established in front of the Dachau crematorium by Phillip Auerbach, a Jewish German businessman who had survived the camps and returned to Munich to head the Bavarian Office of Restitution.[28] Auerbach, who was just completing his doctoral thesis on German resistance against the Third Reich, identified himself more with the political resistance in Germany than with Jewish survivors per se, although as their Jewish advocate he clearly sympathized with the latter group as well.[29] A short time after he began a fund-raising drive for the figure, because of negative feedback he had received, Auerbach abandoned the prisoner-*pietà* and selected another sculpture by the same artist: a solitary, shorn inmate in the typical camp garb (fig. 10).[30]

The "unknown concentration camp inmate," as the subject of the sculpture has come to be known, wears an overcoat, pants, and clogs, so that only his gaunt face betrays emaciation. The accusatory right hand of the earlier group is now buried in the coat pocket; the knit brows and focused gaze have been raised in a dreamy, undirected look. This new design without the naked, emaciated second figure represents a dramatically different meaning from the one expressed in the first sculpture. The accusatory presentation of the inhumanity that reigned in the Nazi camps and the solidarity among the prisoners have been replaced by a detached, isolated, unimposing figure. The combined political and Jewish holocausts represented in the first statue vanish in favor of a vague and palatable representation of a victim of a relatively "clean" camp. It appears that Auerbach, in his desire to gain acceptance from the wider German populace, had chosen a statue with which that group could also identify.

This new monument was dedicated in September 1950 in front of the Dachau crematorium, where it still stands today. The transition from the graphic depiction of the earlier sculpture to the restrained mood of the second reflects the second development in the late 1940s and 1950s which facilitated the break from the older memorial tradition: the cessation of commemorative activities for the Nazi holocausts. During the 1950s the history of the Dachau camp itself, as well as the history of the Leiten gravesite and an exhibition in the crematorium/gas chamber building, illustrated the attempt to recast the former concentration camp as the "clean" camp that it had never been.

The first Nuremberg trial, one of whose purposes had been to inform the German people about the atrocities committed under the Nazi regime, ended in October 1946. The United States conducted a subsequent series of trials at the international court there, while at

Dachau a U.S. military court tried Germans accused of crimes against Allied personnel until 1947.[31] By that time tensions between the United States and the Soviet Union had become increasingly manifest, and the emerging superpowers began to relax their hard-line punitive stance toward occupied Germany.[32] In the spring and summer of 1948 the remaining Dachau internees received amnesty and were released in droves, a precursor of the "release" of images of the holocaust from West German collective memory.[33]

In 1949 West Germany became the semisovereign Federal Republic of Germany. This gave its national leaders more autonomy in setting the country's commemorative agenda. Until 1955, when Chancellor Adenauer concluded an agreement bringing home German prisoners of war from the Soviet Union, West German recollective activities focused on these absent men, and public officials avoided holocaust commemorations as much as possible.[34] To give just one example: from 1951 to 1955 a national "Week of the Prisoners of War" was celebrated with lavish support from government agencies.[35] Although this memorial week was first held in late October, it was moved in 1952 to the first week of May, when the anniversary of the liberation of the concentration camps was usually celebrated.

In Dachau, as the internment camp emptied, Bavarian authorities speculated about uses for the complex once it reverted to German control. In January 1948 the Bavarian legislature unanimously passed a bill calling for the use of the Dachau camp complex as a work camp for the many "asocial elements" in pre–currency reform Germany. The language of the bill unselfconsciously echoed the official descriptions of purportedly "clean" concentration camps during the 1930s.[36] As the stream of refugees from the East mounted in the spring of 1948, however, the legislature decided instead to convert the concentration camp barracks into apartments and create a refugee settlement (fig. 2).[37] This plan was realized, in spite of more cost-effective alternative proposals having nothing to do with the former camp, whose Nazi-era history the printed reports and official correspondence regarding the decision studiously avoided.

The history of the Leiten gravesite after the rejection of the temple project offers another example of the passage of the holocaust into West German recollective oblivion in the late 1940s. When

Knappe's monumental temple project was officially abandoned in January 1946, a commission was formed by Bavarian prime minister Hoegner to find a new solution.[38] The commission's recommendation, released in March 1946, closely followed the suggestion proposed by Knappe's critics: "At the gravesite an architectonically framed sculptural group should be set in a memorial grove as a monument of remembrance and warning. Such a solution would have the advantages that it would be free of false and exaggerated pathos . . . , and would require only a very moderate quantity of material."[39] This recommendation was publicly announced in June 1946, and by September, twenty-one entries had been submitted. The jury deemed none of them acceptable, and decided to request new designs from the creators of the four most promising models.[40] They now specified more precisely that submitted projects should have "the character of a cemetery," so that they would "resemble neither a museum nor a place for an outing." A room for ritual activities and private commemorative markers was to be included, as was a "living and meaningful connection to the surroundings," such as a bell tower. These conditions were set exclusively by state officials; survivors of the camp had no input into the process. In the ensuing months the State Chancellery and the Ministry of Culture did not allocate the funds for the new competition, and the entire project was forgotten by the bureaucracy until 1949, when an international scandal catapulted it back on to the public agenda.

In the summer of that year, a steam shovel mining fine sand at the base of the Leiten Hill exposed several skeletons.[41] Although it was later determined that the skeletons predated the Nazi era, the disinterment spotlighted the negligence of state and local authorities in maintaining the gravesite atop the hill. When the story broke, no one could recall the precise location of the concentration camp graves, nor even the approximate number of corpses: the first estimates ranged wildly, from 2,000 to 20,000 (in reality there were about 5,600). Even the searing experience of seeing farm wagons laden with decomposing corpses being led through the town had not anchored the gravesite in collective memory. Local residents may have privately remembered the macabre processions, but even in the short span of four years, the lack of public recollection had helped to isolate these images from their historical context and strip them of their significance for the collectivity.

To rectify the impression of past neglect, the state mounted massive public relations efforts in 1949–50, including the final realization of the Leiten memorial project begun in 1945 and the renovation of the exhibition in the crematorium which had been installed in 1945–46 during the first Dachau war crimes trial (fig. 13).[42] The descriptions of the new Leiten project reveal that little change had occurred in the ahistorical recollection typical of the immediate postwar period. In December 1949, the Dachau county governor declared that "a kind of interdenominational pantheon with several altars for the various religions" was to be erected.[43] In February 1950, when a new competition for it was officially initiated, the guidelines prescribed a design symbolizing "the religious and national idea of sacrifice on behalf of peace."[44] The text of the document sealed in the cornerstone of the Leiten Hall confirms the official wish to associate the commemoration of the victims of the Nazis with self-sacrifice for high ideals:

> May this place, in memory of the dead of many nations and denominations who died for their belief in honor, freedom, and justice, become not only a site of reverence, but a sign of warning to all humanity.
>
> May this place of hatred become a place of love, serving to promote understanding and peace in the world![45]

According to the reasoning implicit in this text, since the Dachau deaths were meaningful, their commemoration would not renew old hatred against the Germans but promote Germany's integration into the international community. Such government-formulated conceptions excluded the suffering, barbarity, exploitation, and senselessness of the inmate experience in the Nazi camps. They also flew in the face of the popular image of the camps as "clean" correctional penal institutions for "asocial" inmates. As the seventy-four-year-old mayor of Dachau would tell a British journalist in late 1959: "Please don't make the mistake of thinking that only heroes died in Dachau. Many inmates were . . . there because they illegally opposed the regime of the day. . . . You have got to remember there were many criminals and homosexuals in Dachau. Do we want a memorial to such people?"[46] In the limelight of international attention a decade earlier, however, it was not expedient for German officials to recollect this image, so they limited their historical pronouncements to vacuous generalities and proceeded to select artistic designs that would not offend local sensibilities.

When the artistic competition concluded two months later, a newspaper reviewer summarized his impression of the 175 entries as follows:

> There are not only modified churches of every age, Roman forts, Gothic citadels, and neo-German colonial castles [*Ordensburgen*], but especially shows of strength in homeland-style [*Heimatstil*] and transparent industrial halls, and even idyllic Biedermeier garden pavilions, constructions reminiscent of the monument to the Battle of Nations [*Völkerschlachtdenkmal* in Leipzig, 1898–1913], and neoclassical theaters and halls of fame.[47]

This roster indicates the powerful hold these older commemorative traditions still had on the artistic community—and not only on them. When the jury met to examine the entries, it found the following characteristics most appealing because they were "rooted in the local tradition" (*heimatverbunden*): octagonal ground plan, stained glass windows, and careful landscaping.[48]

Considerations of cost—the original projection of 1–2 million marks had been reduced to 600,000 for both landscaping and construction—dictated a relatively simple memorial. Ultimately the third-place entry by architect Harald Roth and sculptor Anton Hiller, subject to some alterations, was selected (fig. 7).[49] Construction was delayed until spring 1951 because funds had not been budgeted,[50] another example of the bureaucratic foot-dragging that characterized the treatment of the Dachau project from 1946 to 1949.

The memorial hall ultimately constructed on the Leiten in 1951–52 has some telling similarities to the monumental tradition of its 1945 predecessor, the 35-meter-tall *Temple of Liberation* (figs. 5 and 8). The eight-sided hall of rough-hewn basalt is only 10.5 meters high and 9 meters in diameter, but its bronze doors, torch mounts, and thirty-three national coats of arms are reminiscent of both the 1945 Knappe project and more traditional heroic monuments such as the eight-sided Tannenberg (1924–27) and Annaberg (1938) monuments, and the German soldiers' memorial erected at El Alamain in Egypt at roughly the same time.[51] Today the Leiten's pseudo-Germanic hall is concealed by trees, hidden from public attention like the graves of the camp victims themselves. When the octagonal hall was completed in 1952, no public ceremony marked the event.

Another element of the public relations effort in the wake of the Leiten scandal was the renovation of an exhibition installed in the rooms of the crematorium building by survivors in late 1945. The original display included mannequins re-creating scenes of torture, and graphic pictures, including a series of photographs of prisoners reenacting the cremation procedure with real corpses after liberation (fig. 13).[52] A major redesign in 1950 removed the mannequins and replaced most of those pictures by charts, statistics, and photographs of postwar commemoration (fig. 14). This exhibition did not last long, however. In 1951 Phillip Auerbach, who had been the only Bavarian state official advocating commemoration in Dachau, was accused of embezzlement, arrested, and put on trial. After he was convicted of several unrelated minor offenses, he committed suicide in August 1952. Responsibility for the Dachau memorial site was transferred to the Ministry of Finance, and at the next opportunity, right after the eighth anniversary of liberation in 1953, Bavarian authorities removed the exhibition.[53] Subsequently, plans were floated to close and tear down the crematorium building, and demolition of the watchtowers actually began.[54]

In the late 1940s and early 1950s the recollective programs of two groups coincided: some survivors, such as Auerbach, who saw the camps as places of senseless death and wanted to turn them into quiet parks to honor the victims; and those Germans represented by the Bavarian Ministry of Finance (which owned the site) and the local county governor's office (which worked to end public access), both of whom professed to remember the camps as "clean" institutions for the retraining of the "work-shy" and wanted to remove evidence to the contrary. The neat landscaping in the crematorium area and on the Leiten Hill in Dachau today date from this period.

The West German attempt to recollect the "clean" camps did not end with the creation of the memorial parks, however. It also affected the overall appearance of the memorial site in the former concentration camp itself (compare figs. 1 and 2). By 1955 the marginalization of organizations of former political prisoners and the eradicatory measures of the early 1950s had prompted survivors to take action and lobby for the creation of a historically concrete memorial site. However, time and again the Bavarian government forced them to modify their plans in such a way as to reduce historical concreteness.[55] Although the survivors planned to retain some or all of the barracks in the memorial site, for instance, state officials argued that because of dilapidation and subsequent modifications, all wooden structures on the site would have to be demolished. From 1962 to 1964 all of the prisoner barracks were torn down, as were the rabbit hutches, kennels, greenhouses, infirmary, canteen, library, disinfection building, chapel, brothel, and the many other buildings that had made up camp life. As a compromise, the two barrack buildings immediately adjacent to the roll-call square—the infirmary and canteen—were reconstructed as sleeping barracks, but with cement floors, locking doors, and tightly fitting windows. One reconstruction remained empty. The other was fitted with typical furnishings from three periods in the camp's history. Still missing was the relatively comfortable quarters where the barrack elder slept; only one set of toilets and lavatories was reconstructed.

By 1965 this compromise between Dachau survivors and Bavarian authorities had yielded a minimalist solution, a reduction of "Dachau" to the barest designators of the "Holocaust" in the narrow sense: an enclosed compound with an entry gate, watch towers, some barbed-wire fencing, two barracks, a gas chamber, and a crematorium.[56] The rest of the camp was strewn with light-colored pebbles, and the locations of the other thirty-two barracks marked by low concrete curbs. These remain today. Thus the memorial site symbolically reincarnates the propaganda image of the "clean" camp, with a few icons of the early political camps and the later extermination centers superimposed upon it. There is no indication that some barracks had been enclosed by barbed wire fences; that Czechs lived in one barrack, Frenchmen in another, Polish priests in a third, German priests in a fourth with a chapel; that two others housed the so-called punishment company, or that medical experiments were conducted in yet another. Attentive visitors to the memorial site might notice that only thirty of the thirty-four barrack outlines have numbers. Nothing indicates that the remaining four housed the infirmary, canteen, and prison library, which had held thousands of books. The complexities of the universe of the Nazi camps were erased from Dachau's memorial topography.

While this historical neutralization may be difficult to understand in retrospect, it may have been a necessary didactic step at the time. First the holocaust in its most general meaning had to be reestablished as a historical fact in the face of repression and denial; only then could its complexity, internal contradictions, and nonlinearity be explored and represented. There are other examples of this "flattening" of history as well. Originally, large letters on the roof of the service building (which had housed storerooms, the camp kitchen, and showers, and now contains the museum, offices, and archive) mockingly proclaimed virtues such as obedience, sobriety, cleanliness, and industry as the "milestones to freedom" to the prisoners standing at attention twice daily in the roll-call square below (fig. 4).[57] But this inscription, a cynical outgrowth of the Nazi-era "clean" camp ideology, was never reconstructed. Another example of didactic simplification was a sign put up at the entrance to the gas chamber in 1960, explaining the word *Brausebad* (showers) stenciled over the door (fig. 16): "This room would have been used as an undressing and waiting room if the gas chamber had worked. The sign 'showers' served to deceive the prisoners." However, the gas chamber had indeed worked: it was tested with Zyklon B gas and possibly combat gasses as well.[58] But it had never been used for the systematic murder of prisoners; perhaps because by the time it was completed, deaths due to mistreatment, malnutrition, and disease already surpassed the capacity of the crematorium. The explanation offered was probably an overly sensitive reaction to claims that no one was ever gassed at Dachau.[59] Such pseudoacademically argued denials highlighted the need for definitive research about the Nazi holocaust. As this literature gradually accumulated in the 1960s and 70s, a number of groups worked to enshrine their images of the holocaust in memorials.

The commemorative buildings erected by various groups in Dachau in the 1960s illustrate a fundamental principle about the political aesthetics of holocaust memorials: they have more to do with the politics and worldview of the recollecting group than with the historical events they purport to represent. The first of these monuments in Dachau (coincidentally one of the last to be completed) was an international memorial initiated with a symbolic cornerstone-laying in 1956 by the International Dachau Survivors' Committee (Comité International de Dachau), the umbrella organization of Dachau survivors.[60] Most of the group's members had been imprisoned for political reasons; but the German and non-German organizations held widely disparate views of the concentration camps. While most of the German members of the committee had been political opponents of the Nazi regime, arrested in the early 1930s and treated preferentially by the SS, the other foreign groups had experienced the camps during the exacerbated conditions of the war years and had endured much harsher treatment. Thus, while the German survivors saw the camps as places where heroic resisters had struggled valiantly against overwhelmingly powerful opponents, the foreigners tended to see them as places of barbarous cruelty and senseless death.

As the project moved slowly toward realization—the 2,000 individuals and families living in the former camp first had to be relocated—the differences between these two collective memories began to surface. In 1959 an international competition brought in sixty-three entries from eighteen countries.[61] The Belgian and French national committees, which had dominated the leadership of the Comité International de Dachau since its reestablishment in 1955 (it had existed as a secret resistance organization during the final months of the camp), favored a sculpture by Yugoslavian artist Glid Nandor in which stylized emaciated bodies with barblike hands were interwoven to resemble a barbed-wire fence (fig. 17). The West German committee, in contrast, liked a model by a German architect in which a slender, 35-meter column of jagged, interconnected strands towered over a large and a smaller stone triangle thrusting in opposite directions (fig. 18).[62] These designs reflect the collective memories of each group. The dynamic, vertical German design would have honored stalwart resistance under adverse conditions, as symbolized by the hunched, thrusting triangles. The jagged tower, in addition to the importance expressed by its height, connoted the deadly, essentially insurmountable ascent to victory over the Nazis. The Yugoslavian design, which was the one ultimately erected, expressed the inhuman treatment of human beings, the nameless, faceless mass death of people penned up in enclosures like worthless animals.

As a compromise between the two groups, before the memorial was completed in 1968 a second sculpture was added within the ramplike base of Nandor's design to symbolize the international solidarity of the prisoners within the camp. This bas-relief consists of three huge links of a symbolic chain. Adorning the links are triangles glazed in the colors of the badges identifying various groups in the concentration camp (fig. 19). However, several of the colors used in the camps are omitted: the green of the "professional criminals," the black of the "asocial elements," and the pink of the homosexuals. Whereas the absence of the first follows a reasonable logic, the lack of the other two colors reveals the prejudices and limits of solidarity of the more politically oriented survivors. The black badge was sometimes assigned by the SS as an additional humiliation, and homosexuals, with their pink badges, were victims as innocent as Jews, whose yellow double triangles are amply represented in the sculpture.

If the chain insignia represents the groups assembled in the Comité International, not the concentration camp, it still refers explicitly to the historical experience. In contrast, Christian religious commemoration at Dachau draws on traditions much older than, and often completely unrelated to, the Nazi holocaust. Constructed in less than six months and dedicated in August 1960, the Catholic Chapel of the Mortal Agony of Christ was the first religious building to be built within the camp perimeter for specifically commemorative purposes (figs. 17 and 21). This cylindrical structure, 15 meters tall and 15 meters in diameter, is located on the central axis of the camp, at the end opposite the roll-call square. A wide opening from top to bottom of the side visible from the camp reveals a raised altar, above which hangs an abstract crucifix. Suspended under the inset conical roof is a huge abstract crown of thorns woven from iron rails reminiscent of the heat-twisted girders and truck chassis used as grates for burning corpses. A ring of lawn and a circle of oak trees surround the chapel (fig. 1). This greenery is a last remnant of suffragan bishop Neuhäusler's 1960 plan for the entire memorial site: a grove of trees without any remnants of the camp.[63] Neuhäusler was allowed to realize his plan only in the immediate vicinity of the Catholic chapel because of protests from the German survivors, who by that time were more interested in historically concrete commemoration than Auerbach had been in the early fifties.

The Mortal Agony chapel illustrates the Catholic recollection of the holocaust, within the Christian system of belief, as an element of a divine plan. The celebration of Mass and the crown of thorns linking Jesus to a concentration camp victim turn the commemorative ritual into a religious affirmation. If the chapel had been located elsewhere, hardly anything would indicate its specific commemorative significance. This is only slightly less true for the other Catholic commemorative building in the camp, a convent just behind the chapel.

The convent, Sacred Blood of the Carmelite order, built in 1963–64, is entered through a gate broken into the base of a watchtower (fig. 1, at top). Plans to construct a cloister at Dachau go back to the weeks immediately after liberation, when freed priests tried to win U.S. general Patton to their plan to construct a church around and over the crematorium, which would have become a kind of crypt in this religious edifice.[64] The situation at the time precluded the immediate carrying out of the plan, which was forgotten in the flurry of West German reconstruction. However, after the completion of the Mortal Agony chapel in 1960, the plan was revived. As the prioress of a Carmelite convent near Bonn wrote to the Archbishop of Munich in 1962:

> The name Dachau will always be connected with man's most terrible cruelties. The site of such ill deeds, where so many human beings bore unspeakable pain, should not be lowered to become a neutral memorial site, or, worse, just a tourist attraction. Rather, at Dachau surrogate penance [*stellvertretende Sühne*] should be performed through the sacrifice of Our Lord Jesus Christ and, in connection with that, through the sacrifice and atonement of human beings who follow the suffering and atoning Lord in love and obedience. The Carmelite order is, in a special manner, appointed to prayer, sacrifice, and atonement.[65]

This is a clear formulation of how the holocaust was to be made part of this group's identity: as part of a path to salvation in which liturgical practice mirrors divine sacrifice without tangible links to the holocaust, thus reinforcing religious identity, not historical consciousness.

Yet another Catholic chapel was erected by Italian survivors of Dachau in the early 1960s on the slope of the Leiten Hill.[66] Fundraising for the votive chapel "Maria Pacis" (Mary, Queen of Peace), modeled after the Roman Pantheon by Italian architect Ehea Ronca, began in 1955. Ground was broken in August 1960, when Bishop Neuhäusler's Mortal Agony chapel was dedicated. The Italian chapel was finished in September 1962 and dedicated after the completion of stone stations of the cross along the path leading up to it a few weeks later. It, too, contains no references to the history of Dachau or the concentration camps but serves solely as a place of worship for Catholic pilgrims. These purely religious stations contrast sharply with the purely secular stations of the induction into concentration camp life that mark the descending path in the memorial at Buchenwald (fig. 3).

After the completion of the Mortal Agony chapel in the memorial site in 1960, considerations of religious equity prompted Bishop Neuhäusler to call for the construction of Jewish and Protestant memorials as well. When he first invited the Organization of Bavarian Jews and the German Protestant Church to erect memorials of their own, he suggested simple columns with a cross and a star of David, but both groups ultimately decided on more elaborate memorials.[67]

For the Jews, Dachau was a dead place, and they did not want to erect a house of God there.[68] After initially acquiescing to a simple star of David, they decided that a nonliturgical memorial building would be more suitable. The Jewish architect Hermann Gutmann, who had designed postwar synagogues in Düsseldorf and Hannover, was commissioned to design the project, for which a cornerstone was laid in June 1964.

The Jewish memorial in Dachau is wedge-shaped in the horizontal and vertical planes, a kind of trapezoid with a parabolic perimeter (fig. 21). The entrance to the building is on the open side of the parabola; an 18-meter ramp leads from ground level downward to the interior 2 meters below. The roof of the building, which begins above the bottom of the ramp, slopes upward toward the rear. The ramp, bordered above ground on both sides with pickets of stylized barbed wire, ends at a gate of barbed bars in the 10-meter-wide opening of the building. A vertical strip of light marble set in the apex of the parabola extends through a small round hole at the highest point of the roof, where it is crowned by a menorah. The column of light entering from the hole in the roof symbolizes not only the chimney that was the sole exit for Jews who descended the ramps of the gas chambers, but also hope, salvation, and freedom. The marble strip was hewn at Peki'in in Israel, a place where at least one Jew is supposed to have been living at all times in biblical history. It thus symbolizes the continuity of Judaism and its connection with Israel. The menorah represents the salvation that is the goal of the continual Jewish hope, in contrast to the unbounded hopelessness Jews experienced in the concentration and extermination camps, the ghettos and mass shootings. The Jewish memorial in Dachau emphasizes aspects of contemporary relevance with little historical justification, although it does include unmistakable icons of the extermination camps: the barbed-wire enclosure, the ramp, the underground gas chamber, the chimney.

The German Protestant Church initially responded negatively to Bishop Neuhäusler's call to erect a Protestant chapel in the Dachau memorial site.[69] Since the Catholic chapel had no explicitly denominational attributes, Protestant Church leaders first thought it would suffice if they donated an item to help furnish that chapel. When in 1961 Dutch survivors requested a specifically Protestant place of commemoration of the concentration camp victims in Germany, German Protestant leaders saw Bergen-Belsen, located in a predominantly Protestant area of West Germany (in contrast to Catholic Bavaria), as a more suitable location for such a project. If Bergen-Belsen was too isolated, they suggested, the chapel might be located in Frankfurt, a hub of foreign traffic to Germany. Finally, after the Dutch suggested that a former concentration camp would be a more appropriate location than a commercial center, and after Jewish groups protested against the Belsen site because so many Jews were buried there, Dachau was chosen as the location.

A cornerstone was laid on November 9, 1963, the twenty-fifth anniversary of the 1938 anti-Jewish pogrom. This date was found convenient because a high Church official could announce it during his trip to Israel in late October. In his consecration speech, Church Council president Kurt Scharf emphasized the role that the Dachau church was to play in the group identity of contemporary German Protestants:

> With the construction of this church we want not only to honor the sacrifice of our Protestant brothers and sisters, but also to attest to our solidarity with all victims of the National Socialist regime of violence. Here, where people were scorned, insulted, humiliated, and tortured, and where life was exterminated, [the

> words of] Jesus Christ shall be preached, He who is the brother of the miserable and the persecuted, and He who calls upon us to show solidarity with them. He exhorts us to change our ways and offers us forgiveness for all of our guilt; He gives us His peace and shows us the way to reconciliation among ourselves, and to deeds of peace among other peoples.[70]

Scharf's speech makes clear that the recollection of the past was to affirm a Protestant agenda in the present.

The naming of the planned church, too, shows the close link between commemoration and group identity. The original suggestion, Church of Atonement (*Sühnekirche*), was rejected, because it excluded the participation of foreign Protestants and camp survivors in the project but also because it was misleading: "because the crimes were so horrible that no expiation is possible," as one church leader put it.[71] The name Church of Christ's Expiation (*Sühne Christi-Kirche*), which was used in the official announcement of the project in November 1963, was later deemed unsatisfactory because it too closely resembled the name of the Catholic chapel, Church of the Mortal Agony of Christ (*Todesangst-Christi Kapelle*), and because non-German Protestant survivors saw their sufferings in the following of Christ's, so that they did not need His expiation.[72] The troubling implications of the holocaust for the non-camp-survivor collective German subconscious are manifest in other suggested names: Church of Penance and Supplication (*Buss- und Bittkirche*) and Church of Judgment and Mercy (*Gericht- und Gnadekirche*). The potential awkwardness of these names was recognized, however, and by the time the building was dedicated in May 1967, the name Church of Reconciliation (*Versöhnungskirche*) had been chosen.

This Protestant church is by far the most complex religious memorial in the Dachau memorial site (fig. 22). Its design was found through a limited competition in which seven architects were invited to submit plans.[73] The winning entry by Mannheim architect Helmut Striffler, published in the summer of 1965, sought to break the orthogonal symmetry of the camp with a curving outer wall of unfinished concrete, which was also intended to link the church, a parsons' quarters, a meeting room, and a central courtyard into one enclosed, protected space.[74] Unlike the tall Catholic chapel, which was built amid a number of other buildings in a camp full of barracks, the Versöhnungskirche, designed after the barracks had been torn down in 1964, had a low-lying, varying contour, "in complete contrast to the pathetic flatness of the camp," as the architect put it. Thus, its architectural form already reflected the sanitized memorial site around it.

About two-thirds of the building is below ground level. A broad, open stairway narrows as it leads down from street level to the enclosed courtyard with the meeting room on the left and the austere chapel straight ahead. All surfaces except the carpeted floor of the meeting room and the glass window are unfinished concrete, creating an impression of barrenness. The building can be exited through the sanctuary, on an ascending ramp leading from the glass doors separating the courtyard from the sanctuary to a heavy bronze portal at the rear. Visitors coming from the crematorium, a short distance away, read a multilingual inscription on the outside of the massive door: "Refuge is in the shadow of Your wings."[75] This biblical quotation reflects the architect's conception, which was to "afford a short breathing space, a gesture of help, to visitors to the camp as they make their way through it."[76]

Not only the architecture and naming of the building suggest that the German Protestant Church conceives of the holocaust as a legacy that calls for active atonement. The activities that take place in the building also confirm this impression. The meeting room, or "community room," is not merely another means by which "breathing space" is provided; its primary purpose is to "anticipate the impartial questioning of the young" and make available information about the activities of the Protestant Church during the Nazi era. A clergyman residing full time in the Church of Reconciliation was to support this educational mission.[77] Since 1979, volunteers from the Protestant youth group Aktion Sühnezeichen (Operation Sign of Atonement, now renamed Operation Sign of Atonement/Services for Peace) have been doing year-long internships at the memorial site. They organize exhibitions, discussions, and lectures, and guide tour groups through the site.

Since this younger generation began taking an active role in holocaust commemoration in the 1970s, the nature of recollection in Dachau has changed. This generation gap in collective memory was eloquently formulated by Ludger Bült, one of the first group of Operation Sign of Atonement resident volunteers in Dachau in 1979–

80. In a speech he gave on the tenth anniversary of the youth group's continuous work in Dachau in 1989, Bült criticized official Church commemoration for emphasizing self-referential themes such as "sadness," "hurt," and "deep inner shock," because they used the concentration camp experience for religious ends.[78] Instead of these "metaphors of pain," he called for "education about the causes and goals of National Socialism," and for the investigation of hitherto ignored dimensions of the holocaust, such as the use of prisoner labor by German firms and the fates of homosexuals in the camps.[79]

The effects of this generational shift are not immediately apparent in the outward appearance of the Dachau memorial site, but they have left some marks. In the 1970s, while no new memorials were established, more subtle changes were made: the exhibition was expanded to include the Jewish Holocaust, regular showings of a documentary film about the concentration camp were instituted, and a catalog of the museum's exhibition was published.[80] The number of young people visiting the memorial site, most of them on organized school field trips, climbed sharply during that period, so that by the 1980s a host of changes were necessary.[81]

A number of large maps and photographs on billboards were erected throughout the memorial site in an attempt to convey a visual impression of what life in the camp had been like. In the 1980s when the Dachau town administration continued the eradicatory work begun in the 1950s with the demolition of several structures—World War I factory buildings that had been part of the original camp in 1933,[82] the commandant's villa,[83] and railroad tracks leading from the town into the camp—several local groups mobilized to prevent the disappearance of this historic material. Although these groups succeeded in rescuing only one small section of the rail line, their public relations work did help to anchor the former concentration camp in public recollection.[84] Within this relatively secure enclave of local public memory other dimensions of the concentration camp experience are being explored and recollected, such as the existence of homosexuality and prostitution in the camps and inmate collaboration with the SS.[85] In earlier periods public discussion of these issues would have jeopardized public commemoration of the holocaust and exacerbated the marginal status of camp survivors.

Traces of this new multidimensional conception of the holocaust can be found in several places. In 1985 the Dachau memorial site inaugurated an annual journal, the *Dachauer Hefte,* to publish new research and inaccessible source material. Its thematic issues have explored, for example, slave labor in the camps, women's experiences as prisoners, and medical experiments in the camps. In the memorial site itself, a kind of architectonic inertia set in with the dedication of the international memorial in September 1968, so that this new multidimensionality has not yet found artistic expression. A move in this direction, an attempt to erect a plaque commemorating the homosexual victims of the concentration camp, ended in 1985 in a standoff between the survivors in the Comité International and the young initiative group.[86] For a number of years the granite slab was displayed in the semiprivate space of the Protestant Church of Reconciliation's meeting room, until finally in 1995 it found a permanent home in the museum's hall of commemoration, where other private plaques and ribbons from commemorative wreaths are exhibited.

Also since 1989, a number of towns along the route of the deadly evacuation marches of April 1945 erected memorials to recollect their town's personal contact with the Dachau camp. In 1996, the same year that construction was begun on a youth hostel in the town, the Bavarian Minstry of Culture and the Comité International de Dachau decided that a complete overhaul and reconception of the thirty-year-old exhibition was necessary for it to adequately represent the evolving recollection of the holocaust. In Buchenwald, whose memorial site was also reconceived after the fall of East Germany in 1989–90, a monument has been erected to commemorate the systematic murder of the Sinti and Roma, a group that was hitherto ignored in all German memorial sites.[87]

Such memorials for marginalized groups and forgotten aspects of the holocaust have begun to enliven holocaust commemoration in Germany. Coupled with continuing efforts to eradicate remains, they reveal that public recollection is a dialectical process of remembering and forgetting, and collective memory a contested entity shaped by symbolic battles over the signification of events giving meaning to our lives.

APPENDIX: CHRONOLOGICAL OVERVIEW OF MEMORIALS AT DACHAU

1945	May	Two 15-meter columns crowned by a cross and a star of David are proposed for the roll-call square
	November	Karl Knappe's proposal for a 30-meter-tall *Temple of Liberation* is released to the public
		Around this time a first exhibition is opened in the larger crematorium building
1946	April	A grave marker for the Dachau uprising is dedicated at the city cemetery
	October	The prize committee receives twenty-one new proposals for the Leiten memorial
1947	September	A plaque for the "Dachau Uprising" sponsored by Dachau survivors is dedicated on the savings bank opposite city hall
1949	August	Phillip Auerbach proposes a prisoner "pietà" by Fritz Koelle as a memorial for Dachau
		A mining operation uncovers human bones at the base of Leiten Hill
	December	Provisional dedication of the restored Leiten cemetery takes place
1950	April	The second Koelle statue of the "unknown inmate" is unveiled near the crematorium
		Designs for the Leiten memorial hall are shown and the cornerstone laid
		The exhibition is renovated
	September	The shell of the memorial hall on Leiten Hill is dedicated
		Newspapers and magazines print criticism of the renovated exhibition
1953	May	The exhibition is removed from the crematorium shortly after survivors' commemoration
1955	May	On the tenth anniversary of liberation, a Belgian plaque is placed at the crematorium, the International Survivors' Committee (Comité International de Dachau) is reestablished, and Italians begin raising funds for a chapel
	July	The Bavarian parliament considers a motion to close and tear down the crematorium

continued

1956	September	The Comité International de Dachau dedicates the cornerstone for an international memorial
1957		Demolition of the watchtowers is halted at the last minute
1958	September	A large international memorial, with a tower 50 meters high, is dedicated in Buchenwald
1959	January	The design competition for the Dachau international memorial elicits 63 entries from 18 countries; the design by Yugoslav sculptor Glid Nandor is selected
1960	July	The Comité International installs a temporary exhibition in the crematorium
	August	Fifty thousand people attend a commemoration in the camp during the Eucharistic World Congress
		The Catholic Chapel of the Mortal Agony of Christ is dedicated
1961	July	A memorial bell tower from Austrians is dedicated next to the Catholic chapel
1963	April	Ground is broken for a Carmelite cloister at the west end of the camp
	July	The Italian chapel (a miniature Pantheon) is dedicated on Leiten Hill; German president Lübke and Italian premier Segni attend
1964	April	A German survivors' organization dedicates a memorial to Soviet prisoners of war in Hebertshausen
		A Jewish memorial by Dieter Aldinger is dedicated in the city cemetery
		Demolition of camp-era barracks begins
	June	The cornerstone of a Jewish memorial building in the camp is dedicated
1965	May	A new museum in the former service building is opened and reconstructed barracks completed
		Cornerstone is laid for a Protestant church and meeting room
1966		Some 332,000 people visit the new museum
1967	May	The Jewish memorial building and Protestant Church of Reconciliation are dedicated
1968	September	An international memorial is dedicated on the roll-call square
1970	April	A Social Democratic youth group in Dachau proposes a commemorative agenda for the town

		Bavarian state police move into the former SS camp after the U.S. army moves out
1972	August	Commemorations are held during the Munich Olympic Games
1978	May	The museum publishes German- and English-language versions of its catalog; French follows in November 1979
1980	February	Volunteers from the Protestant group Operation Sign of Atonement start regular work
1981		Adult education courses about the Nazi era are offered in Dachau township
		State police use CS-gas and rubber bullets in the neighboring former SS camp
1983		The first summer youth camp is held, and the first three schoolteachers begin work
		Some 924,000 people visit the museum
1984	January	Museum begins closing Mondays
1985	April	Dachau is considered unsuitable for U.S. president Ronald Reagan to visit
		World War I–era buildings that were part of the camp in 1933 are torn down
1986	June	Social Democratic parliamentary proposal to establish a memorial in Dachau subcamps is rejected
1987	June	The Dachau camp commandants' villa from 1938 is torn down
		Local Christian Socialist Union party officials vow to "fight to the last drop of blood" to prevent a youth center
1988		A section of railroad track leading from town into the former camp is dedicated as a memorial
1989	April	Some towns along the route of the evacuation "death marches" dedicate memorials
1992	May	U.S. liberators of Dachau dedicate a plaque on the former gatehouse
1994	June	Departing Soviet soldiers build a Russian Orthodox chapel
1995	June	Plaque commemorating the persecution of homosexuals is moved from the Protestant chapel to the museum
1996	June	Plans for a $7.7 million renovation of the museum and memorial site are proposed

continued

1997	October	Bavarian parliament cuts funding for renovation by 40 percent
1998	May	International Youth Guest House is dedicated

Michael R. Marrus

The Future of Auschwitz: A Case for the Ruins

AUSCHWITZ-BIRKENAU, SITE OF THE LARGEST NAZI CONCENTRATION camp complex and graveyard for more than a million of its victims, is partly in ruins today, decaying and crumbling into the marshy Polish soil on which it was built more than a half-century ago. But after decades of neglect or inadequate attention, particularly from the standpoint of the Jewish victims and their survivors, conservation is now proceeding apace, part of the transformation of virtually every aspect of life in Poland following the collapse of communism in 1989. What rules should govern the process now under way? Specifically, might there be a danger of too *much* conservation at Auschwitz—too exhaustive a restoration, too aggressive a reconstruction, too zealous an effort to recapture in physical form the greatest death factory the world has ever seen? In August 1993, these questions were put to the Auschwitz State Museum authorities by a group of about thirty museologists, philosophers, social scientists, historians, and other experts. From North America, Western Europe, and Israel, we assembled in Oświęcim for a three-day conference entitled "The Future of Auschwitz." This paper is my brief personal report on that meeting, together with my own assessment of the broad direction that conservation should follow.

Let me first underscore what I think was obvious to every participant in our three-day conference: we were grappling with one of the most difficult of conservation problems, one for which there are no easy answers and perhaps no fully satisfactory ones. In its present condition as a memorial, a historical site, and a museum—to which tens of thousands of visitors flock annually, from near and from far—as in its past manifestation as a concentration, slave-labor, and death camp, Auschwitz is in a class of its own. Emblematic of the Nazi Holocaust in the West, but also the most important center for the commemoration of Polish suffering at the hands of the Nazis during the Second World War, Auschwitz is a place where several symbolic universes coexist and do not always complement one another.[1] As with the search for its historical significance, so it is with the challenges the camp poses to museologists and conservators: in the case of Auschwitz precedents do not readily apply and guidelines do not easily suggest themselves. As one conference organizer, the British anthropologist and Auschwitz authority Jonathan Webber, properly reminded us at a difficult moment in our deliberations, "We are all feeling our way."

Consider just the diverse origins and massive scale of the place.[2] Auschwitz-Birkenau is at the center of a huge camp complex, including detention facilities for political prisoners and slave labor camps, as well as machinery for mass murder. At the height of the Nazi empire the complex included more than forty camps scattered throughout the Upper Silesian countryside, in territory incorporated into the Reich after the defeat of Poland in 1939. Begun in June 1940 with the establishment of *Konzentrationslager* Auschwitz or Auschwitz I (also referred to as the *Stammlager,* or core camp), this system soon extended to a vast enclosure known as Auschwitz II, built on the nearby site of the ruined Polish village of Brzezinka, which the Germans called Birkenau. It was to that camp, beginning in 1942, that Jews from every corner of Europe were deported, almost all of them to be gassed and their bodies burned in specially constructed gas chamber–crematorium complexes specially built for the purpose.

After the war, the area that came under the jurisdiction of the State Museum at Auschwitz, organized in 1947, amounted to nearly 200 hectares, or 2 million square meters. Of these, over 200,000 square meters were within the *Stammlager,* with its famous "Arbeit macht frei" iron gateway, three-story brick barracks, and reconstructed gas chamber and crematorium; and some 1.7 million square meters fell within the immense confines of Birkenau, with its originally fenced-off interior subcamps, its rows of wooden and also stone barracks, its guard towers, storehouses, and other facilities, and the ruins of four huge gas chamber and crematorium complexes. In 1947 these two camps included over 150 buildings and other structures in various states of disrepair, plus kilometers of barbed wire, ditches, and other grim paraphernalia.[3] According to the careful investigation of Auschwitz State Museum historian Francizek Piper, as many as 1.3 million people were deported to this place during the period 1940–45, and some 1.1 million of them were murdered—about a million Jews, but also Poles (between 70,000 and 75,000), "Gypsies" (21,000), Soviet prisoners of war (15,000), and thousands of people of other nationalities.[4]

Crudely built in 1941–43, originally intended to house Soviet prisoners of war and then devoted to the Nazis' "Final Solution" of the Jewish question, much of the Birkenau complex was poorly constructed at the start—intended to last only for the short time the Nazis would take to complete their murderous project. Wooden barracks, for example, were set directly on the ground rather than on a foundation of stone, gravel, or brick. Many of these huts collapsed or were removed immediately after the evacuation of the camp, the materials being used for firewood or to construct shelters elsewhere. For more than ten years the remaining structures deteriorated owing to natural causes. They also underwent substantial alteration as a result of the complete or partial dismantling of buildings by former inmates and local inhabitants.

Conservation did not begin until more than a decade after the camp was liberated. But even after restoration began, parts of the camp complex suffered from continued vandalism. The museum grounds were officially demarcated as state property only in 1958, and a protection zone established around Birkenau in 1962. By 1978, according to Polish authorities in their application to UNESCO to list the camp as a World Heritage site, fewer than 20 percent of the original structures of Birkenau still survived. Since then, the deterioration of the site has continued. Moreover, some of the ruins in Birkenau, notably of the wooden barracks, are not "original" ruins but structures that were rebuilt in the 1960s and have subsequently collapsed. The postliberation perimeter of Birkenau has never been completely closed, and for years people have come and gone and cattle have grazed where more than a million people were once tortured and slaughtered. As of 1993, disruptive visitors remained part of the local landscape at Birkenau: in particular, fictional filmmakers, who not only added their own measure of destruction but also implanted a few new structures—such as guard towers and a barracks—intended to round out their picture of the camp during its time of operation. Happily, museum authorities decided in 1993 to prevent any such indignity to the camp site in the future by banning such films altogether from the camp's grounds.

What is the comprehensive conservation strategy for Auschwitz-Birkenau? Repeatedly, participants asked this of the Auschwitz State Museum authorities at our 1993 conference, suggesting that specific issues of preservation could only be resolved within the context of what museologists call a "curatorial plan" or "design philosophy," or what lay people might think of as a generally agreed-upon vision about the purpose of a place. Such an overarching scheme, several participants insisted, was sadly missing, and they found it difficult to move forward in the absence of such a clearly articulated, global conception.[5] Unencumbered by commitments to past decisions at the Auschwitz-Birkenau site, the critics tended to think in terms of broad options and diverse possibilities.

Museum authorities, on the other hand, seemed ill at ease with this line of thought and reluctant to define their guiding principles more narrowly than in the past. My own sense is that the 1978 statement prepared for the UNESCO authorities largely applied in 1993 as well: "While conserving its character of a monument to the suffering and struggles of nations, the museum serves as a historical exhibition and research institute with archives; it is also the largest cemetery in the world. By virtue of its activities, the museum makes an important contribution to the struggle for world peace and security."

One should also note the repeated commitment of the museum staff in recent years to take into account, in a way that had pointedly not been done before, Auschwitz-Birkenau's special significance for Jews. In part because more Jews were murdered in Auschwitz than in any other Nazi camp (although Treblinka with some 900,000 victims is a close second), in part because the Jewish victims of Auschwitz came from every corner of Europe and not just from Poland or Eastern Europe, and in part as well because there are tens of thousands of survivors of the Auschwitz complex and a rich memoir literature testifying to its horrors, this place has become virtually emblematic of the Holocaust (outside the former communist world, at least). In the past, the failure of the site and the museum to register this significance constituted a major bone of contention. It aroused protracted, intense polemics in the late 1980s, following the establishment of a Carmelite convent in a derelict building just outside the walls of Auschwitz I.[6] The resolution of this controversy to the satisfaction of most, together with the repeated and sincere statements of museum authorities, has removed the matter from the center of attention. Concerns about balance and emphasis still exist, to be sure, and even continuing unease on this issue in some quarters, but competing views about the place of Jewish victimization at Auschwitz did not play a visible role in our debate over a comprehensive conservation plan.

My own impression is that the reluctance of the museum authorities to define fixed curatorial goals springs in part from their discomfort with the notion of enshrining a single conception as official doctrine—an understandable apprehension for an institution emerging from an externally imposed, communist-dominated system that operated within a strictly defined ideological framework. In reaction to this past, the museum has embraced a resolutely pragmatic approach. As one official insisted, there *is* an overall conception at Auschwitz: it is a "mixed conception." "Mixed conception" apparently means that no single pressure group is allowed sway over the others; no single goal predominates; no single school of conservation thought sets the overall tone.

Two other forces may be at work in the museum's vagueness. The first factor is a reluctance to rebuke an older curatorial direction—forty years of sometimes painstaking labor on the part of sincere and committed museum employees, operating with insufficient means and in a national environment that treasures any record of Polish creativity and achievement. More than once, museum officials reminded us of the many years of constructive work staff members had previously invested in the museum under difficult conditions: cataloging artifacts, attempting to preserve exhibits, and rebuilding crumbling structures. Rethinking basic goals might impugn such faithful service and undermine time-tested, worthwhile efforts at conservation. The second factor is the staff's understandable apprehension of outside criticism, which rains freely on the museum from numerous quarters, national and international, some of them flagrantly insensitive to local concerns and responsibilities. Embracing one philosophy, they might well fear, particularly one worked out in consultation with intellectuals from outside Poland, would guarantee alienating proponents of other views. It might also diminish the commemoration of the suffering of the Poles themselves at the hands of foreign invaders—a highly sensitive point inevitably raised with the assertion of the Jewish significance of Auschwitz-Birkenau. Certainly the position of the museum officials in the sometimes intense debates over alternative courses was hardly enviable. It is not surprising that, with resources extremely limited, with a crumbling infrastructure, with lines of authority for decision-making sometimes blurred, and facing sometimes powerful competing interests, the authorities resisted a radical rethinking of their activity. "We're doing the best we can under very trying circumstances," they seemed to be saying.

Sympathetic and understanding as we outside critics may be, I think we must nevertheless press the case for a comprehensive review of existing priorities and signal our unease about some courses of action that have been proposed. In my view, the failure to work out an overall philosophy of conservation makes it difficult to set what Bohdan Rymaszewski, chair of the International Auschwitz Council's standing committee on conservation, referred to in our discussions as "a hierarchy of [conservation] tasks." Further, there is some danger that some currently contemplated restoration work could disrupt the unique atmosphere of Birkenau in particular, and could interfere with both its commemorative purpose and the interests of historical authenticity. Among the most remarkable aspects of that camp is the mood it evokes because of what James Young of the University of Massachusetts has called "the magic of ruins"—places "haunted by the phantom of past events, no longer visibly apparent, but only remembered."[7] Many of us at the conference, including me, felt that serious consideration should be given to preserving at least some of these ruins *as ruins,* particularly in Birkenau, which presents itself to visitors today as a unique place of horror.

From the guard tower at the southern entrance to that camp, through which the trains of deportees passed in 1944, Birkenau now appears both different than what it was under the Nazis and at the same time evocative of crimes of unimaginable magnitude. To the first-time visitor in particular, the camp seems vast, empty, desolate, quiet—quite unlike other tourist sites, and capable of communicating to most, I think, a deep sense of loss. Many hundreds of thousands were murdered here, the visitor learns, or recalls. Looking across the empty landscape one may learn little of how or why this happened, but the scale of the crime starts to sink in, together with another sense: that this is a place unlike any other, and therefore a place where the chatter of explanations may fail to get to the bottom of it all. The inescapable reaction, I think, is a feeling of awe and horror at what some people did to others.

Starting there, let me recommend that a test be applied to any conservation work planned for the camp: Will the changes detract in any serious manner from this sense of desolation, from the capacity of ruins to evoke dismay and revulsion in the face of terrible crimes? In other words, will the proposed restoration and reconstruction, intended to achieve clarity, make it more difficult to grasp the murderous enterprise as a whole? If the answer is yes, then the proposal fails the test.

The plans to reconstruct the twenty wooden barracks remaining at Birkenau—originally Wehrmacht horse stables intended as makeshift accommodations for inmates and set on the bare ground without proper foundations—illustrate well how well-meaning people's effort at reconstruction may hinder the search for historical authenticity. According to current plans, the twenty remaining wooden barracks at Birkenau, themselves reconstructions from the late 1960s and now in very poor condition, are to be turned into exact replicas of the originals through extensive repair and rebuilding. Work has already begun. Painstaking and laborious, this project involves carefully drawing, photographing, and dismantling the structures, replacing some wooden elements and reinforcing others, and finally setting the reassembled barracks on solid foundations, so as to prevent deterioration in the future. The entire process takes about six months for each barrack. But the result, from my standpoint, is less than satisfactory: a sanitized, well-reinforced stable, scarcely capable of evoking the filthy, flimsy structures into which inmates were packed like sardines and where they suffered agonies of hunger, illness, and exposure to the elements. The result, indeed, is so remote from the barracks described or remembered by former inmates as to call into serious question whether it is worth the effort. Indeed, unless properly set in context, the result may be deleterious: the introduction of a palpably "fake" element that will detract from the fidelity of the site. The danger, as James Young puts it, is that "even a well-intentioned conservation will begin to infect the surrounding area with the fiction of its own inauthenticity." Far better, I conclude, to rely upon the imagination of visitors as it operates amid the present-day ruins, perhaps assisted by models or photographs available of similar barracks during the Nazi period or at the time of liberation in 1945.

I cite this one example to advance some general opinions about reconstruction at the Auschwitz and Birkenau camps. Over the course of our discussions at the conference, we heard various plans and proposals for restoration—in effect for the construction of replicas of what is known to have existed under the Nazis. As of 1993, extensive work had been completed on the railway lines and platform built in Birkenau for the arrival of Hungarian Jews in the spring of 1944. For reasons that were unclear to me, expensive restoration had also been completed at one of the camp's sewage treatment systems, and work continued on the second. A second generation of repairs and reconstruction (the first was in the mid-1960s) was proceeding at the "Zentral Sauna," the building through which prisoners not immediately killed entered the camp as inmates. Substantial repairs were under way for the stone barracks and other structures. And there were proposals for the rebuilding of camp kitchens, infirmary barracks, and even part of the system of gas chambers and crematory ovens.

What is the likely effect, one should ask, of all this activity? In my own view, it is a mistake to try to replicate Auschwitz-Birkenau as it was under the Nazis—the apparent intention of much of the work mentioned above. For, to state the obvious, even the most faithful and most lavish of reconstructions could not include the mud, the filth, the stench, the noise, the cries, the smoke, the barking of dogs, not to mention the hordes of emaciated inmates and their tormentors. And so the result will invariably diminish the horror, render the place more "familiar," and hence more distant from historical reality.

Replicas will always be replicas. We should not invite visitors to evade the challenge to their imagination, and confuse our handiwork with the real thing. To be sure, much can and needs to be done at Auschwitz-Birkenau. Serious consideration should be given to freezing in place some or all of the ruined structures that remain. Some carefully selective reconstruction, or the use of models, or appropriately placed panels and photographs, might help visitors grasp what the original structures looked like and how they functioned. I and other participants appreciated the proposals of the Auschwitz State Museum officials that pointed in precisely this direction. There are many ways to help visitors to gain an understanding of the camp. But truth demands that they also appreciate how time and circumstances separate us from the years when hundreds of thousands suffered and perished in Auschwitz-Birkenau. Perhaps the best piece of advice—offered by participants awed by the difficulty of the task and aware that, whatever we do, future generations will contemplate the site differently than we do—was: Go slowly, cautiously, and do not pretend that we can see or understand it all.

Nathan F. Cogan

A Commentary on the Video-Documentary *The Last Remnants of Lithuanian Jewry:* The Narrative of a Holocaust Survivor

IN 1994 I PRODUCED THE VIDEO-DOCUMENTARY *THE LAST REMNANTS OF Lithuanian Jewry* (Berkeley, Calif.: Magnes Museum, 1995), using a script that had evolved out of my aunt Fanya's survival as a nun during the Holocaust. My son David M. Cogan edited and coscripted the film, adding footage of survivor interviews I had done in Lithuania in 1991 and 1992. Our hope was to shed light on the nearly total destruction of Lithuanian Jewry during the Nazi occupation and to provide students with a sense of the stark contrast between what the Holocaust world of Eastern Europe was once like and what it is today. That fewer than 200 Holocaust survivors still live in Lithuania, primarily in Kaunas and Vilnius (or what were once Kovno and Vilna), is a tragic reminder of the horrendous and inhumane murder of nearly 220,000 Lithuanian Jews, or Litvaks—that is, 93 percent of the total Jewish population of the country following the reannexation of the Vilna region from Poland in 1939. Indeed the number of victims murdered in Lithuania is as great as the total of Jews killed in France, Belgium, and the Netherlands combined. Against a background of nearly complete genocide, then, Fanya's testimony or narrative of survival provides a contemporary perspective and human focal point for comprehending an enormous loss.

Fanya's story is especially compelling for several reasons. First, she was rescued by a farmer named Luksha and then by an anonymous group of nuns and priests within the Church; more accurately, she "hid" as a nun, as Sister Theresa, going through conversion simply to save her life. She then spent the war years without papers in a series of monastic convent homes for the sick and elderly in Telšiai, Panevežys, and Anixčiai, Lithuania. Second, since the war, she has lived out her life in rural Lithuania, strongly aware of her Jewish roots but also self-consciously divided by her need to be assimilated in a society that was trapped in antisemitic Sovietism. Third, her story is uncommonly well documented. It emerges from three sets of interviews during her brief visit to the United States in the spring of 1989, Telšiai during my first visit in August through September 1991, and while I was teaching under a Fulbright grant at Vilnius University during the fall of 1992. In addition there are her letters in Yiddish and Lithuanian to America, first to my mother (1946–50), then after I initiated communication with her (1961–95). Her account also includes photos of family and friends retrieved from a photographer in Varniai (Vorne in Yiddish) after the war.

As the only member of my father's family in Lithuania to survive the Holocaust, Fanya remembers that lost world, even though she does not bear direct witness to mass murder. Fanya, like most survivors, did not remain unscathed. The enormity of loss affected her as much as it did all of the survivors I met there in 1991 and 1992, most of whom had become orphans during the war. Indeed, behind her spirited, pixieish personality is a woman who deeply remembers and understands Holocaust realities: loss of family, community, and childhood friends and the decimation of Lithuanian Jewish culture. Of the three Kagan siblings who did not make it to America before World War II, she alone could tell the story of that lost community.

Short and buxom, barely five feet tall, with dyed, deep brown hair tinged slightly red and sad though intelligent brown eyes, Fanya would laugh and speak of herself as the *alte makhsheyfe,* the "old witch," a strange, somewhat self-deprecatory, crude, yet comic Yiddish expression without a Lithuanian equivalent. If the word "pixie" more accurately describes her usually upbeat personality, her choice of terms probably conveys something more. Naming the self "witch" both protects and accounts for her outsider role in the Lithuanian world of Telšiai, where she has lived for decades as one of the few remaining Jews. During Soviet rule (1944–91), she essentially remained a Lithuanian citizen, singing Lithuanian folk songs with a deep-felt passion in a local choral group, or at home sharing her music with her son and daughter and her son's three children. Fanya's sense of Jewish culture shows up in her daughter's cooking, but her identification with the Jewish survivor community in Kaunas (formerly Kovno) and rural western Lithuania has not been passed on: her children are more aware of Jewish roots than Jewish identity.

Fanya has lived for more than forty years in Telšiai with her husband, Leon Kentra, whom she married in 1953. Her two children—Juozas (born 1946) and Vanda (born 1950)—live in Kaunas. All her immediate family of ten that remained in Lithuania when the Nazis arrived—mother, brother, sister and her husband, and six nephews—were murdered in the area of Telšiai (then Telz) by the Nazis and their Lithuanian cohorts in 1941.

The only child of Jakov Kagan and his second wife, Leah Moshovich Kagan, Fanya was born in Pavandine (Povondina in Yiddish), in western Lithuania, on July 11, 1918. Jakov's first wife—my father's mother—Rachel Feves Kagan (born ca. 1870), mother of the six elder Kagan children, had died in 1912 from traumatic bleeding. The three older sons, my father included, had immigrated to the United States by 1914, leaving behind two sisters and a brother. In 1928, Jakov (ca. 1867–1939), who had remarried in 1915, was about sixty years of age when he moved his family and shoe repair business from Pavandine to the village Varniai (Vorne). Of the four children still at home, Molly (Malke), born 1912, immigrated to the United States in 1936. Vorne, a shtetl with a Jewish population of several hundred, had one synagogue and a 250-year-old Jewish cemetery, which still stands. Both Jakov and his first wife, Rachel, are buried there. Only Dora Kagan Tallat-Kelpsiene, a survivor and the keeper of the Varniai Jewish cemetery and a close friend of Fanya's, lives there today.

From 1928 to 1939, Jakov continued his primary occupation of boot making and shoe repair in Varniai, though with help from his eldest daughter, Sora Mira (born ca. 1907), he also managed as a small farmer, keeping two milk cows at the Lithuanian farm of a Mr. Luksha, six kilometers from Varniai. Luksha later was directly responsible for saving Fanya after the Nazis invaded Lithuania. A significant irony: the Soviet occupation in 1940 prevented Fanya's family from marking her father's grave in the Varniai cemetery after Jakov died in 1939.

According to Fanya, her mother, Leah Kagan, suffered from bad health and was often bedridden. Fanya at the age of twelve was described by my own father during his only return visit to Lithuania in the summer of 1930 as a "bright young girl with a fine singing voice and a wonderful aptitude for languages." This link with America is ingrained in Fanya's memory, in part because my father, a trained cantor from the Shavel (Shauliai) yeshiva, had recognized her natural talent as a soprano and encouraged her to take lessons. Fanya remembers Hershele, twenty-eight years her senior, was "like a father to me." She strongly recalls his *davening* (chanting) in the Vorne synagogue, and her three American cousins—my eldest siblings—who were the same age and younger.

In describing "life before the war," Fanya remembers the dowry which Hershele had given to Sora Mira's husband, a delivery truck confiscated in July 1940 by the Soviets for military use. Though her half-sister Molly had immigrated to America in 1936, Fanya recalls with deep bitterness the Canadian government's rejection of Sora Mira and her family's emigration application in 1938, a denial based on the "fact" that "Jews were not farmers," a story that my mother (1897–1983)—who was born in Lithuania but who had emigrated in 1907—corroborated. When Jakov died in 1939, Fanya, then twenty-one, was responsible for caring for her often-ill mother. As the younger sister, she assisted Sora Mira with the care of her six young boys, two of whom were twins, born about a year earlier. Fanya still woefully mentions her older brother Meyer (born 1905), a tradesman and local violinist who, she proudly remembers, had made his own violin. Meyer, unmarried, lived at home too. Sora's husband, a delivery trucker, remained in that post during the year of Soviet occupation (1940–41). The sole photograph of Sora Mira's six boys appears in the video-documentary *The Last Remnants.*

Fanya also volunteered as a Hebrew teacher in a local *heder,* an after-school "Jewish" school. Earlier she had graduated from the local Lithuanian gymnasium in 1936. In 1940, after the Soviets occupied the country, Fanya continued to work as a clerk in a local food store in Varniai. She vividly recalls her father as an honest boot maker whose boots were admired by Lithuanians and Jews alike. She does not recall encountering antisemitism growing up, though she was well aware that Hitler's anti-Jewish propaganda had influenced life in rural western Lithuania in the late thirties.

Operation Barbarossa—Germany's attack on the Soviet Union on June 22, 1941—is vivid in Fanya's memory. (The collaboration of *Einsatzgruppe* A soldiers and Lithuanian militia in mass murder is one of the unbelievable horrors of the genocide of the Jews.[1] It is represented in my documentary with selected film and photo clips.) She also recalls that on July 2, "a Lithuanian farmer named Luksha turned me back in the middle of the day from visiting the farm outside of town" where she and other Jewish families in the area of Vorne had kept milk cows. "He warned me that the German army was within sixteen kilometers, and he and others already knew the Germans were killing Jews. He said I could stay on his farm." That day was to change the rest of her life. Her escape left behind her sixty-three-year-old mother, Meyer, Sora Mira, and Sora's husband, and their six boys. In our interviews Fanya reported, with visible pain yet restraint, that she could not save any of the boys though she desperately wanted to: western Lithuania was cut off, and they had known for days from radio reports that the Nazis were moving into Lithuania and driving out the Russian army. She indicated that anti-Jewish propaganda on the radio had been prevalent in her part of Lithuania. Fanya went into hiding, first with Mr. Luksha and his family.

The Nazis overran Lithuania in late June and by July had moved Jews into the Telz ghetto from her region. Fanya's *tragishe geschikhte* —the horror of "walking away" from her doomed family—became the never-ceasing "nightmare" of her lifetime. Within two hours' time on July 2, she pleaded with and begged Sora Mira to let her take one of the six boys, ages two to nine, but, as Fanya tells it, Sora Mira said, "For you to hide a circumcised Jewish boy [would mean] instant murder for the boy, for you, and for your Lithuanian protectors." She recalls a clandestine visit to the Telz ghetto to say goodbye to her mother, who had been moved there from Varniai. "I remember my mother waving to me, telling me to stay in hiding away from the ghetto."

Fanya's story, so often a series of discontinuous short narratives and rarely chronological, links memories about her family and friends with life after the war, when she was desperate to survive in war-torn conditions. While discussing her memories of survival during the war years, Fanya is very helpful just so long as she is not forced to deal with what Lawrence Langer would call "deep memory,"[2] the kind of memory that allows one to recall the details of humiliation and loss. For the most part, it has been simply too painful for her to deal with the memory of the loss of her immediate family, especially Sora Mira, who functioned as her mother. Although Fanya is excellent in telling stories about the war—acquired as postwar knowledge—she can describe details of her convent experiences in only the most general terms. She emphasizes how "lonely" she often was and how "fearful" she was lest her Jewish identity be discovered. She speaks of the countless and monotonous hours spent washing clothes of the elderly and sick. It is not clear whether her role as a nun—she never really believed in the baptism that she was forced to undergo—ever provided her solace in the sanctuary of the monastic system.

Leaving barefoot in 1941, she began a three-year escape into the makeshift "underground" world, first of farms and then of the Catholic monastery system, beginning in Telšiai as Sister Theresa, wearing a habit and constantly moving when Lithuanian fascists threatened the sanctity of the Catholic hospice settings where she worked. She admitted she was "baptized" formally, but never felt Catholic in her heart. "I used to think to myself, Why do I have to fake all that religious and Christian belief, when I know that my family is just as good?" From Telšiai she began a two-and-a-half-year journey across Lithuania, first in Panevyžys, later in Anyxčiai by mid-1942, caring for the sick and elderly. She occasionally joked about her role as Sister Theresa, singing Catholic hymns and then breaking into comic relief with "Rose Marie, I Love You," a song she may have learned from popular radio in the thirties. She shrugs when commenting on leaving the convent in late 1944, after the Soviets had driven out the Germans: "The priest and the mother superior asked me if I would like to stay on, and I said no." By the beginning of 1945, she had finally left the convent behind.

Fanya attributes her survival to the central critical fact that she could speak Lithuanian without an accent. Her survival in the Catholic monastic underground, by hiding in a series of shelter homes without papers or passport, had very much to do with the help of the priests. She still remembers the liturgy she had sung in Latin; once she broke out with bars from the "Ave Maria," perhaps to prove she had been there. And while she herself survived the war, she could not escape the tragedy of genocide. Fanya admits to having feared that Jewish lives were endangered in the outside world, but not until the war's end did she fully realize the horror of nearly total genocide. Not until the Soviet reoccupation of Lithuania in the late summer of 1944, while she was still working as a nun in a home for the aged in Anyxčiai, did she begin to learn of the mass murders. Her hiding obviously saved her life, but it distanced her from the actual pogroms and murders that took place throughout the country.

One anecdote she tells is revealing of her "escape" into the convent world. "I remember the German prisoners there [in Panevežys] in the [late] summer of 1944 after the Soviets took over the country. I don't like to tell this story to Jewish people because they would curse me for what I did, but the Germans who were starving begged me for food. I felt sorry for them and gave them bread. I asked them, 'Do you know who I am?' And one of them answered, 'Yes, you're a village girl.' And then I said, 'Nein, ich bin eine Judin.' One of them crossed himself. I knew he felt guilty. He said, 'We're members of the Wehrmacht, the regular army. We didn't hurt the Jews.'"

When Fanya returned to Varniai in early 1945, "there was nothing left: no house, no family, no records, no papers," and presumably no cemetery. Her friend Dora began restoring the Jewish cemetery in the late 1980s; by 1992 it had become a significant site of memorialization, drawing visiting Jewish emigrés from America, South Africa, and Israel. The survivors in the area of Telšiai, including those who had fled to Russia, today number perhaps twenty people; a marker recalling "14,000" now stands on a memorial sign adjacent to the Telz cemetery.

Fanya's postwar fate was burdened with hardship. By 1950 she had survived the loss of two husbands. Her first husband, whom she met in 1945, abandoned her in 1948, leaving her with a two-year-old. Her second husband, Vanda's father, died in June 1950 from tuberculosis, hardly two months after the second child was born. Leonas Kentra (born ca. 1923), a Lithuanian whom she married in 1953, became a "real" father to both Juozas and Vanda. Leonas, a furnace operator, helped raise her two children. They have always called him Father. Parenthetically, Fanya confided in 1992 that my correspondence from the United States to her family in the sixties had worried her immensely because she feared that her son Juozas's status as a student at Kaunas Polytechnic Institute might be threatened by her having an American relative.

Fanya's 1989 visit to the United States was remarkable. It was a reunion for a woman who had not seen external family members since 1941. After several days of "normal" culture shock she began, spontaneously, to break into impromptu Yiddish songs and, since she came at Passover time, even Passover songs in Hebrew that she had learned in the 1930s when many Lithuanian Jews had become active Zionists. In Yiddish, songs like "Dovid'l mein sohn" and "Mein yiddishe mamele," as well as dances that clearly suggested a physical ease with folk dancing, were a natural part of her repertoire. (Later, in 1991, we would videotape her dancing with her youngest granddaughter at her son Juozas's home in Kaunas.) Her Yiddish songs may also reflect her connectedness to other Jewish families that lived in Telšiai up to 1990 but have since moved to Israel. Today there are few Jews left in this town that boasted a major yeshiva and a Jewish population of over 1,500 in 1940.

In 1991 during my first visit to Lithuania, I drove with Mark Zingeris, a Lithuanian-Jewish poet and interpreter, to Anyxčiai, Fanya's convent setting, once a series of homes for the sick and elderly. I took photographs and interviewed an elderly lay sister who recalled how some townspeople of Anyxčiai had hid the town pharmacist, Katz, and his family during the war years, before they migrated to Israel. She did not recall a Sister Theresa. Fanya, who left in early 1945 and never returned, would say, "There is no one left who remembers me."

Across Lithuania in the second half of 1941, 175,000 Jews were murdered, mostly in pits and ravines set up by the Germans but handled by willing Lithuanian militias. What happened in Anyxčiai repeats the pattern. Rivka Lozanskaya Bogomolna, a woman who lives in Vilnius and who survived the slaughter of Jews in her town of Butrimonis, tells essentially the same story of cold-blooded murder by Lithuanian militia and Nazi soldiers. At Rainiai and Geruliai outside of Telšiai, where there are memorials to the dead, Fanya and her friends Dora and Rafael relate similar stories of mass shootings. Some of the killing fields remain unmemorialized though not unidentified.

Fanya took us to the "killing fields" outside of Telšiai on September 1, 1991, a day that symbolically commemorates the fiftieth anniversary of the destruction of the Telz (Telšiai) ghetto. From Varniai, Fanya's home, "Jews were transported to the Telz ghetto, and from there they were taken to killing fields and pits in Geruliai (the men) and Rainiai (women and children), and shot to death." Fanya's friend Dora Kagan Tallat-Kelpšiene, who was hidden by seven different Lithuanian farm families, had escaped the Telz ghetto in order to survive. Still a schoolteacher in Varniai, she describes the march from Laukuva to the Telz ghetto in July 1941 where her own mother was interred.[3]

In her reflections on the war, Fanya showed us two pictures of "Shainala" Glass, which are displayed in the video *The Last Remnants.* Fanya spoke fondly of her very attractive girlfriend whose striking "good looks caused young Lithuanian cadets to turn their heads in admiration" in the late thirties. Fanya commented that Shainala erred in marrying a Jewish pharmacist from Panevyžus because she gave up a potential singing career at the Riga Conservatory. A photograph that Fanya recovered from a photographer in either Varniai or Telšiai after the war testifies to the fresh, healthy looks of a woman murdered in the killing fields near Panevyžus in 1941 by Nazis and Lithuanian "Jew-shooters."[4] From a political perspective, Jewish Lithuanians, including Dmitri Gelpernas, who survived the Kovno ghetto and resides in Vilnius today, look back with nostalgia on the interim government of Smetona and a "free and democratic" Lithuania, where some Jews were able to serve in the Lithuanian military and be admitted to the university.

Essentially, Fanya survived both Hitler's war on the Jews and forty-seven years of sovietization in Lithuania by keeping quiet about controversial issues. This is not to say her life was dull: indeed, she had taken up Lithuanian folksinging after her marriage to Leonas in 1953. Despite a diploma for work in pharmacy school, she spent nearly three decades as a clerk-manager of a Soviet-operated store in Telšiai, raising two children and retiring on a microscopic pension in 1989.

Fanya's hiding as a nun is a classic example of passive resistance. The trauma, the horror, the humiliations, the fear of being caught, and, most significant, the loss of her entire immediate family—these are elements of her Holocaust experience. To what extent she feels guilty about being one of the lucky 7 percent, we cannot know, given her ability to mask her feelings, which is a constituent element in her survival. Two topics that emerged in the interviews seem, on the surface, to contradict each other but actually illuminate her self-divided role as a Jew and as a woman assimilated into Lithuanian cultural life. These topics are the role of Lithuanians in the murder of the Jews and the place of memorials that signal her lost past.

What becomes problematic in interviews with Holocaust survivors in Lithuania is the topic of Lithuanian complicity in the killing of Jews. Fanya's response that "there were good Lithuanians and there were bad Lithuanians" is conditioned, in part, by an innate fear of "talking bad" about her neighbors in rural western Lithuania. Yet the nightmarish fact of Lithuanian involvement with the Nazis is part of her consciousness. Naturally she had not written about it in her letters, and she was very cautious about addressing that topic in 1991 and 1992 partly because there is no reason to fault *all* Lithuanians. After all, her Lithuanian husband, Leonas, is a good husband to her and a good father to Juozas and Vanda. But there is an acceptance—perhaps a rationalization—on her part that she can live among the "good" Lithuanians. Two other female survivors whom I interviewed—both married to Lithuanian men—convey the same ambivalence as Fanya in their comments on the complicity issue. But in all three instances, they were rescued by Lithuanians or harbored in their homes. Fanya made these observations: "If you are a Jew among non-Jews, you can be an angel. But if you do anything wrong, they'll remind you of who you are. . . . But I have very good relations with the Lithuanians; our friends bring mushrooms and berries as gifts. Even when I became engaged to Leonas [in 1953]—a woman of a different nation with two kids—I felt 'different.' However, they soon discovered that I too was a real person, and I became accepted by everyone in his family." Fanya was reluctant to talk about Lithuanian complicity in the killings of Jews. The reemergence of Lithuanian nationalism at the end of Soviet rule in Lithuania in the period 1991 to 1992 added an impediment to talking openly about what she knows of Lithuanian involvement.

Mark Zingeris, the son of a Kovno ghetto survivor, was also troubled by my question of Lithuanian involvement. Like Fanya, his family claims deep historic roots in Lithuania, and he is quick to remark that Vytautas Magnus in the fourteenth century allowed Jews in. Mark would rhetorically ask, "How do blacks in America feel about the lynchings that took place in the South? Don't the blacks continue to live among those who killed their grandparents?" However reasoned, it is still not easy to understand how survivors can remain in that vast graveyard with the knowledge of such extensive Lithuanian involvement. Malke Sher Pelziene is a widow born in 1914 whose entire family escaped intact to Russia and Tashkent during the war. In 1994, after living in Plunge (1945–94), a town in northwestern Lithuania close to Fanya's Telšiai, she moved to Vilnius to be with her children, whose commitment to Jewish culture and identity makes them one of the last intact "Jewish" families in Lithuania. In an interview in December 1992, Malke told me that she did not trust her Lithuanian neighbors precisely because she knew exactly what role many Lithuanians played in the mass killings of Jews in Plunge and elsewhere.

Fanya's personal view of the genocide of the Jews is significant. Unlike survivors who have left for Israel, Fanya remains on the physical and emotional soil of Lithuania. Her memory of the past has been transformed into memorialization through annual visits to the Varniai cemetery and to the killing fields of Rainiai and Geruliai. During my first visit to Varniai and Telšiai in 1991, Fanya took us (my wife and adult son David were with me) first to the family graveyard in Varniai and then to the vast unmarked graves at Geruliai, Rainiai, and locations nearby—the area outside Telšiai where her entire family was shot and buried after the mass shootings in the late summer of 1941. Rafael Genas, a Litvak who also lives in Telšiai, accompanied us; he had survived as a sixteen-year-old recruit in the Soviet Sixteenth Division. Graveyard markers erected in the post-Soviet era indicate that fourteen thousand Jews were murdered in that region. (Earlier signs reading "14,000 *Soviet* citizens" were replaced by 1992–93.) Unlike Holocaust survivors in the United States, Fanya can go directly to the memorialized sites of the dead and grieve; in this sense the killing fields in Lithuania become objective correlatives of the grief survivors feel. Geruliai and Rainiai, with their unmarked graves of fourteen thousand, symbolize both memory and memorials. Fanya has adapted her life to postwar conditions in a country where large parts of the Lithuanian populace had participated in the killing of Jews. In the fifty years since she left the convent to return to civilian life, she has achieved a level of inner peace, having raised her two children during the Soviet occupation. If Fanya is symbolic of the surviving Jews of Lithuania, it is because she knows how to survive. Just as her new friend Jana Ran Čarny had not only disguised herself as a Nazi as she fled the Vilna ghetto in September 1943 but even became adept at playing the role of a Nazi secretary,[5] so Fanya had become skilled at seeming a nun. Louis Begley's young hero in his novel *Wartime Lies* describes this phenomenon of disguise in terms of "cheating": Tania "hated cheating, *except to avoid capture* . . . Tania said if it was my nature to be a cheat it was too bad that I was not at least original and clever at it."[6] Clearly, a high degree of cleverness was necessary to the survival of people such as Fanya and Jana.

The killing fields at Rainiai and Geruliai, where her family lies in unmarked graves, are significant for Fanya, but they are not on the map in the way Ponar and Fort IX are. In Fort IX near Kaunas, upward of 80,000 were executed, including trainloads of French Jews. In October 1992, when I told Fanya I had planned to visit Fort IX, it was difficult for her: "Why do you want to visit Fort IX?" she asked me incredulously. Perhaps she found my interest morbid. I had to ask myself, was there too much horror and tragedy in her consciousness already? In other words, was she asking: What more could I, her American nephew, possibly learn about the nature of the *Katastrophe* (the Lithuanian word for the Shoah) at Fort IX? Weren't Geruliai and Rainiai and the neighboring fields enough for anyone to deal with? Or was she asking me to mourn exclusively for *her* Holocaust dead rather than all the victims of the Lithuanian genocide? Both Fanya's marriage and assimilation into Lithuanian culture provide her with a degree of stability in a country once heavily dominated by antisemitic Sovietism. She has refused to be psychologically imprisoned by history, hatred, genocide, rejection, and even antisemitism. There is a profound existential reality about her: she is neither self-pitying nor apologetic. To have raised her children in such complex political, economic, and historical circumstances—without the choice of leaving and starting over—argues for a strong, surviving individual. Yet the Holocaust in Lithuania—as elsewhere—staggers our ability to comprehend the nature of the tragic murder of nearly 220,000, especially when we consider the extent to which Lithuanian nationalists, often neighbors, participated in the butchery. There were, of course, good Lithuanians who hid Jews—like Luksha, the farmer who enabled Fanya to escape into the monastic world. Fanya's story—that of a rescued person—differs from the realities faced by Jewish partisans like Dmitri Gelpernas or Jana Ran Carny, or others whose testimony is recorded in such significant film documentaries as *Partisans of Vilna*.

For some people, Fanya's story seems a bright and unique note in the midst of a very grim war. To some, Fanya's "survival" story seems so precious precisely because she hid as a nun. Yet these people, despite the graphic contextual and historical notes that accompany *The Last Remnants,* make the grave intellectual and/or emotional error of distorting Fanya's story by decontextualizing her survival from the realities of genocide. To gloss over her tragic experience by sentimentally appropriating an abbreviated, less painful version of the Holocaust—that is, viewing her as a nun—is unfair to the lesson to be learned from it. Indeed, her story, taken out of context, falsely provides an audience with what may be an emotionally satisfying, illusory fable. But no serious observer can afford to create a psychological safety zone that separates Fanya's hiding as a nun from genocidal brutality. To do so is equivalent to creating an ahistorical understanding of her story and a falsified view of rescue that overlooks its nightmarish elements, including guilt and personal angst. Similarly, students who reduce Anne Frank's diary to a painless exit from Holocaust realities also create a false intellectual highway.

It is necessary for students of the history and the literature of the Holocaust to reconnect individual biography to social and psychological realities. Fanya's role as nun hides some frightening truths, not only about her survival but also about the terrible statistics that underscore it. Sarah Neshamit, who has reported on rescue efforts in Lithuania, points out that "less than one-half of one percent of those who survived" were rescued by Lithuanians.[7] While Fanya did not experience crematoria, smoke, and ashes, she has had to deal with the pain and anguish of memory for over fifty years. Moreover, the idea of a Jewish woman disguised as a nun—without reference to historical atrocity—is an unfortunate psychological misappropriation, a distillation of joyful news without the necessary and compassionate understanding of another's tragic worldview. The psychological need to appropriate a happy, more promising story instead of its functional reality, indeed, is a distortion of truth. If some readers do not engage in the inquiry necessary to determine what happened to real people in the Holocaust, it is perhaps because they are psychologically not prepared to do so. Furthermore, to separate anyone's survival story from Holocaust realities is to minimize the horror of war and genocide. Fanya's urgent realization that necessity forced her to hide, to act out a dramatic role with precision, or otherwise face instant execution at the hands of the Nazis or Lithuanian sympathizers is *her reality.*

In *The Last Remnants of Lithuanian Jewry,* Fanya is a symbol of the Jew as survivor, someone we can touch and be touched by, yet someone whose survival forces us to confront the horror of genocide. As an affirmation of her being she provides us with a link to a past not quite forgotten. Perhaps the human conscience can only absorb so much horror at one time, and so we can add Fanya's story to several other film stories of survival, including *Weapons of the Spirit* (1985), about the good people of Le Chambon, France, and Steven Spielberg's *Schindler's List* (1993), based on Thomas Keneally's novel. We can also recognize that the level of fear that so understandably underscores the condition of the young hero of Louis Malle's *Au Revoir les enfants* has its analogue in the fearful world of the monastic convents where Fanya once hid. *Europa, Europa* (1991) provides a rich study of youthful survival in Nazi-occupied Eastern Europe.

As students of the Holocaust, we need to confront the horrible and at times unfathomable brutalities of genocide. We can also reflect on Fanya's survival as a measure of good will shown by an unknown handful of priests and sisters willing to save one life. How different from the perpetrators and bystanders, the indifferent, those who looked the other way: the handful of rescuers in the Lithuanian Catholic Church were critical participants in a disturbing commentary on genocide. About them we know so little. That Fanya survived disguised as a nun does not make history easier; it forces us to ask why so few opposed the racist policies of the Nazis. Had Fanya lived in Denmark, she would have witnessed a radically different response to those policies, as Hannah Arendt describes Danish resistance in *Eichmann in Jerusalem* (1962).

The Lithuanian nationalist or fifth-column involvement with the Nazis in the genocide of the Jews is horrifying. Despite some rescue attempts, the pogroms in Vilnius and Kaunas alone during the Soviet evacuation on June 22, 1941—just days ahead of the arrival of the Germans—paints a disheartening, excruciating picture of pro-Nazi Lithuanian complicity in evil. The brutal murder of over 220,000 Jews in Lithuania, the events at Babi Yar and elsewhere in the Ukraine and Poland, the incomprehensible murder of thousands of children, occurred long before the machinery of the Holocaust had become associated with crematoria, gas ovens, Auschwitz, and train journeys.

In the context of genocide in 1941 to 1944, the story of Fanya

Kagan Kentriene sheds lights on brutal events in Eastern Europe. She is clearly one of the lucky. We cannot, though, allow ourselves the luxury of mythifying her survival and making it emblematic of rescue. There are so few stories of rescue and survival in Lithuania that one would be guilty of distorting history to say otherwise.

Lithuania itself has paid an enormous price for its acceptance of Nazi authority in 1941 to 1944. Soviet occupation and the ensuing civil war (1944–51) led to the disappearance and death of 15 percent of the Lithuanian population. In the Devil's Museum, in Kaunas, there is a sculpture of Stalin and Hitler, each with devil's horns, Stalin chasing Hitler over a field of skulls, that "vast graveyard."

Fanya remains a survivor of the Holocaust world. In *The Last Remnants of Lithuanian Jewry,* I have attempted to give meaning to a lost culture, without irony and without sentiment, by focusing on memory and memorialization. Fanya as symbol of the survivor connects us to the Nazi destruction of Eastern European Jewry, a past we cannot afford to forget. She also connects us to survival in a small Baltic state trapped in its own self-destructive history. If the goal of the new republic of Lithuania is to reestablish and accept ethnic diversity as a civilizing value, then the present generation needs to acknowledge that history.

Scott Denham

Schindler Returns to Open Arms: *Schindler's List* in Germany and Austria

SCHINDLER'S LIST MADE SUCH A PUBLIC IMPRESSION IN GERMANY AND Austria that one hardly need review here the details of its unprecedented positive reception. It was a blockbuster hit, capturing over 4 million German viewers in its first eight weeks.[1] From American news magazines describing Richard von Weiszäcker and Steven Spielberg together at the film's gala opening in Frankfurt,[2] to the German debates on the film reported in the *New York Times,*[3] to Marion Dönhoff's letter to the *New York Review of Books,*[4] the reception was well documented in March of 1994 when Oskar Schindler returned home in such style. The private European premier, in Vienna on February 16, 1994, complete with Simon Wiesenthal, Austrian president Kleistil and chancellor Vranitzky, and other VIPs,[5] received less press coverage in the United States, but the effect was the same: the inauguration of a huge hit. In this essay I reflect on *why* the film was greeted so warmly in Germany and Austria, and I analyze the ignominious fate of three representative reviewers who dared criticize it.

A month before the Frankfurt opening on March 2, Andreas Kilb praised the film in a front-page editorial in *Die Zeit.* "Spielberg succeeds in doing what no other American or European director has yet achieved: transforming the history of the ghettos and concentration camps into a cinematic fiction without distorting it by way of kitsch or cheap brutality."[6] Second, he asserts, this movie puts to rest the basic aesthetic question of whether the Holocaust can be portrayed on film, especially because the hero is a German. This brings up a third point for him, one to which I will return: why is it that none of the important Holocaust films come from Germany?[7]

In mid-February both *Bunte* and *Der Spiegel* also introduced *Schindler's List* before it opened, *Bunte* in a scoop interview with Schindler's widow, Emilie,[8] and *Der Spiegel* with a striking cover story on "The Good German"; the cover—a close-up of Liam Neeson, who plays Schindler in the film, with the words "Der gute Deutsche" across his chest—was later reproduced in *Newsweek*'s story on the movie's success in Germany.[9] The *Spiegel* subheading proclaims that Spielberg's film "does justice to this great theme with seriousness, forcefulness, and passion."[10] The lengthy *Spiegel* story is mainly background information and does nothing but praise Spielberg and the movie; it canonizes the film as a teaching tool, as required viewing for everyone. And just this, of course, has happened: both German and Austrian schoolchildren by the thousands have seen the film and viewed the screenings with rapt attention.[11] Like the first *Spiegel* story, *Bunte* and a flashy piece in *Stern* also say nothing critical about the film in their preview publicity articles, but provide only sensationalistic supporting information: *Bunte* goes to Argentina to chat with Emilie,[12] and *Stern* talks with *Schindler-Juden* in Israel and elsewhere.[13] Likewise, a second *Spiegel* article concentrates on the testimonials of Schindler Jews.[14] Lots of photos all around.

The flood of reviews and editorials began the first week of March. One of the most striking is Frank Schirrmacher's in the conservative daily paper of record in Germany, the *Frankfurter Allgemeine Zeitung*. In a front-page editorial, Schirrmacher can't conceal his surprise that Spielberg, of all people, has made an "emotionally powerful" film that is "deeply nonideological" and concrete and thus effective. It "rescues history from abstraction and turns it into a vivid process." Spielberg, he says, "shows that art is educating and, even in our visually overstimulated age, capable of astonishing power." He closes with the sentence: "Everyone should see this film."[15] The movie was praised as well at the other end of the political spectrum, by Sylke Tempel in *Die Wochenpost* and Sabine Horst in *Konkret*.[16] Tempel's argument about why the film is good is far more subtle than most. She argues, after praising the "nuances" of Spielberg's technique, that this "hero who isn't one," this obnoxious, drunken playboy, sets a very basic standard for action:

> People such as this destroy the self-pardoning assumption that no act of resistance was possible under the Nazis' totalitarian system. . . . It's no accident that no film about Schindler has been made in Germany . . . [and that] embarrassingly low pensions are paid to those who helped the oppressed and high pensions to the SS widows. . . . It is apparently easier to portray the horrible deeds than to put up a monument for those who didn't look away, who were able to get around a murderous system, to remain decent, to resist.[17]

The film suits her since it condemns, implicitly, the inaction of most Germans. For Schirrmacher of the *Frankfurter Allgemeine,* on the other hand, the film celebrates a German hero and so all Germans share in his triumph.

Can we know why so many Germans saw the film? Was it to see a German hero and thus feel good about a German who saved Jews? Or was it to get yet another shot of collective guilt: why didn't others save Jews the way Schindler did? I doubt that either reason was primary in the minds of German filmgoers. I think that Schindler's story drew German viewers because of its famous director, and because of all the hype and press that preceded the film. It was marketed brilliantly, and not only through a subtle advertising campaign. The front-page—rather than culture section—placement of press coverage, the many television discussions, documentaries, and gala premiere photo ops, the fact that this was, after all, Hollywood, together served to fix this movie in the minds of the public to a vastly greater degree than some other comparable cultural event like, say, Reitz's *Heimat* or the uproar surrounding Christa Wolf's *Was bleibt?* or the *Historikerstreit* (the now-famous "Historians' Dispute" of the mid-1980s). As Wim Wenders put it in a recent interview, *Schindler's List* "is a truly remarkable film, but if it bore the name of Andrzej Wajda and not Steven Spielberg, nobody would care about it. It's a Polish film, beautifully shot by a Polish team, and judged by its style could have been made by Wajda, in which case it would have been an art film, it would have been shown with subtitles, and about 1 percent of the people who see it now would have seen it."[18]

I think that more German viewers, once drawn into the theater, "liked" (approved of, were moved by, felt good about) the film because it is essentially a movie about Schindler's redemption, and not about the Holocaust. Schindler's story is so compelling because it is improbable and incredible and at the same time a classic salvation story. Claude Lanzmann called it cathartic for viewers to cry during the film,[19] but in strictly literary critical terms the story is a romance rather than a tragedy, for the hero survives and order is restored to his world. *Schindler's List* is a feel-good movie.

The feel-good aspect is what the *Wochenpost*'s other reviewer, Sigrid Löffler, finds fundamentally troubling with the film. (And with Löffler we move into a discussion of the dissenting reviewers and their surprising fates.) "Film as Indulgence" ("Kino als Ablass") she calls her devastating review, in which she first agrees that Spielberg has made a high quality film. "But," she asks,

> is good taste with respect to this subject really a critical category? Is the aura of authenticity, the documentary wash and newsreel quality of the black-and-white footage, really a virtue? Does showing per se have any educational value? Can one really influence the filmgoer positively by way of empathy and feelings of understanding, really change opinions and attitudes? If so, then the millions of kids who got their training in how to love foreigners and outsiders thanks to *E.T.*'s sappy emotionality would have had to grow up to be pure xenophiles and protectors of minority rights. Unfortunately, it seems as if the opposite has taken place: [*Schindler's List*] functions as a spiritual laundromat, instant absolution, an emotional quickie. . . . The movie ticket becomes an easy ticket of indulgence.[20]

She further makes the point that Spielberg's now-famous Auschwitz shower scene will surely play into the hands of the Holocaust deniers: it was water after all, they can say.

Other negative views of the film were voiced most prominently by Will Tremper in the conservative *Die Welt,* and by Günther Rühle in the Berlin daily *Tagesspiegel.* Tremper's critique that the film was "pure Hollywood," Rühle's that "lots of people are making lots of money with Schindler right now," and Löffler's are nothing new: anyone reading the reviews in the United States, or just discussing the film among friends, will have heard all these arguments.[21]

For me the fascinating point about the film's reception in Germany has to do not so much with a very few dissenting voices but with the fact that Henryk Broder—a well-known commentator on German-Jewish issues and a kind of Mr. Moral Jewish Voice in Germany—caustically censured these three critics with charges of anti-

semitism. His prominent article, "Kritik der dummen Kerls: Spielbergs Widersacher" (loosely, "Dumb Guys Criticize Spielberg"),[22] appeared in the *Frankfurter Allgemeine*—the same paper where Schirrmacher had encouraged the whole country to see this great movie, and where in past years the conservative side of the *Historikerstreit,* the condemnatory blow to *Europa, Europa,*[23] the right-wing view of the Bitburg controversy, and similar sentiments had been put forth. Although Broder can easily be an absolutist on paper, has a poison pen, and never seems hopeful about human relationships, he often has good points to make about things German and Jewish in Germany. Yet why this hostile, condemnatory reaction to the few critical voices about the film?

First, it is important to note that Broder had previously written on the film, using arguments similar to Tempel's outlined above, in a prominently placed "Theme of the Week" essay in *Die Woche,* a newish middle-brow weekly with a big national circulation. Here he writes on March 3, 1994: "[Schindler] proved that it was possible to remain decent in a dictatorship. One didn't have to be a hero or a saint, just a person with a normal sensibility for what one may do and what one may not."[24] Schindler's story provokes, he goes on to say, because it raises the uncomfortable questions "Why weren't there more Schindlers?" and "Why did my parents and grandparents always say that one couldn't do anything, whereas someone like Schindler is proof to the contrary?" For Broder, the film has a moral and educational value: its story can force useful, even productive thought about other scenarios of (potential) individual action in the face of evil—in Sarajevo, to use his own example.[25] Yet not even two weeks later he returns to the film in a much less useful manner, it seems to me, in a vicious attack on the three dissenting voices mentioned above.

In his response to Tremper, Löffler, and Rühle, Henryk Broder accuses all three of having given voice to an antisemitic subtext: "All three critics express their disappointment in such a way as to make one suspect that the film is the last thing on their minds. A latent discontent seems to have been waiting for a respectable occasion to be articulated."[26] When Löffler condemns *Schindler's List* implicitly, because it will not or cannot teach and effect action since it is just a typical Hollywood tear-jerker, when Rühle contends that lots of folks are making money on Schindler, when Tremper complains about the "Wild West-like" aspects of the ghetto liquidation scene or the fictional sex scenes or the film's propagandistic aspects, Broder sees these complaints as subtle attacks on the normal commercialism of Hollywood and veiled repetitions of clichéd accusations of "Jewish wheeling and dealing."[27] Broder also finds in their critiques the well-known antisemitic argument that the Jews are using the Holocaust for their own gain, to make money.

To be sure, Will Tremper's "review" of the film, which he dubs "Indiana Jones in the Cracow Ghetto," was hardly a review at all, and it is indeed reckless and self-serving. Tremper claims, using a long quote from Himmler's famous Posen speech of October 1943, that "real" SS soldiers would have been much better behaved during a ghetto liquidation than were Spielberg's. Maybe so, but this isn't the point. So Tremper deserves a thrashing (and he was taken to task by others as well),[28] but not, I think, Löffler or Rühle, whose concerns about the film are legitimate. Broder's essay concludes: "Where others spray 'Juden raus!' on walls and gravestones, some write a [film] critique. Which is to say that the vandal says what he thinks, while the critic just acts as if he were discussing a film."[29]

As Broder's and other similar responses show, a kind of "politically correct" censorship is at work here. As one commentator puts it: "Some Germans seem to believe that Germans are necessarily forbidden from thinking that films about German crimes are bad."[30] Broder's vicious attack inspired three further interesting responses, both directly aimed at damage control, at keeping discussion of this film from becoming another Bitburg affair, in my view. In the *Frankfurter Allgemeine Zeitung* Michael Wolffsohn appealed for calm, measured discussion about the film, specifically for a bit more caution in using such terms as "antisemitism" and "extreme right."[31] For, he says, to call a critic an antisemite, rhetorically, leaves us with no words for real, violent, neo-Nazi xenophobic skinheads. He, too, is put off by Löffler's and Tremper's pieces. Yet "whoever calls Will Tremper and Sigrid Löffler 'antisemites' doesn't know the brutality and racism of real antisemites. . . . Gulfs lie between such terribly self-important or off-base critics and the old-new antisemites," says Wolffsohn.[32]

Klaus Rainer Röhl in *Die Wochenpost,* who also reviews Broder's attack and condemns it as irresponsible,[33] Andreas Kilb in *Die Zeit,* who dismisses the Tremper-Broder spat as irrelevant bickering,[34] and Wolffsohn all point out that Broder is essentially creating a climate of political correctness around the discussion of the film and the whole topic. By this they mean, of course, that Broder is prohibiting debate by implying that any dissent from the "correct" view is a sign of, at best, latent antisemitism. Kilb tries to deflate the matter by stating that there is no crisis: "Unlike the series *Holocaust* several years ago, Spielberg's film has *not* initiated a dispute in the German papers."[35] With this bizarre statement, we can only conclude that Kilb wants everyone to say simply, "Great film," and leave it at that. And in fact, this is what most Germans have done.

All this raises two main issues. First, we see again that the past is still far from "mastered," as so many would have it. As the *Historikerstreit* of the eighties would do once more, the showing of the television miniseries *Holocaust* in 1979 opened up German public discussion about the Holocaust in many interesting ways. Most striking was the degree to which discussions of guilt (national, collective, and individual), complicity, and resistance were carried out in the public sphere of television, radio, and the print media. The series *Holocaust* had several especially interesting results. New, above all, was the degree to which it created understanding and opened up repressed emotions, emotions that until then had, it seemed to many, never been expressed or had never been allowed to be expressed in the face of textbook data, documentaries, and other mainstream public portrayals of the Holocaust. The series also unleashed a new flurry of talk about the "educating potential of the media in general and the fictional film specifically, and about the limited effects of documentary films."[36] Many commentators discussed the troubling fact that the viewers (themselves included) reacted to the emotions and characters and narrative, but not at all to what is actually a very problematic portrayal of historical fact.

We see, of course, the same phenomenon lurking in the background of the discussion of *Schindler's List.* Yet it is as if the Germans have tired of real debate on the issue, and a kind of Americanist non-debate has set in. Good movie, they say; don't spoil the affair by showing the world that we don't appreciate a German hero when given one; let's agree that this movie will teach our schoolkids how to be better citizens, to do the right thing like good old Oskar did. It has indeed been easy for the German public to see this movie as something it is not. The film is really about Schindler and his salvation, set against the backdrop of the sadist Goeth (played by Ralph

Fiennes) and the unmitigated evil of the Hollywood SS extras. The film is not about the Holocaust, it's about a happy end in the gas chambers. It's water, after all, for righteous Schindler's Jews.

That the German press has almost univocally praised this film, and that several prominent commentators have tried either to quell dissenting voices or to paper over the stains of possible debate, seems to me to show how the German community has taken a slightly different message from the film than has ours. In Andreas Kilb's preview commentary in *Die Zeit* he raises the question about why none of the important Holocaust films have come from Germany; Broder asks this same question in his first discussion of the film. Arthur Brauner, a major producer in Germany, for years did in fact try to make Schindler's story into a film, but could get no funding.[37] And what if he had? How might the world have understood a film from Germany telling the heroic tale of a good Nazi who saved the lives of Jews, regardless of the truth or legitimacy of the story? It would never have worked. But let a Hollywood master who also happens to be Jewish make the film—indeed he says he rediscovered his Jewish identity in doing so—and let it be done (arguably) tastefully, tactfully, with a gripping plot and technical brilliance, and let it offer an unambiguous condemnation of Nazi evil and a call for action in the face of terrible odds, and to top it off let its final image—Spielberg's actors and Schindler's Jews filing past the righteous man's grave—be one of hope and reconciliation. Send this to Germany and what do we expect?

As a picture of the Holocaust, *Schindler's List* is a distortion, but as the story of Oskar Schindler it's as compelling a tale as many have heard in a long time. The German trick in watching this film is this: conflate these two subjects, the Holocaust and Schindler, into one, and then conclude simply, gratefully: "Great film; thanks, Spielberg." What was it Richard von Weiszäcker said to Spielberg after the Frankfurt premiere? "It needed you to do it."[38]

A BIBLIOGRAPHY OF *SCHINDLER'S LIST* PRIMARILY IN THE GERMAN AND AUSTRIAN PRESS

Ackerman, Gwen. "Premierengäste kämpften mit den Tränen." *Die Welt,* March 3, 1994.

Acklin, Claudia. "Wieder ein Mammutunternehmen: Zu *Schindler's List* von Steven Spielberg." *Tages Anzeiger,* December 22, 1993.

"Als ob es gestern war: Premiere von *Schindlers Liste.*" *Süddeutsche Zeitung,* March 3, 1994.

"Ansturm ungebetener Besucher: *Schindlers Liste* brachte Ungemach für Schindlers Witwe." *Oberösterreichische Nachrichten,* January 25, 1994.

"Arthur Cohn über *Schindlers Liste.*" *Baseler Zeitung,* April 2, 1994.

Bauschmid, Elisabeth. "Kronzeuge Himmler: Der neue Relativismus der geistigen Welt: Schindler, Spielberg und die Zumutung des Erinnerns." *Süddeutsche Zeitung,* March 3, 1994.

Berger, John. "Die Grenzen des Erfolgs: *Schindlers Liste* oder Widerstand aus dem Geist unserer Zeit." *Frankfurter Rundschau,* April 30, 1994.

Blair, Jon. "Der grosse Gatsby von Polen: Steven Spielberg über die Entstehung seines Filmes *Schindlers Liste.*" *Profil,* January 17, 1994.

Bremer, Jörg. "Ist der Holocaust in Bildern darstellbar? Grosser Respekt, aber auch Kritik: Steven Spielbergs Film *Schindlers Liste* wird in Israel diskutiert." *Frankfurter Allgemeine Zeitung,* March 4, 1994, 33.

Broder, Henryk. "Deutsche Ausreden." *Die Woche,* March 3, 1994.

———. "Kritik der dummen Kerls: Spielbergs Widersacher." *Frankfurter Allgemeine Zeitung,* March 15, 1994, 33.

Bruckmoser, Josef. "Der Spieler und Nazi-Kumpan rettete 1200 Juden das Leben." *Salzburger Nachrichten,* February 14, 1994.

Buchka, Peter. "Der Schwarzmarkt des Todes: Das Unfilmbare filmen: Steven Spielbergs *Schindlers Liste.*" *Süddeutsche Zeitung,* April 3, 1994.

Busche, Jürgen. "Zeitgeschichte, im Fernsehen diskutiert: Ein positiver Held?" *Süddeutsche Zeitung,* March 29, 1994.

Cheyette, Bryan. "*Schindler's List.*" *Times Literary Supplement,* February 18, 1994.

"Club 2 Diskutiert *Schindlers Liste.*" *Wiener Zeitung,* March 1, 1994.

"Deutschland: Bombendrohung bei Premiere von *Schindlers Liste.*" *Vorarlberger Nachrichten,* March 5–6, 1994.

Dönhoff, Marion. "Dissent on *Schindler's List.*" Letter to the Editor. *New York Review of Books,* June 9, 1994, 60.

"Ehrentafel für Schindler." *Tages Anzeiger,* February 12, 1994.

"Entspannung: Drei weitere Berliner Kinos zeigen *Schindlers Liste*." *Der Tagespiegel,* March 11, 1994.

Epstein, Jason. "A Dissent on *Schindler's List*." *New York Review of Books,* April 21, 1994, 65.

Frank, Michael. "Kein Lächeln für einen liederlichen Helden." *Süddeutsche Zeitung* (March 10, 1994): 3.

Frank, Niklas. "Der Deutsche, der uns rettete." *Stern* 10 ([March] 1994): 197–205.

Furler, Andreas. "Poker mit Mördern." *Tages Anzeiger,* March 4, 1994.

Gangloff, Tilmann P. "Falsch Dargestellt: Zur Kritik an *Schindlers Liste*." *Stuttgarter Zeitung,* February 7, 1994.

"Ganz anders als Hollywood: Steven Spielberg kam zur Premiere von *Schindlers Liste* nach Wien." *Tiroler Tageszeitung,* February 17, 1994.

Gemünden, Gerd. "I No Longer Trust the Power of Images: A Conversation with Wim Wenders." Unpublished interview. March 1, 1994.

"Gesinnungsstreit über *Schindlers Liste*." *Vorarlberger Nachrichten,* April 2–3, 1994.

Gierig, Monika. "Abgrund der Erinnerung: Was amerikanisch-jüdische Kritiker an Spielbergs neuem Film 'Schindler's List' bemängeln." *Frankfurter Rundschau,* January 15, 1994.

Göttler, Fritz. "Bilder töten die Imagination: *Schindlers Liste* in Claude Lanzmanns Sicht." *Süddeutsche Zeitung,* March 5–6, 1994.

Gourevitch, Philip. "A Dissent on 'Schindler's List.'" *Commentary* 97.2 (1994): 49–52.

"Grenze für Greuel." *Der Spiegel* 11 (March 14, 1994): 192–206.

Grissemann, Stefan. "Hollywoods Notizen zu einer Industrie des Todes." *Die Presse,* March 4, 1994.

Gross, Alan G. "Filming the Holocaust." Letter to the Editor. *Times Literary Supplement,* March 18, 1994, 16.

Gross, John. "Hollywood and the Holocaust." *New York Review of Books,* February 3, 1994, 14–16.

Günther, Egon. "Spielbergs Juden." *Neues Deutschland,* March 23, 1994.

Gympel, Jan. "Das Kino ist keine moralische Waschanlage: Will Tremper und der immer heftigere Streit um den Film 'Schindlers List.'" *Tagesspiegel,* March 20, 1994.

Hanisch, Michael. "Das Mädchen im roten Mantel." *Neue Zeit,* March 3, 1994.

Hasler, Thomas. "'Ein Tribut an die Menschlichkeit': Spielbergs *Schind-*

ler's List läuft in Zürich mit grossem Erfolg—Beobachtungen im Kino Le Paris." *Tages Anzeiger,* March 21, 1994.

Heim, Christoph. "Den Horror zeigen, davon erzählen." *Baseler Zeitung,* March 4, 1994.

Heinlein, Peter. "Suche nach dem wahren Oskar Schindler." *Die Welt,* February 25, 1994.

Heinrich, Ludwig. "Bei Spielberg fehlt keiner." *Oberösterreichische Nachrichten,* February 16, 1994.

Heller, Edith. "Ich will nicht sehen, wie meine Eltern starben." *Tagesspiegel,* May 1, 1994.

Hertneck, Marcus. "Wenn alles in einen Topf geworfen wird: Anmerkungen zu zwei Dokumentationen über Oskar Schindler und Spielbergs Dreharbeiten." *Süddeutsche Zeitung,* March 8, 1994.

Hirsch, Helga. "Wohltäter aus Angst?" *Die Zeit* 11 (March 18, 1994): 14 (foreign edition).

Hoberman, J., et al. "*Schindler's List: Myth, Movie, and Memory.*" *Village Voice,* March 29, 1994.

Hoffman, Rainer. "*Schindlers Liste:* Reaktionen in Deutschland auf Spielbergs Holocaust-Film." *Neue Zürcher Zeitung,* March 15, 1994.

"Hoffnung statt Hoffnungslosigkeit: Benefizgala von *Schindlers Liste* in Wien." *Wiener Zeitung,* February 18, 1994.

Horlächer, Pia. "Arche der Hoffnung: 'Schindler's List' von Steven Spielberg." *Neue Zürcher Zeitung,* March 3, 1994.

Horst, Sabine. "'We Couldn't Show That.'" *Konkret* 3 (March 1994): 40–42.

Hütter, Frido. "Lektion aus Hollywood: Steven Spielberg Holocaust-Film *Schindlers Liste* wurde gestern in Wien vorgeführt." *Kleine Zeitung,* February 11, 1994.

———. "*Schindlers Liste.*" *Kleine Zeitung,* March 5, 1994.

———. "So ist *Schindlers Liste* in Polen gedreht worden." *Kleine Zeitung,* February 26, 1994.

Jackson, James O. "Schindler Schock: Speilberg's Film Stuns the Two Lands of the Holocaust, Germany and Israel, Annoying Some Critics but Overwhelming Viewers." *Time,* March 14, 1994, 53 (European edition).

Jansen, Peter W. "Das Mädchen mit dem Roten Mantel: Ein Film über Erinnerung, Massenmord, Menschlichkeit: Spielbergs Meisterwerk *Schindlers Liste.*" *Der Tagesspiegel,* March 1, 1994.

Jerzabek, Günther. "Schindler war ein Sudetendeutscher." Letter to the Editor. *Süddeutsche Zeitung,* March 2, 1994.

Joffe, Josef. "*Schindlers Liste.*" *Süddeutsche Zeitung,* March 19–20, 1994.

Jörges, Hans-Ulrich. "Ein Film packt die Deutschen: *Schindlers Liste* konfrontiert die Nation auf neue, erschütternde Weise mit ihrer Nazi-Vergangenheit." *Die Woche,* March 3, 1994.

Karasek, Hellmuth. "Die ganze Wahrheit schwarz auf weiss." Interview with Steven Spielberg. *Der Spiegel* 8 (February 11, 1994): 183–86.

Kilb, Andreas. "Des Teufels Saboteur." *Die Zeit* 10 (March 11, 1994): 13–14 (overseas edition).

———. "Stichelei: Noch einmal zu Schindlers Liste." *Die Zeit* 13 (April 1, 1994): 13 (foreign edition).

———. "Warten, Bis Spielberg Kommt." *Die Zeit,* January 28, 1994, 1 (foreign edition).

"Kinoaufführung durch Klatschen gestört." *Frankfurter Rundschau,* April 8, 1994.

Klein, Hanna. "Spielbergs Film und die österreichischen Retter." *Volksstimme,* March 11, 1994.

Knopf, Michael. "'Viele wollen nichts wissen': Ratlosigkeit nach dem Entsetzen: Wie Jugendliche auf Spielbergs *Schindlers Liste* reagieren." *Süddeutsche Zeitung,* March 9, 1994.

Koar, Jürgen. "Grauen in schlichtem Schwarzweiss: Steven Spielbergs Film 'Schindlers Liste' beschwört dokumentarisch die Wirklichkeit des Holocaust." *Süddeutsche Zeitung,* December 18, 1993.

Kögel, Annette. "'Auch wenn ich was auf die Nase kriege: Dafür lohnt es sich': *Schindlers Liste*—eine fesselnde Schulestunde mit Ignaz Bubis." *Der Tagesspiegel,* March 17, 1994.

Kölle, Ingrid. "Spielberg greift sich 'Golden Globes': *Schindlers Liste:* bester Film, bestes Drehbuch, beste Regie." *Stuttgarter Zeitung,* January 24, 1994.

Körte, Peter. "Reserveroffiziere, Haarspalter und Ratlose: Zwei Talkshows zu *Schindlers Liste.*" *Frankfurter Rundschau,* March 29, 1994.

———. "Sterns Liste oder: Die vergebliche Erinnerung." *Frankfurter Rundschau,* March 1, 1994.

Krause-Burger, Sibylle. "Die Vergangenheit ist nicht zu bewältigen." *Der Tagesspiegel,* March 13, 1994.

Lanzmann, Claude. "Holocauste, la représentation impossible." *Le Monde,* March 3, 1994, Arts & Spectacles, i, vii.

———. "Ihr sollt nicht weinen: Einspruch gegen *Schindlers Liste.*" *Frankfurter Allgemeine Zeitung,* March 5, 1994.

———. "Man hat kein Recht, den Holocaust zu zeigen." *Der Standard,* March 4, 1994.

"Lanzmans Einspruch: Reaktionen auf *Schindlers Liste.*" *Frankfurter Allgemeine Zeitung,* March 4, 1994.

La Roche, Emanuel. "Siehe da: Man kann davon erzählen! Erste deutsche Reaktionen auf Steven Spielbergs Film 'Schindler's List.'" *Tages Anzeiger,* March 5, 1994.

Leiss, Peter. "Verdrängt, halb vergessen, verharmlost und Schlimmeres." *Frankfurter Rundschau,* May 24, 1994.

Lepiarz, Jacek. "Beifall mir Vorbehalt." *Neue Zeit,* April 5, 1994.

Leuken, Verena. "Ein Gerechter: Dokument des Wahrhaften: Spielbergs Film *Schindlers Liste.*" *Frankfurter Allgemeine Zeitung,* March 3, 1994, 33.

———. "Die Wiederverwertung der Betroffenheit: *Hitlerjunge Salomon:* Verlogener Streit um einen schlechten Film." *Frankfurter Allgemeine Zeitung,* January 29, 1992, 27.

Löffler, Sigrid. "Kino als Ablass: Spielbergs misslungener Holocaust-Film." *Wochenpost,* February 24, 1994.

"Mahnmal Gegen Völkermord." *Oberösterreichische Nachrichten,* December 15, 1994.

Maslin, Janet. "Minus Suspense Factor, Oscars Cut to the Chase." *New York Times,* March 23, 1994, B3 (national edition).

Menasse, Eva. "Ausschaffen und abschieben: Ein Schweizer Polizeihauptmann rettete Juden vor dem Holocaust und büsste dafür ein Leben lang." *Profil,* January 17, 1994.

Mika, Bascha. "Schindler und die Schüler: Geschichtsunterricht im Kino." *Tageszeitung,* March 15, 1994.

Mommert, Wilfried. "Brauner verlor gegen Spielberg." *Leipziger Volkszeitung,* March 4, 1994.

[Mrt]. "Die Versuchung." *Tages Anzeiger,* March 16, 1994.

Nagorski, Andrew. "*Schindler's List* Hits Home." *Newsweek,* March 14, 1994, 77.

———. "Spielberg's Risk: The Director Takes a Chance with a Holocaust Drama Shot in Black and White." *Newsweek,* May 24, 1993, 60–61.

Neumann, Hans-Joachim. "Blick in den Abgrund: *Schindlers Liste* von Steven Spielberg." *Zitty* 5 ([March] 1994): 8–11.

Neuwirth, Christian. "Uneinigkeit über Gratis-Kinokarten." *Salzburger Nachrichten,* March 5, 1994.

Niroumand, Mariam. "Der widerspenstigen Führung: Frankfurter Staatsakt für Spielbergs *Schindlers Liste.*" *Tageszeitung,* March 3, 1994.

Noack, Frank. "Darf ein Heiliger vulgär sein? *Schindlers Liste* und die anderen Spielfilme über den Holocaust." *Tagesspiegel,* March 22, 1994.

Omasta, Michael, and Andreas Ungerbock. "Waschanlage für die Seele." *Falter* 6 (1994).

Ostwind, Paul. "'Ich hätte mehr retten können': Steven Spielbergs Film *Schindlers Liste* ist das bemerkenswerte Beispiel für die Kraft und Lebendigkeit des amerikanischen Kinos." *Volksstimme,* March 10, 1994.

Osswald, Dieter. "Spielertyp, Showman, Mensch: Im Gespräch mit Liam Neeson über seine Darstellung des Oskar Schindler." *Leipziger Volkszeitung,* March 4, 1994.

Pätzold, Kurt. "Zufall oder entschlossene Tat?" *Neues Deutschland,* March 11, 1994.

Philipp, Claus. "Hollywood, redlich und 'wertvoll': Drei Golden Globes für Steven Spielbergs Holocaust-Epos *Schindlers Liste.*" *Der Standard,* January 24, 1994.

Plank, Karl A. "Focus of 'Schindler's List' Too Christian." *Charlotte Observer,* February 28, 1994.

Pfeiffer, Annette. "*Schindlers Liste* erschüttert." *Stuttgarter Zeitung,* March 5, 1994.

Pressel, Gustav G. "'Es ist mir bis heute unerklärlich, woher er den Mut genommen hat': Elisabeth Tont, einst Sekretärin Oskar Schindlers in Krakau, errinnert sich an ihren Arbeitgeber, dem Steven Spielbergs neuer Film gewidmet ist." *Frankfurter Rundschau,* January 26, 1994.

"Pressestimmen" (collection of reviews, excerpted). *Kulturchronik* 3 (1994): 34–35.

"Proteste gegen *Schindlers Liste.*" *Tiroler Tageszeitung,* March 19–20, 1994.

Purtscheller, Wolfgang. "Klar war's ordentlich." *Profil* 13 (1994).

Riepe, Manfred. "Beklemmend nüchtern: 'Oskar Schindler.'" *Frankfurter Rundschau,* March 2, 1994.

———. "Noch zur rechten Zeit: 'Oskar Schindler—die wahre Geschichte.'" *Tageszeitung,* February 26, 1994.

Riepe, Manfred, and Stefan Müller. "Tränen zur Deutschlandpremiere." *Tageszeitung,* March 3, 1994.

Rinke, Moritz. "Schindlers Hühner: Über das Scheitern einer Deutschen Diskussion." *Baseler Zeitung,* May 2, 1994.

Röhl, Klaus Rainer. "Broders Liste." *Die Wochenpost,* March 30, 1994, 12.

Rosenthal, Ruvik. "Ein Mann wie Noah: Schindlers 'Kinder' erinnern sich." *Frankfurter Rundschau,* March 26, 1994.

Ruggle, Walter. "Kinoerfolg—wie einst im Mai." *Tages Anzeiger,* March 21, 1994.

———. "Der Kinoknabe ist aus den Träumen erwacht." *Tages Anzeiger,* March 3, 1994.

Rühle, Günther. "Nachruhm." *Tagesspiegel,* March 10, 1994.

Rybarski, Ruth. "Hollywood und Nazigreuel: Steven Spielbergs neue Produktion *Schindlers Liste* provoziert heftige Kontroversen über die Darstellung des Holocaust." *Profil,* January 17, 1994.

Schenk, Ralf. "Porträt eines Retters im Stakkato des Grauens." *Neues Deutschland,* March 1, 1994.

"'Schindler' Targeted in Germany." *International Herald Tribune,* April 7, 1994.

"*Schindlers Liste:* Deutschland-Premiere am 1. März in Frankfurt." *Frankfurter Rundschau,* January 27, 1994.

"*Schindlers Liste* Deutschsprachige Premiere in Wien." *Die Welt,* February 18, 1994.

"*Schindlers Liste* für Tiroler Jugend." *Tiroler Tageszeitung,* March 1, 1994.

"*Schindler's List:* Ein beliebiger Film?" *Baseler Zeitung,* April 2, 1994.

"*Schindlers Liste:* Verfilmung des Stoff war bereits 1965 geplant." *Frankfurter Rundschau,* February 3, 1994.

Schirrmacher, Frank. "Schindlers Liste." *Frankfurter Allgemeine Zeitung,* March 1, 1994, 1.

Schnitzer, Vivianne. "Blanca Reicher, eine der 'Schindler-Frauen.'" *Tages Anzeiger,* March 23, 1994.

———. "Eine Stadt im Schindler-Fieber: In Mähren war der Retter von 1200 Juden bis vor kurzem kein Thema. Heute sind die Erinnerungen an ihn zwiespältig." *Profil,* March 15, 1994.

Schoefer, Christine. "Geschichtsstunde im Kino: *Schindlers Liste* schlägt Wellen in den USA." *Freitag,* February 11, 1994.

Schönberger, Reino. "'Schindler hat erst nach dem Krieg kapiert, was er getan hatte': Der Mann, der mehr als 1200 Juden rettete, lebte nach dem Krieg verarmt in Frankfurt / Steven Spielberg setzt ihm in seinem Film ein Denkmal." *Frankfurter Rundschau,* January 26, 1994.

Schröder, Julia. "Nach dem Melodram die Debatte: *Schindlers Liste* von Stephen [sic] Spielberg—ein Film und seine Folgen." *Stuttgarter Zeitung,* March 18, 1994.

"Schüler sollen *Schindlers Liste* kostenlos sehen." *Die Welt,* February 4, 1994.

Schütte, Wolfgang. "Wie Schindler unter deutsche Liste kam." *Frankfurter Rundschau,* April 30, 1994.

Schutt, Hans-Dieter. "'Wirklich, ich bin froh, dass ich so weit weg bin.'" Interview with survivor Richard Weinstein. *Neues Deutschland,* March 3, 1994.

"Schweigen und Tränen: Premiere *Schindlers Liste.*" *Frankfurter Rundschau,* March 3, 1994.

Seesslen, Georg. "Shoah, oder die Erzählung des Nichterzählbaren." *Freitag,* March 4, 1994.

———. "Endlich erwachsen." *Deutsches Allgemeines Sonntagsblatt,* March 4, 1994.

Sereda, Elisabeth. "'Ich musste heulen': Steven Spielberg über sein Holocaust-Drama *Schindlers Liste.*" *Die Woche,* March 3, 1994.

Shelleim, Jochanan. "'He was a mensch': Morgen läuft *Schindlers Liste* in Basel an, Am Dienstag stellte Steven Spielberg seinen Holocaust-Film in Frankfurt vor." *Baseler Zeitung,* March 3, 1994.

Sila, Roland. "Judagsindl in *Schindlers Liste.*" Letter to the Editor. *Vorarlberger Nachrichten,* April 12, 1994.

Silver, Eric. "Der gerechte Schurke." *Süddeutsche Zeitung,* December 23, 1993.

"Spielberg-Europapremiere in Wien: *Schindlers Liste* als Benfizgala." *Wiener Zeitung,* February 16, 1994.

"Spielberg-Film in Frankfurt: *Schindlers Liste* erschüttert das Premierenpublikum." *Leipziger Volkszeitung,* March 3, 1994.

"Spielbergs Erfolgsliste verlängert: *Schindlers Liste* dominierte die 51. Verleihung der 'Golden Globes.'" *Oberösterreichische Nachrichten,* January 24, 1994.

Spudlich, Helmut. "'Es gibt sechs Millionen Geschichten zu erzählen.'" *Salzburger Nachrichten,* February 17, 1994.

———. "Ins Todeslager Auschwitz und zurück." *Salzburger Nachrichten,* February 16, 1994.

Stadler, Michael. "Bilder gegen das Wegschauen, Worte für das Unsagbare, ein Film gegen das Vergessen." *Salzburger Nachrichten,* March 5, 1994.

"Starke Reaktion auf *Schindlers Liste.*" *Oberösterreichische Nachrichten,* February 18, 1994.

Steiner, Ulrike. "Hoffnung ist der rote Faden: Steven Spielberg beweist mit

Schindlers Liste seine Meisterschaft als Erzähler." *Oberösterreichische Nachrichten,* March 5, 1994.

Stopka, Christoph. "Ich bin Frau Schindler." Interview with Emilie Schindler. *Bunte,* February 17, 1994, 22–25.

Tempel, Sylke. "Handeln im rechten Moment." *Wochenpost,* February 24, 1994, 21.

Thomson, David. "Presenting Enamelware." *Film Comment,* March–April 1994, 44–50.

Tok, Hans-Dieter. "Ein Profiteur wird zum Lebenretter." *Leipziger Volkszeitung,* March 2, 1994.

Tremper, Will. "Indiana Jones im Ghetto von Krakau." *Die Welt,* February 26, 1994.

"Tumult in US-Kino bei Holocaust-Film." *Salzburger Nachrichten,* January 21, 1994.

"Two Cheers for Schindler." *Tikkun* 9.2 (March–April 1994): 7–9.

Tycner, Janus. "Bei Schindlers Polen." *Die Zeit,* March 18, 1994, 24.

———. "Oskar Schindler: Lebemann und Lebensretter." *Kulturchronik* 3 (1994): 31–33.

"Ursprünglich Hätte Gert Fröbe Osker Schindler Spielen Sollen." *Salzburger Nachrichten,* January 26, 1994.

"Verbot aufgehoben: *Schindlers Liste* in Malaysia." *Neues Deutschland,* March 31, 1994.

"VIP Parade: Wunderkind." *Kleine Zeitung,* January 17, 1994.

"Vom grossen Morden." *Der Spiegel,* February 21, 1994, 168–83.

Von der Leyen, Katharina. "Beispiellos, *Schindlers Liste.*" *Die Woche,* April 3, 1994.

"Vorbehalte gegen *Schindlers Liste.*" *Tagesspiegel,* March 24, 1994.

Wallnöfer, Isabella. "*Schindlers Liste* in Wien." *Die Presse,* February 17, 1994.

Wallnöfer, Pierre A. "Das ergraute 'Wunderkind' sehr oft missverstanden." *Salzburger Nachrichten,* February 16, 1994.

Wesemann, Arnd. "Ein Staatsakt made in Hollywood: Der globale Start für *Schindlers Liste* und die Frankfurter Premiere." *Der Tagesspiegel,* March 3, 1994.

White, Armond. "Toward a Theory of Spielberg History." *Film Comment,* March–April 1994, 51–56.

Whitney, Craig R. "Tears and Praise at German Premiere of 'Schindler's List.'" *New York Times,* March 2, 1994, B1, B6 (national edition).

"Wiesenthal voll des Lobes für *Schindlers Liste:* Präsentation von Steven Spielbergs Film über die Judenverfolgung." *Süddeutsche Zeitung,* February 18, 1994.

Wilder, Billy. "Man sah überall nur Taschentücher." *Süddeutsche Zeitung Magazin,* February 18, 1994.

Wolffsohn, Michael. "Der eingebildete Antisemit: Die Kritiker von *Schindlers Liste* gehören nicht in die rechte Ecke." *Frankfurter Allgemeine Zeitung,* March 19, 1994.

———. "Gute Deutsche?" *Die Welt,* March 4, 1994.

———. "Wo bleibt der Mut zum Widerstand?" *Rheinischer Merkur,* March 4, 1994.

Wulf, Dieter. "Wer sich nicht erinnert, stirbt ab." *Neue Zeitung,* March 31, 1994.

"Zutiefst erschütternde Totenklage: Spielbergs *Schindlers Liste* in unseren Kinos." *Wiener Zeitung,* March 3, 1994.

Judith E. Doneson

Is a Little Memory Better than None?

AUTHOR, HOLOCAUST SURVIVOR, ICON OF "BEARING WITNESS" NOT only to his own experienced horrors during the Final Solution but also to the killing fields of Cambodia and the ethnic cleansing in Bosnia, Elie Wiesel was to speak at Temple Shaare Emeth in St. Louis, Missouri.[1] The speech was scheduled for seven in the evening. By 5:30 P.M., police were diverting traffic on the packed roads to a parking lot several blocks away where buses were waiting to shuttle the crowd to the temple. Inside the auditorium, the permanent places had been filled since 3 P.M. "Latecomers" were scrambling for what remained of the makeshift seating. It was a stunning and surprising reception by the citizens of St. Louis.

At last, maybe twenty minutes late, the honored guest began. As Mr. Wiesel shifted from the notion of instantaneous gratification that permeates society to religious fundamentalism to the war in Bosnia, the lady to my right, fidgeting continuously some five minutes after Wiesel commenced, suddenly poked me. "Did you see him on Oprah?" she queried. I nodded. "He was much better on her show, don't you think?" An amazing comment on the impact of the media on society.

Even more astonishing was Wiesel's appearance on the *Oprah Winfrey Show,* one of numerous talk shows covering, among other subjects, Lorena Bobbitt the husband mutilator, Michael Jackson as child molester, mothers who steal boyfriends from their daughters, and so on. Why did Wiesel, an outspoken opponent of most commercial renditions of the Holocaust, agree to appear on a program that so often trades in sensationalism?[2]

The answer came from Oprah herself during her hour-long 1993 conversation with Wiesel, when she referred to a well-publicized poll claiming that 22 percent of American adults doubt that there was a Holocaust. She also spoke of a poll stating that one out of three adults and half of all high school students have never heard of the word "Holocaust." The discussion then cut from Wiesel's library, a venue that allowed Wiesel the luxury of not presenting himself on the same set where the aforementioned guests are taped, to filmed, on-the-street interviews. Young girl: "I'm not familiar with the word 'Holocaust.'" Young boy: "I heard this guy was killing lots of them because he didn't like them or something." Girl: "'Holocaust'—Nothing comes to mind right now." And when the *New York Times* published reports of the survey, they quoted Wiesel: "What have we done? . . . We have been working for years and years. I am shocked that 22 percent—oh, my God."[3]

Since the summer of 1994, however, we have learned that there were serious flaws in the phrasing of the questions in that poll, and the percentage of Americans who repudiated the actuality of the Holocaust—the thrust of the poll was to determine the number of Holocaust deniers in the population—is far less than previously believed. The reanalyzed data informs us that committed deniers number approximately 2 percent, with some 10 percent or less expressing uncertainty as to the Holocaust having happened, on the basis of their own lack of information.[4] Elie Wiesel's appearance on the *Oprah Winfrey Show* nonetheless remains as a reminder of his acquiescence to the authority of the media over the minds of the American public. This fact draws our attention if only because of Wiesel's previously unyielding stance regarding most film and television representations of the Holocaust as trivializing the event they depict.[5]

As time passes and the Holocaust recedes deeper into history, it seems that the media have come to occupy a dominant position in translating the destruction of the European Jews to the American people. More so than in the past, American film and television, from feature films to telefilms to talk shows to tabloid programs, and the print media, including popular magazines and newspapers, often focus on some aspect of the Holocaust. Do they serve an important function, by counteracting propaganda spread by Holocaust deniers and racist diatribes? What is their role in trivializing the Holocaust? Can we learn this most important history, albeit a diluted version, through the media, even though periodically their accounts rest on tertiary and semi-informed sources? In attempting to answer these questions, we might illuminate some of the polemics inherent in popularizing the Holocaust, but we will also better understand the role the American media play in helping to commemorate the destruction of the European Jews.

This discussion, therefore, will be not a lament but rather an acceptance of the realities of the lure of mass culture on American society. My focus is neither on the varying techniques of talk shows, feature films, and telefilms, nor on the styles of popular journals referring to the Holocaust, nor is it on the theoretical debates concerning history and memory, the limits of representation, or why the fascination with the Holocaust. Instead, my goal here is to present an overview of recent depictions and references to the Holocaust in the media—with emphasis on the popular media—and their potential to inform. Perhaps we can then better understand why we unexpectedly find Elie Wiesel revealing his story on one of the most popular talk shows on television.

Historian Saul Friedlander, responding to the increase in media references to the Holocaust since the late 1960s, has observed that none of this has "led to any compelling framework of meaning as far as public consciousness is concerned."[6] Perhaps, however, it might be suggested that, at least in the United States, portrayals of and references to the Holocaust in the media have cumulatively served to assimilate the Holocaust into the American sensibility, ultimately constructing a distinctive framework, or a paradigm, that assists the population, when confronted by starvation in Somalia or ethnic cleansing in Bosnia or internecine fighting in Rwanda, to respond with more compassion and sometimes even a plan of action.[7]

In studying the image of the Jew in nineteenth-century German popular literature that ultimately came to haunt German Jewry in the 1930s, George Mosse came to the conclusion that

> anti-Jewish feeling only acquires particular relevance when it is combined with political issues or when Jewish group interests conflict with other powerful interests, but none of this would be of significance in an age of mass politics without the support and preconditioning of popular culture.[8]

Let us therefore begin by scanning only a few of the anti-Jewish harangues that were fed to the public through various media modes, in

1993 and 1994. Popular talk show emcee Sally Jessy Raphael hosted a young girl who called the Jews agents of the devil and proposed their elimination from the earth. Two well-liked St. Louis disc jockeys were fired for, among other things, asking listeners to call in and guess whether a celebrity was Jewish on the basis of his or her last name. Renowned singer Dolly Parton felt that Hollywood studios rejected her proposal for a film on a Southern gospel singer because "people in Hollywood are Jewish. And it's a frightening thing for them to promote Christianity." A professor at William Patterson College in New Jersey faces student complaints for telling his sociology class that more people were killed in factories run by Nazi industrialists than in the concentration camps. Khalid Abdul Muhammad, assistant to Minister Louis Farrakhan and the Nation of Islam, in his widely communicated, now infamous speech on the campus of Kean College in New Jersey, included in his remarks: "Everybody always talk about Hitler exterminating six million Jews. But don't nobody ever ask what did they do to Hitler." Minister Farrakhan, under intense pressure from mainstream black leaders, appeared on the Black Entertainment Network and condemned Muhammad's tone but not his words. Farrakhan added: "Why is it that we have so many stories about a Jewish Holocaust? . . . Why is it that we can see a *Schindler's List* but there is nothing that is said of the holocaust to black people, which was a hundred times worse than the Holocaust of the Jews?" Arsenio Hall, a former talk show host in the late night arena, gave Farrakhan a forum to explain his remarks, at which time he continued his accusations of a media—read Jewish—conspiracy against him. One public access cable channel, an outlet intended as a soapbox for the people, has a Thursday night television program in Manhattan led by a swastika-sleeved neo-Nazi who calls the Holocaust a fiction. And a young, supposedly Jewish denier took a video camera to Auschwitz, where he "confirmed" that the only use of gas chambers was to fumigate clothing and mattresses in order to preserve the health of inmates.[9]

In her study on Holocaust deniers (also known as revisionists), Deborah Lipstadt writes of Montel Williams—one more in the bevy of talk show emcees—and his attempts to persuade her to appear on his program and "debate" the deniers.[10] Lipstadt refused, as she rightly tells us, because there is nothing to debate; the reality of the Holocaust is not an opinion. But notwithstanding her correct posture, millions of viewers will tune into Williams and similar programs; far fewer will read Lipstadt. In his review of Lipstadt's book in the *New York Times,* Walter Reich blames the Holocaust deniers for Americans' doubts about the Holocaust.[11] Reich speaks on the basis of the poll that first claimed that one-fifth of Americans are ignorant of the Holocaust. But whether the percentage of the population who questioned the actuality of the Holocaust is larger or smaller, might it be true that ongoing media representations of the Holocaust serve as an antidote to deniers and somewhat inform those who are uninformed about the Final Solution? As Elie Wiesel related to Oprah Winfrey: "If you convinced me to be with you today it's . . . partly because of you, but partly because of the statistics that I heard. It means we have to do something more, something better, something else."[12] He reiterated these thoughts on *Charlie Rose,* a discussion program on public television, even after the egregious statistics had been altered.[13]

Yet, in an earlier article critical of popularizations of the Holocaust and those who found in them some redeeming value, Wiesel, in an explicitly acrimonious voice, writes: "But then the 'experts' will ask, how do we transmit the message?" Michael Marrus suggests, in his inclusive survey on "The Use and Misuse of the Holocaust," that those engaged in Holocaust research may help counter some of the abuses found in popularizations of the Holocaust in the same manner that scholarly writing on the French Revolution helped to shape popular French perceptions two hundred years later. But we have to remind ourselves that the French Revolution belongs to French history, whereas the Holocaust is a refugee event in America, and knowledge of it at best *may,* in the long run, only function at the level of metaphor or paradigm.[14] Elie Wiesel concurs with Marrus when he advises: study texts, read the Warsaw diaries of Emmanuel Ringelblum and Chaim Kaplan, study the works of historians Raul Hilberg and Lucy Dawidowicz, see films such as Alain Resnais's *Night and Fog* and Claude Lanzmann's *Shoah,* and "stop insulting the dead."[15]

One finds oneself in a perplexing predicament. It can be difficult and painful, and seemingly facile, to counter the feelings of survivors like Wiesel with one's own beliefs and opinions, emerging from a generation born after the event in question. Who would place the moral fortitude, the penetrating poignancy, or the historical value of

Ringelblum's or Kaplan's diaries, composed while they struggled to bear witness and survive in the Warsaw ghetto, on a par with a melodramatic television drama? There is no logic in invoking such incompatible illustrations as a basis for comparison. More to the point, what would encourage a media-hungry population to read Emmanuel Ringelblum's *Notes from the Warsaw Ghetto* or Raul Hilberg's volume *The Destruction of the European Jews?* Elie Wiesel understood the rhetorical nature of query when he decided to appear with Oprah Winfrey as well as on other, perhaps more highly regarded interview programs such as *Later* with Bob Costas and *Charlie Rose.*[16] In fact, when Rose asked Wiesel why he had not spoken out against Pope John Paul II's bestowal of a papal knighthood on former Austrian chancellor and accused Nazi war criminal Kurt Waldheim, Wiesel underscored the power of the media in his retort: "I am just one person. I don't have your program. I don't have a column in the newspaper."

Around the time of the appearance of *Schindler's List,* the popular late night news show *Nightline* held a discussion on Steven Spielberg's film.[17] In the opening segment, a filmed report before the ensuing conversation, while visuals were displayed of the United States Holocaust Memorial and publicity shown for *Schindler's List,* reporter Tom Foreman declared in voice-over that this was being called "the year of the Holocaust."

We've seen these 'years' before, at least in the media. They seem to materialize every decade since Anne Frank's diary was adapted into a play and a film in the 1950s. That decade was followed by the Eichmann trial and the film *Judgment at Nuremberg* in the 1960s; by the watershed 1978 telefilm *Holocaust* on NBC/TV, perhaps the impetus for bringing the Holocaust qua Holocaust, that is, the attempted destruction of European Jewry, to public consciousness as well as for the attacks on popularizations of the Final Solution that came after; by a spate of telefilms in the 1980s; and by the opening of the United States Holocaust Memorial Museum and the appearance of *Schindler's List* in the nineties.[18]

In the current flow of media interest revolving around the destruction of the European Jews, a majority of television programs are geared to a mass market. For instance, on *Charlie Rose* there have been heated discussions about *Schindler's List* as well as interviews with stars from the film, thereby focusing attention on both the film and the Holocaust. Some telecasts are modeled on tabloid sensationalism, as when Geraldo Rivera hosted a program entitled "The Angel of Death Mystery," dealing with the suspected demise of Mengele, the infamous doctor of Auschwitz. In his exposition, Rivera includes the on-screen testimony of a survivor who was a victim of Mengele's experiments. Obviously, this type of tabloid show lends itself to criticism, becoming for some a vulgarization of the subject. But devotees of tabloid television, whose numbers are many, and who are unlikely to read a historical text or a survivor's account, thereby discover information that might well have otherwise remained absent from their mind. Jerry Springer, the talk show host who does not hesitate to mention on the air that he lost many family members to the Holocaust, followed an hour on reformed Ku Klux Klan members with the recommendation to viewers that they see *Schindler's List.* The fact is that good box-office receipts—or higher Nielsen ratings—result in awareness. This, in turn, helps offset negative imagery of Jews in the media and helps counter Holocaust deniers by informing people through a format with which they are comfortable.

Oprah Winfrey opened her conversation with Elie Wiesel by telling her audience, "My guest today has a story to tell that may be the most important anyone will ever hear." And Wiesel told his tale, in his own idiom, to millions of viewers who were just then discovering his existence.[19] The list of programs engaged in some manner with the Holocaust is long. For many critics of popular representations, it is too long. But for a majority of Americans, such programs remain a source, often the only one, that allows them a hint of realization, of memory as it were, of the Final Solution.

Interestingly, the memory precipitated by the media is not necessarily more specious or simplified than the memory of many within the Jewish community. Omer Bartov, in his insightful study "Intellectuals on Auschwitz," maintains that American Jews know as little as their gentile counterparts about the history of the tragedy of European Jewry.[20] Ignorance, however, does not prevent the Holocaust from often becoming the rallying cry of unity within the Jewish community. Even in Jewish fundamentalist circles, especially among those who have recently "returned" to strict adherence of Jewish laws, the Holocaust serves a function: it represents God's wrath against the Jews for straying from His ways. One is reminded of a convert from Christianity to strict Jewish observance who speaks frequently throughout the United States. For his talk in St. Louis, sponsored by a group that specializes in "proselytizing" among "heretic" Jews, he appeared bedecked in the long coat, hat, and sidecurls associated with extreme Orthodoxy (though he was tailored in gray rather than black). He "informed" the audience that because the German Jews were more "Aryan" than the Germans, because they gave up their religion, there was a Holocaust. And the listeners applauded his vulgarization of history with vigor.[21]

In a different vein, a ceremony was held in Warsaw in April of 1993 commemorating fifty years since the Warsaw Ghetto Uprising. Among the several thousand guests were Yitzhak Rabin, prime minister of Israel, Lech Wałęsa, president of Poland, and Albert Gore, vice president of the United States. The tribute was held at the monument to the fighters of the uprising. It was described in the pages of the *New York Times* as follows: "After the speeches, a light-and-sound [sic] show staged by a Polish director, Isabela Sywinska, enveloped the monument. . . . Theatrical smoke rising from the back of the memorial simulated the destruction of the ghetto by fire. The noise of a train signified the cattle cars that took about 300,000 Jews from the ghetto to the Treblinka death camp."[22] Vulgarization? Trivialization? Or just a heartfelt attempt—utilizing a popular, visual tourist device for relating history—to memorialize the extraordinary actions of a people battling their death sentence?

Glancing at the print media, two popular travel magazines have recommended the U.S. Holocaust Memorial Museum as a spot to visit. Neither one contained a comprehensive article revealing the essence and substance of the museum. The endorsement in *Travel & Leisure* appeared on a page of short travel suggestions. There was a blurb guiding travelers to Dick Lee Pastry for dim sum in San Francisco. There was a hurrah for Marshall Field's department store in Chicago, which had emerged from bankruptcy and refurbished its downtown store. And there was a headline: "Uproar over a New Museum: Stark, Sober and Meant to Shock," about Washington, D.C.'s, Holocaust Memorial Museum.[23] *The Traveler* has a page called "Word of Mouth." For Monaco, they tout a restaurant where Prince Albert eats spaghetti. For Europe, they discuss seats for the great jazz festivals. And for Washington, D.C., in bold print: "The Prisoner Is You," followed by a two-sentence description of the manner in which one tours the museum. Are these magazines trivializing the museum by the manner in which they bring it to our attention: a tourist attraction like any other? Or are they simply providing the reader with information within the framework of the established format of their journals?

Elie Wiesel has frequently protested that we are living through a period of general desanctification of the Holocaust which inevitably leads to trivialization. He cites the comparing of Hitler's crimes with Stalin's, the Bitburg affair, the likening of Israeli soldiers to Nazis.[24] How simple it is to add recent examples. Feminist lawyer and law professor Catherine A. MacKinnon compares pornography against women to Nazi atrocities against the Jews. While speaking to a rally of young Roman Catholics in Denver, Pope John Paul II has second thoughts and strays from his prepared text, which would have likened abortion to the Holocaust. During the Golden Globe ceremony, an award ceremony sponsored by the foreign press in Hollywood, in his acceptance speech as best actor for his role as an AIDS victim in the film *Philadelphia,* Tom Hanks refers to AIDS as the current Holocaust.[25] But are these instances of desecration or ignorance?

What is at the core of the dilemma? Abuse of the Holocaust? Desanctification? Lack of knowledge? Vulgarization? Trivialization? Too much memory? Too little memory? Whom do we please? Which survivors? At every juncture, one discovers what on the surface, especially within the situation of imagining the unimaginable or speaking the unspeakable, that is, the rigid obedience to the inviolableness of this most tragic episode in human history, seem to be breaches of the sacredness of the Holocaust. But where is the understanding of the limitations of most of us in grasping this event at the level for which it begs?

Some time ago, Leon Jick described an invasion in the United States in the 1970s of "popularizations in varying degrees of vulgarity" dealing with the Holocaust. This culminated with the American telefilm *Holocaust* in 1978, about which Jick writes: "The flaws in the production were overlooked by most Jewish groups who were delighted with the exposure."[26] His voice was one of many, most pronounced in academia, who saw in this nine-and-one-half-hour docudrama the embodiment of trivialization of the Final Solution.

Nonetheless, there was much praise for the production, including the accolades of Holocaust survivors. This production and its impact have been debated extensively.[27]

Most of us are aware of Hollywood's affinity for sentimentalizing and simplifying complex situations. Many of us have struggled with the uniqueness of the Holocaust. The truth is, however, a majority of people do not and will not engage in this philosophical inquiry. Without doubt, at the time of its appearance, *Holocaust,* an uncomplicated vision of the events in question but a morally honest one, served as the catalyst for a mass awakening of public awareness of the destruction of Europe's Jews, especially in the United States and Germany. *Holocaust* and similar representations allow a glimpse into a history that might otherwise elude many of us.

In a discussion of *Schindler's List* on *Nightline,* literary critic Leon Wieseltier summed up his view of the problem when he said that "there is a sense, and the reception of Spielberg's film confirms this, in which one thing doesn't have reality in this culture until Hollywood says it does."[28] In a *Charlie Rose* conversation on *Schindler's List,* Melvin Jules Bukiet, a writer for the liberal Jewish magazine *Tikkun,* expressed his deep concern that the better the movie, the more it will transmute history; indeed, the movie will *become* history for a vast majority of the people who see it. Responding to this, Janet Maslin, film critic at the *New York Times,* pointed out that the logical consequence of Bukiet's argument is that you cannot make any movie about the Holocaust without violating it in some way. In her estimation, *Schindler's List* is worthwhile in being a three-hour film that people take seriously, that moves them and makes them see things they did not previously think about.[29]

Essentially, *Schindler's List* has become the *Holocaust* of the 1990s, occasioning higher critical praise than the latter but no less controversy. And the reception of Spielberg's film has commandeered the media, just as *Holocaust* did in 1978.

Schindler's List details the story of Oskar Schindler, a German from Czechoslovakia who made his fortune during the war and lost it in his successful attempts to save some 1,100 Jews from the clutches of the Nazis. The film is not without problems, especially in that it follows an established pattern in Holocaust films of portraying Jews as victims who cannot act on their own behalf but are dependent upon Christian/gentile assistance for survival. As in Raul

Hilberg's classic *Destruction of the European Jews,* Spielberg has presented the Holocaust largely from a German perspective. The Jews are seen as passive victims of this history, when in fact they risked their lives daily by keeping diaries, opening schools, printing underground newspapers, and offering assistance to those in need. In the Cracow ghetto, where the film begins, there were in reality several welfare organizations, an underground newspaper, and a Jewish fighting organization that carried out acts of sabotage outside the ghetto. But will the omission of these facts impair the audience's ability to learn something about this tragic period from the film? Not likely.

One woman who survived the Holocaust through Oskar Schindler's list expressed her feelings about the film: "We were praying that someone would make a picture like this. . . . Now I'm going to be very nervous waiting for the Oscars."[30] The Academy Awards, Hollywood's grandest celebration honoring its perceptions of the best in film for the year, accorded *Schindler's List* twelve Oscar nominations. Does the glitter and glamor of a ceremony lauding a film on the Holocaust in any way trivialize the event or lessen the impact of the film? For Schindler's Jews, it seems not. Because of the film, "millions of moviegoers and even their own families can at long last understand the pain they bore by themselves," according to David Margolick in the *New York Times.* And for their children and grandchildren, "the movie has had more impact than any book they had read, any stories they ever heard from their parents."[31]

After the film appeared, Thomas Keneally's book on which the script was based acquired a place on the *New York Times*'s paperback bestseller list and held it for months. As part of their punishment for the attempted bombings of synagogues and plots to ignite race wars by attacking black churches and Jewish leaders, a group of skinheads was forced to listen to Holocaust survivors and to see *Schindler's List;* in a complete turnabout, one of them remarked: "I don't think I could ever be angry at someone because of the color of their skin or their religious beliefs—and it is because of what I saw these past three days."[32] And antisemitic orator Khalid Abdul Muhammad also saw *Schindler's List.* After the screening he admitted to being moved, but not to changing his mind about Jews.[33]

Without question, the effect of *Schindler's List* has been demonstrated worldwide. In Germany, for example, once more an American film is crossing the ocean to explain events in the country where it all began. The movie premiered, according to a *New York Times* headline, to "tears and praise." The article states that German critics had been previewing the film for months prior to its opening. And it quotes the German weekly *Der Spiegel:* "*Schindler's List* is great beyond all expectations. . . . No book, no documentation, no film can grasp the horror and the incomprehensibility of the Holocaust. But *Schindler's List* shows what it is possible to do."[34]

Schindler's List advances the concern among historians that history is becoming the charge of the media. During the past thirty years in particular, history as entertainment has become the trend. In the words of Michael Kammen, in *Mystic Chords of Memory:* "Although some segments of American society were inclined to take the past seriously . . . in mass and popular culture national history became a diversified form of entertainment." The 1994 controversy over the Disney historical theme park that was to be built in Virginia accents this view.[35] The image of the American West is currently being revised in films such as Clint Eastwood's *The Unforgiven,* disdaining the violence of the past, but surely a metaphor for the present.

In this context, Saul Friedlander reminds us: "The representation of the Nazi epoch cannot be considered as already beyond the pale of relevant historical consciousness. It remains an imperative knowledge not only for its own sake or for understanding the scope of criminal human potentialities, but more directly in terms of present-day political responsibility."[36]

In 1993, the "year of the Holocaust," the tie-in between the destruction of Europe's Jews and the ethnic cleansing in Bosnia became a major thrust of media focus. At the ceremony for the opening of the U.S. Holocaust Memorial Museum, broadcast live on television, Elie Wiesel invoked the present when he suggested that as a Jew, he must do something about Bosnia.[37] During the discussion of *Schindler's List* on *Nightline,* Leon Wieseltier reminded viewers that though there had been no satellites to peer into the concentration camps during World War II, the pictures of Bosnia were now clear.[38] And psychiatrist Robert Lifton, who has written extensively on Hiroshima, the Holocaust, and other twentieth-century tragedies, noticed that the pictures of the camps in Bosnia symbolically reactivate internalized Holocaust images, bringing us back to Nazi camps, and reminding us of what we did not do for the victims then. Lifton maintains: "As survivors by proxy, can our witness be transformed into life-enhancing action—in Bosnia in this case, but also in other areas of death and suffering such as the famine in Somalia? And can we reassess the potential of television, a medium we imperfectly understand, for contributing to our humanity?"[39] Clearly attuned to the power of television images, Irish writer and politician Conor Cruise O'Brien remarked to journalist Charlayne Hunter-Gault on the *MacNeil/Lehrer NewsHour* that "the politicians don't know what to do until they know how the television audience is reacting."[40] Obviously, not all media depictions of tragedies fall into the category of popularizations, but that element of entertainment so necessary to attract viewers has even slipped into the nightly news.

Jeffrey Schmalz, an AIDS activist who succumbed to the disease, remarked in an article he wrote about AIDS shortly before his death: "The world is moving on, uncaring, frustrated and bored."[41] For memory of the Holocaust, now more than fifty years in the past, how much more so might this be true.

In reflecting on the mystical quality of collective memory, Leon Wieseltier says, "It consists in the unaccountable capacity to remember—not to know, but to remember—things that happened to others."[42] Apropos, in his report on *Schindler's List* for *Nightline,* Tom Foreman concluded: "So, too, many Americans are being affected by what they are seeing in this 'year of the Holocaust.' They are hoping that change in their hearts can somehow help change the world."[43]

In his extraordinary study of one particular battalion of German soldiers, Christopher Browning explains how "ordinary men" became mass murderers and advanced the destruction of European Jewry.[44] Likewise, we must realize that it is ordinary men and women who just might deter future tragedies against humanity, *if* there is some force that continually enlightens them in a comprehensible vernacular. Apparently the media have become the source of this remembrance. "Unless someone remembers 'it,'" Michael Kammen states (in our context, 'it' being the Holocaust), "it might just as well not have happened. Conversely, history hinges upon memory: the necessarily selective, collective remembrance that suits a society.

That's not merely the 'common man's' view; it was the perspective of a sophisticated historian like Carl L. Becker sixty years ago," concludes Kammen.[45] And as Becker's comments might strengthen the case for understanding popularizations of the Final Solution, let us repeat them succinctly: "Without memory no knowledge."[46]

Lawrence Baron

Holocaust Awareness and Denial in the United States: The Hype and the Hope

IN LATE 1992 THE AMERICAN JEWISH COMMITTEE COMMISSIONED THE Roper organization to conduct a survey to measure the extent of the American public's knowledge about the Holocaust. The American Jewish Committee (hereafter AJC) released its findings the following April to coincide with the fiftieth anniversary of the Warsaw Ghetto Uprising and the opening of the United States Holocaust Memorial Museum.[1] The poll revealed that only 61 percent of the adults and 48 percent of the high-school students who were queried correctly described what the Holocaust was. Even more disconcerting was the finding that 20 percent of the adults and 22 percent of the students believed it was possible that the Holocaust never happened. Another 12 percent and 17 percent of the adults and students, respectively, did not know enough to affirm or deny the historicity of the Holocaust. Although a majority of the respondents felt it was important for Americans to learn about the Holocaust, the AJC concluded that the survey underscored "the serious knowledge gap that exists for both adults and youth in the United States with regard to basic information about the Holocaust."[2]

The survey's findings confirmed the gnawing fear of Holocaust survivors that the Holocaust will be forgotten or denied altogether when they are no longer alive to remind the world of its horrors. Benjamin Meed, the president of the American Gathering and Federation of Jewish Holocaust Survivors, called the findings "alarming."[3] The poll prompted Elie Wiesel to appear on the *Oprah Winfrey Show.* When Winfrey asked Wiesel why so many people doubt whether the Holocaust occurred, he dejectedly replied, "Maybe something is wrong with the way we have taught the story. Maybe the story can't be told."[4] Citing the poll's statistics on the extent of Holocaust denial among Americans soon became a recurrent theme among those dedicated to preserving the memory of the Holocaust.[5]

Subsequent polls, however, have discredited the AJC's initial findings about the inroads of Holocaust denial among Americans. The wording of the AJC's question on Holocaust denial was confusing: "Does it seem possible or does it seem impossible to you that the Nazi extermination of the Jews never happened?" To check whether this wording contributed to the high level of Holocaust denial reported by the AJC, the Gallup Organization conducted a poll in January of 1994 posing the question to one group in its original form and to another in a clearer way: "Do you doubt the Holocaust actually happened or not?" While the former produced similar results to the AJC poll, the latter showed that only 9 percent of the respondents doubted the Holocaust had happened. The Gallup poll further asked both groups if the Holocaust definitely happened, probably happened, or did not happen. Ninety-eight percent in the first group and 95 percent in the second replied that the Holocaust definitely or probably happened. Only 2 percent in each group believed that it definitely never happened.[6]

The Gallup findings spurred the AJC to commission a follow-up Roper survey, replacing the original question concerning Holocaust denial with the following one: "Does it seem possible to you that the Nazi extermination of the Jews never happened, or, do you feel certain that it happened?" After the Roper Organization admitted in May of 1994 that the original question on Holocaust denial was "flawed," the AJC hired Tom Smith of the National Opinion Research Center to analyze the data compiled by both Roper polls. His subsequent report revealed that only 1.1 percent of Americans in the second survey believed that it was possible that the Holocaust never happened. Another 8.8 percent said they did not know enough to answer the question. On the basis of this and other recent polls, Smith has concluded that only a "small segment of the population" are "consistent and committed deniers" of the Holocaust and that those who express some doubt about whether the Holocaust happened "do so from lack of information."[7]

The attention paid to the issue of Holocaust denial has obscured other misconceptions about Holocaust education that were fostered by the results of the first AJC poll. Viewed in isolation, the survey's findings have led many people to question the efficacy of Holocaust education in the United States. However, when placed in the broader context of what American students know about history in general, these results reveal that Holocaust education has been relatively successful. Any interpretation of the poll's statistics on students must take two other factors into consideration: first, the slow but escalating pace of institutionalizing the teaching of the Holocaust in public schools; and second, the practical limits imposed on the quality and quantity of existing Holocaust education by insufficient classroom time, teacher training, and resources. The negative publicity generated by the AJC poll also has overshadowed its finding that the majority of Americans *support* Holocaust education and appreciate the positive impact it can have on student attitudes toward minority rights.

Fortunately, there are some recent polls that compare how much Americans know about the Holocaust with what they know about other historical events. In 1990 the Anti-Defamation League (a Jewish organization) hired Yankelovich Clancy Shulman to conduct a poll with a representative sampling of 885 Americans. Those polled were given a list of major historical events and asked how much they knew about each. Sixty-three percent of the respondents said they knew either a great deal or a fair amount about the Holocaust. Only the Vietnam War was better known than the Holocaust among those surveyed. In contrast, only 23 percent of the respondents claimed they knew a great deal or a fair amount about the Russian Revolution. The poll confirmed that younger Americans know less about the Holocaust than older Americans.[8]

In 1995 I designed a questionnaire for San Diego high school students who were the first group to participate in a three-year pilot program enabling students studying the Holocaust to visit the Museum of Tolerance in Los Angeles. The results from the first year of the Building Tolerance Project reveal that even before these students began the unit, they felt they knew more about the Holocaust than about the American civil rights movement.[9]

The Anti-Defamation League poll also asked its pool of respondents to rate the significance of various historical events on a five-point scale, with five being the most significant. Fifty-five percent of the participants gave the Holocaust a five, and 18 percent gave it a four. This composite statistic of 73 percent ranked second only to the 77 percent who believed that slavery in America deserved either a five or a four. Only 58 percent rated the treatment of Native Americans as this significant. When the interviewees were asked to select which of these three events was the worst tragedy, 51 percent chose the Holocaust, compared to 22 percent for slavery and 12 percent for the treatment of Native Americans.[10]

The National Assessment of Educational Progress (hereafter NAEP) provides data on how much American high school students know about the Holocaust as compared with their knowledge of other historical events. In 1986 and 1988 the NAEP developed a National Assessment of History, consisting of 141 questions, and administered it to a representative sampling of nearly 8,000 seventeen-year-olds. The Holocaust appeared in a section of twenty-one historical questions concerning civil rights. Seventy-six percent of the students correctly identified the Holocaust as a reference to Nazi genocide during World War II, placing it fifth in terms of student knowledge of items in this section. The authors of the first AJC poll noted that this figure was higher than the percentage of students correctly defining the Holocaust on the first AJC survey because this question was posed in a multiple-choice rather than open-ended format, increasing the chances of correct recognition or guessing.[11] The extent of student knowledge of the Holocaust ranked in the upper fifth of percentages of correct responses for all of the historical questions posed on the NAEP.[12] On the San Diego survey, there is a section of thirteen multiple-choice questions on the Holocaust, the American civil rights movement, and the Armenian and Cambodian genocides. Prior to taking the Holocaust unit, 92 percent of the students correctly identified what the Holocaust was and 89 percent knew which country was most responsible for it. More students knew that gassing was the main method of killing used during the Holocaust than knew that abolition of segregation was a primary aim of the American civil rights movement.[13]

The AJC poll's findings about student knowledge of the Holocaust partly reflect the limited accessibility of Holocaust education in American public schools. It must be remembered that Holocaust education was not even on the educational agenda of any city school system until the early 1970s.[14] In 1975 Illinois became the first state to recommend that the Holocaust be included in its public school curriculum.[15] As late as 1983 less than 1 percent of America's public high schools had introduced the teaching of the Holocaust into their curricula.[16] Considerable progress has been made over the past decade, with California, Florida, Illinois, and New Jersey now mandating the teaching of the Holocaust, and seven other states recommending that it be taught in their high schools.[17] But whenever boards of education and state legislatures have considered the adoption of Holocaust units into the curriculum, the resolution of the issue has been delayed and sometimes altered either by Holocaust deniers opposing it or by various ethnic and racial groups demanding that past atrocities committed against them also be taught in the public schools.[18] With all due respect to Elie Wiesel, the low level of student awareness of the Holocaust has resulted more from the protracted struggle for Holocaust education than from the pedagogical problems of teaching about the Holocaust.

Indeed, the AJC poll presents some evidence of the success of Holocaust education among students who have had the opportunity to receive it. The current estimate of the number of students who annually learn about the Holocaust in public high school classes is between 2.5 and 3 million. This constitutes about 20 to 25 percent of today's high school enrollment.[19] When asked where they learned about the Holocaust, 59 percent of the students in the first AJC poll attributed their exposure to the subject to school. Multiplying this percentage by the percentage of students who correctly identified the Holocaust in the poll yields a figure of 28 percent. This number approximates the estimate of the percentage of students learning about the Holocaust in public schools and suggests that such education has had an impact on them.[20] Similarly, Tom Smith has demonstrated that the "predominant factor determining knowledge of the Holocaust" among Americans is the amount of formal education they have had.[21]

Nevertheless, the students responding to such polls often lack specific knowledge about the Holocaust. Only 28 percent of the students in the AJC poll knew that around 6 million Jews were killed by Germany and its allies during World War II. Only 42 percent of the students could identify the yellow star as the emblem Jews were forced to wear during the Second World War. A mere 20 percent knew that the Nazis persecuted "Gypsies" or homosexuals too.[22]

These findings probably illustrate other curricular and institutional factors that undermine the teaching of the Holocaust in many school systems. Administrators and legislators frequently do not allocate adequate funds to train teachers and prepare new course materials for Holocaust education. In states recommending that the Holocaust be taught, the prerogative to do so still remains in the hands of local school boards or individual teachers. The Illinois law mandating the teaching of the Holocaust contains the typical proviso that "each school board shall itself determine the minimum amount of instruction time" for satisfying this requirement.[23] Holocaust units are usually taught as part of survey courses such as American History, Western Civilization, World History, or Civics. Holocaust educators estimate that about half of the teachers who introduce the Holocaust into their classes do so for three class days and that only 10 to 20 percent of the remaining teachers devote as much as a week of classes to it. The teaching of longer units or entire courses on the Holocaust is less common.[24] The textbooks used in such survey courses normally treat the Holocaust briefly and superficially.[25] Thus, details about the genocide of the Jews either are never covered or are submerged in an ocean of other facts and topics.

As is often the case, the positive findings in the AJC poll have been the least reported. More than 80 percent of the adults and students surveyed agreed that the Holocaust teaches "that firm steps need to be taken to protect the rights of minorities." Eighty-four percent of the adults and 75 percent of the students felt that "people must speak out against oppression so that another Holocaust will not happen." Seventy-two percent of the adults and 64 percent of the students indicated that it is either essential or very important "for Americans to know about and understand the Holocaust." Conversely, only 2 percent of the adults and 3 percent of the students thought that it is "not important" for Americans to know about the Holocaust.[26]

For all the hand-wringing the AJC poll occasioned, the future of Holocaust education in the United States appears bright. The earlier Anti-Defamation League survey found that 73 percent of those it polled believed it was essential or very important to incorporate the

Holocaust into American education.[27] This represents a remarkable consensus, given the diversity of the American population and other curricular demands on the educational system. Many states that do not yet teach about the Holocaust have educational councils to spearhead campaigns to either recommend or mandate its inclusion in their curricula.[28] Holocaust courses have proliferated at American colleges and universities to such an extent that some Jewish studies specialists fear that students will learn about Jews only through the Holocaust rather than through broader surveys of Jewish history.[29]

Millions more Americans will learn about the Holocaust outside the classroom. The Holocaust Memorial Museum in Washington, D.C., and the Museum of Tolerance in Los Angeles, as well as traveling exhibitions such as "Anne Frank in the World" and "Daniel's Story," have given many people their first major exposure to the Holocaust.[30] Some 10 million people visited the Holocaust Memorial Museum alone in its first five years. That museum also has developed a Holocaust education program for local high school students and faculty to serve as a model for teaching the Holocaust throughout the country.[31] Fascination with the Holocaust shows no signs of abating among journalists, movie directors, novelists, scholars, and television producers. There are hundreds of books on the Holocaust currently listed in *Books in Print.* By comparison there are only ten titles written by Holocaust deniers.[32] The spectacular popularity of the movie *Schindler's List* has added momentum to the efforts to expand Holocaust education in the public schools. Forty-five states have accepted Steven Spielberg's offer to provide study guides and free showings of the movie to high school classes.[33] The second AJC poll reported that the number of Americans who could identify the Holocaust correctly had increased by 7 percentage points since the first poll was conducted. It attributed this improvement in public knowledge primarily to the influence and media coverage of the Holocaust Museum and *Schindler's List.*"[34]

There are a number of caveats to heed before concluding that the growth of Holocaust awareness is an unqualified blessing. Professional educators in particular need to be wary about how well the ability to answer simple factual questions about the Holocaust actually measures understanding of the dynamics and significance of the event. For example, students may learn that 6 million Jews died during the Holocaust but have no idea of how antisemitism and racism evolved over the centuries in Europe. As the teaching of the Holocaust becomes more widespread, the lessons emphasized by teachers and learned from it by students inevitably will become more universalized and varied. Many students and teachers will equate the Holocaust with other contemporary or historical manifestations of ethnic, political, racial, or religious discrimination and persecution, but will fail to comprehend how it differed from these events. As James Young has observed, "In America, the motives for memory of the Holocaust are as mixed as the population at large."[35] For the substantial number of Americans who learn about the Holocaust through movies, novels, and television,[36] the distinction between fact and fiction is likely to be blurred, and the scope of their knowledge about the Holocaust often will be quite narrow. Indeed, this is reflected in the poll conducted by the United States Holocaust Memorial Museum in 1998. Although 79 percent of those questioned knew that millions of Jews were murdered during the Holocaust, 19 percent believed this didn't happen during World War II, and another 19 percent weren't sure![37]

On the other hand, the fear that the Holocaust will be forgotten or denied by a majority of Americans in future generations does not seem credible in light of the developments and polls I have discussed here. The remembrance of the Holocaust ultimately depends on the extensive documentation related to it in research archives, the systematic preservation of eyewitness testimonies recorded for posterity on audio- and videotape and in written depositions and memoirs, the compilation of a large growing corpus of sound scholarly studies on it,[38] and its official integration into the curricula of high schools, colleges, and universities. Although Holocaust educators and survivors should not ignore the falsification of history promoted by the denial movement, they should be more concerned about how the memory of the Holocaust will be distorted by being relativized, simplified, trivialized, or universalized by teachers lacking a background in the subject,[39] journalists penning sensationalistic stories about it, and the arts and entertainment industries exploiting it for its theatrical qualities. In other words, the spread of Holocaust awareness has brought with it many pitfalls. In this sense, the two American Jewish Committee polls demonstrate how far Holocaust education has come in the United States and how far it still has to go.

APPENDIX: BUILDING TOLERANCE PROJECT, RESULTS FOR 1994–95

The Building Tolerance Project is a three-year program that started in the school year of 1994–95. Sponsored by the Jewish Community Relations Council of San Diego, it funds trips to the Museum of Tolerance in Los Angeles for high school classes in the San Diego area that are studying state-mandated Holocaust units. A Holocaust survivor accompanies the students on the trip to and from the museum. In its first year, 711 students participated in the program. Before and after the unit, students received a survey on basic knowledge about the Holocaust, the Armenian and Cambodian genocides, and the American civil rights movement. These latter three subjects were covered because they are also featured in Museum of Tolerance exhibitions.

Ethnic/racial background of students surveyed: 42 percent white, 29 percent Hispanic, 12 percent African-American, 12 percent Asian, 2 percent Native American, 3 percent other.

All figures are percentages, rounded off to the nearest whole number.

How much do you know about these topics?
(NA = no answer, 1 = nothing, 2 = little, 3 = basic facts, 4 = very much)

	NA	1	2	3	4
Holocaust					
Before program	0	6	14	48	32
After program	0	1	5	25	69
Armenian genocide					
Before	2	56	30	9	3
After	1	16	43	33	7
American civil rights movement					
Before	2	5	27	43	23
After	0	2	16	39	43
Cambodian genocide					
Before	2	64	26	7	1
After	0	18	40	33	9

Questions (with correct answer and percentage who answered correctly before and after the program):

The term "the Holocaust" usually refers to: the murder of 6 million Jews during World War II.

Before 92
After 97

The term "genocide" means: attempt to destroy an ethnic, racial, or religious group.

Before 73
After 88

The country most responsible for the Holocaust was: Germany.

Before 89
After 97

The main method of killing during the Holocaust was: gassing.

Before 76
After 89

The Holocaust was planned at a conference held in: Wannsee.

Before 40
After 53

The concentration camp where the most people were killed was: Auschwitz.

Before 77
After 91

The country responsible for committing the Armenian genocide: Turkey.

Before 28
After 55

During what war did the Armenian genocide occur? World War I.

Before 21
After 35

The leader responsible for the Cambodian genocide was: Pol Pot.

Before 3 (Most students gave no answer to this question)
After 2 (Most students gave no answer to this question)

The American civil rights movement primarily fought for the abolition of: segregation.

Before 64
After 75

The best known leader of the American civil rights movement was: Martin Luther King, Jr.

Before 83
After 94

The immediate cause of the Los Angeles riots was: anger over the decision in the Rodney King trial.

Before 89
After 93

Stereotyping someone means: assuming he or she is a certain kind of person on the basis of his or her ethnic group, race, or religion.

Before 85
After 85

IV. D · E · N · I · A · L

Jonathan Petropoulos

Holocaust Denial: A Generational Typology

ALTHOUGH THE DEBATE ABOUT WHETHER TO RESPOND TO HOLOcaust deniers continues without resolution, both sides would agree that there is merit in Sun Tzu's dictum "Know thine enemy."[1] If anything, the urgency of this injunction has increased since Deborah Lipstadt and others have shown that deniers are not mere byproducts of the lunatic fringe in both North America and Europe but a distressingly pervasive group that threatens to influence a significant section of the public. Nonetheless, there have been only limited attempts to attain an accurate or sophisticated understanding of this group, which one might call a subculture.[2] In my view it is a mistake to lump all deniers into one category: they possess different worldviews, agendas, arguments, and resources for propagating their lies. When one analyzes this subculture with the aid of the concept of generations, three fairly distinct groups emerge within the denier population.

The idea of generations can be best understood through three theoretical notions. The first is the "ideal type" construct from Max Weber. Of course, Weber had no interest in idealizing his subjects but sought to establish a "logically precise conception of ideal types." His methodological innovation has been summed up by H. H. Gerth and C. Wright Mills as follows: "Weber's interest in worldwide comparisons led him to consider extreme and 'pure cases.' These cases became 'crucial instances' and controlled the level of abstraction that he used in connection with any particular problem. The real meat of history would usually fall in between such extreme types: hence Weber would approximate the multiplicity of specific historical situations by bringing various type concepts to bear upon the specific case under focus."[3]

The second theoretical pillar is Robert Wohl's meaningful observation in *The Generation of 1914:* "Historical generations are not born; they are made. They are a device by which people conceptualize society and seek to transform it."[4] Clearly, Wohl is not talking about all members of a generation here; for these generalizations to be useful, distinctions and subcategories need to be preserved. As he points out, "Hitler's coming to power and the creation of the Third Reich signified not the victory of the war generation, as the Nazis claimed, but the victory of one part of the war generation over its opponents and the imposition of one interpretation of the war generation's experience on the population as a whole."[5] In short, generations are tricky: they are not as neat in real life as on paper.

Still, clusters of thought and behavior often form in response to significant events, such as wars, and this is why Karl Mannheim developed the third key concept, that of the "generation unit." This he defined as "a widely shared pattern of response to a specific historical situation rather than a concrete group." For him, the crucial point is that such units share (as Wohl paraphrases him) "certain principles or tendencies [*Grundintentionen*]."[6]

The first discernible generational group of deniers comprises old Nazis. Individuals who experienced the Third Reich, they typically feel they made great sacrifices for National Socialism and cannot accept that they were not pursuing some worthwhile ideal. This type, the "old Nazi," denies the crimes of the regime and insists on the good intentions of Hitler and his cronies.

One example is Ernst Mochar, a figure portrayed by Gerald Posner in his book *Hitler's Children.* Mochar's daughter Ingeborg summarizes his thought process thus: "He . . . so very identified with National Socialism, he could not admit for himself that it was an error. . . . He was so very disappointed from the end of the war. His political life had ended. He was very bitter. All his ideas had been defeated, and he collected experiences which supported his feelings like stories of crimes committed by communists."[7] About the Holocaust, many of these old Nazis resort to the cliché of conspiracy theories. Mochar himself has argued: "Well, it wasn't six million Jews, maybe it was six thousand. . . . They overdo it now, they exaggerate it, and all this is written by Jewish newspapers and press—it is not true."[8]

The old Nazi is to be found primarily in Germany and its allied, satellite, or occupied countries. This means, of course, that their geographical area ranges from the Baltic to Belgium. (As an aside, although the Japanese were technically not National Socialists, Holocaust denial and antisemitic conspiracy theories are pervasive in that country, too.)[9] Furthermore, according to Allan Ryan, the former director of the U.S. Department of Justice's Office of Special Investigations, more than 10,000 "Nazi criminals" immigrated to the United States after World War II, and many are alive today, maintaining an active communication network.[10] Within Germany, there are associations of former "comrades." The Auxiliary Fellowship for Reciprocity (Hilfsgemeinschaft auf Gegenseitigkeit, or HIAG), for example, a euphemistically named organization comprised of those formerly in the Waffen-SS, counted 20,000 members in the late 1950s (out of 500,000 Waffen-SS veterans).[11] Well-attended reunions of this sort have taken place now for decades. At one famous meeting in Minden in 1956, 10,000 Waffen-SS personnel showed up.[12] Yaron Svoray and Nick Taylor have chronicled more recent meetings at solstice festivals and other celebrations adopted from the Nazi calendar.[13] Newsletters, magazines, and other publications catering to this audience have facilitated contact for decades: *Der Freiwillige, Der Ausweg,* and *Wiking Ruf* for Waffen-SS veterans, and an English-language journal for former SS members entitled *Siegrunen!* are but a few examples.[14]

That these old Nazis have refused to recognize the crimes of the Third Reich is not due only to their need to stave off the devastating awareness of their own gullibility, of having been personally manipulated into bolstering a criminal regime. There are broader societal forces that contribute to their failure to face the truth. First, in the public sphere, governments fell short in their postwar reeducation campaigns. The surveys of the U.S. high commissioner in Germany from the period 1945–55 reveal in stark, shocking terms the limitations of education.[15] In 1952, for example, 41 percent of those in the Federal Republic saw "more good than evil in Nazi ideas," as against only 36 percent who saw "more evil than good."[16] At that time, 21 percent thought that "the Jews themselves were partly responsible for what happened to them during the Third Reich."[17] In

Austria, public opinion polls on these issues are even more depressing. Bruce Pauley has shown that 20–25 percent of Austrians still have "strongly antisemitic opinions."[18]

Second, on the more personal level, the friends and family of the old Nazis also failed, as they often shied away from the hard work of presenting the truth. Eric Santner notes this in his discussion of mourning: "The legacies—or perhaps more accurately the ghosts, the revenant objects—of the Nazi period are transmitted to the second and third generations at the sites of the primal scenes of socialization, that is, within the context of a certain psychopathology of the postwar family."[19] The patriarchal structure of many German families partly explains the persistence of Nazi views. Posner writes of Ingeborg Mochar's relationship with her siblings and father: "[Her] brothers tried to discourage her from arguing with [her father]. They constantly told her he was a good old man who would not change his opinion and they implored her to 'leave him in peace.'"[20] In certain cases, the propagation of Holocaust lies is closely tied to issues of parental respect and trust. In the years directly after the war, fathers could not admit their errors to their children, believing it would undermine their authority and damage the relationship. The lies then became compounded: not only did the fathers make mistakes during the war but they disgraced themselves by perpetuating disinformation later on. Once one has lied about past behavior, it is extremely difficult to admit one's culpability. (A parallel may be found in the recent statements by Pope John Paul II claiming that the Vatican never helped Nazis escape through the so-called "rat-line." The years of denial by his predecessors and associates have made an honest admission even more difficult.)[21] In short, the old Nazis' refusal to confront the truth of the Holocaust stems not only from their views about National Socialism but also from their behavior in the years immediately following the war.

The second distinct generational type is the young denier: the "angry young man" who typically has limited education and poor job prospects. Such individuals are often active in the neo-Nazi scene. They are consciously racist, xenophobic, and by far the most violent of the deniers. They communicate their views through a specific subculture that includes not only the myriad political parties of the radical right (there are an estimated thirty-three neo-Nazi groups in Germany and hundreds in the United States) but also the punk music scene.[22] For these young neo-Nazis, "oi" music or "race rock" is a more important focus than any one political leader. This music also appeals to an audience beyond the neo-Nazi core. One group out of Frankfurt, Die Böse Oncles ("The Angry/Bad Uncles"), who have produced an average of one album per year since their founding in 1979, reportedly sold 500,000 copies of a recent effort entitled *Heilige Lieder* ("Sacred Songs")—even though sale of the record is prohibited by law and one cannot buy it over the counter.[23] Clearly, it reached a range of German youth beyond the "rightist extremists" in Germany, about 43,000 according to an estimate by the German government.[24]

The young are attracted to Holocaust denial because it is one of the greatest taboos in Western culture. Rebelling against it contributes to a separate identity that they can call their own. One sees this motivation in the controversial film *Beruf Neonazi* by Winfried Bonengel, in which the subject, a twenty-seven-year-old Munich right-wing extremist named Bela Ewald Althans, exposes his life and articulates his views before the camera. Early in the film Althans introduces the audience to his "*Freundeskreis,*" his circle of friends. Clearly, part of the members' motivation is the desire to be a part of a group—to gain acceptance among other "outsiders." Althans and others like him revel in this renegade subculture, to the point that one doubts whether they really want to convince the public of their views. Widespread popularity would undermine their position as outsiders. Still, Althans seeks publicity and aspires to "lead" others. His cooperation with the French filmmaker Winfried Bonengel reflects this ambition, and he attempts to attract supporters by issuing what has become the "party line" among deniers. This is most evident in the scene filmed at Auschwitz, described in *Der Spiegel* as follows: "The yuppie-Nazi stands in the concentration camp and is permitted to hold forth on why, from a technical standpoint, no Jews could have been killed there: 'They have all survived and now cash in with money from us.'"[25] Significantly, Althans casts himself and other Germans as victims: they are the ones being duped and exploited.

Still, the primary motivations behind these views are the wish to shock mainstream society and to establish a group bond by violating this taboo. This search for a distinctive identity is combined with an effort at self-empowerment: young deniers feel strength within their group, and they emphasize historical themes, such as Germany's military prowess, that alleviate feelings of vulnerability. They are the most lost of what many perceive to be a lost generation—or what one young neo-Nazi described as "the victims of a restless *Zeitgeist*."[26] The discussion in the United States of a "Generation X" points to the analogous nihilism endemic among American youth.[27] In both American and European societies, the weakening of moral structures and of material prospects has led not only to desperate efforts to establish a viable identity, but to increased violence. Even Great Britain in 1993 reportedly experienced 130,000 racially motivated incidents, of which 32,000 were classified as violent—a clear sign of the problems of generation throughout the West as a whole.[28]

In between the young and the old is the third variant: the middle-aged denier. As with the other two groups, members of this category are typically male (this is another demographic issue worth investigating, although National Socialism and other extreme right-wing ideologies have always appealed more strongly to men). Individuals in this third category differ from those above by tending to have better education and greater social respectability. Middle-aged deniers represent the most serious threat, in that their arguments are more sophisticated and their financial resources greater than those of the other denier generations. One is reminded of José Ortega y Gasset's observation (about a different era) that "at any given moment, historical reality was composed of men between the ages of thirty and sixty, because this was when individuals enjoyed the perquisites of power."[29] The most prominent deniers fit into this middle category, including Arthur Butz (born in the mid-1940s), David Irving (born 1938), Ernst Zundel (born 1939), and Fred Leuchter (born in the early 1940s).[30] That such people are neither burdened with Nazi party affiliation from the Third Reich nor part of outlawed neo-Nazi groups makes it easier for them to mask their intentions and present a facade of respectability. The apparently most dangerous figure discussed by Svoray and Taylor is Wolfgang Juchem, in large part because he does not have the extra baggage of party affiliation.[31]

This generation of deniers owes its success to several additional factors. First, its members are astute at exploiting, even hijacking, certain common attitudes in our society. One of these qualities is suspicion, and these deniers play on a widespread public sense of having been duped repeatedly. The media thrive on such fodder: from the John F. Kennedy assassination to UFOs, our culture is saturated with people asserting and accepting that they have been the victims of lies. Within academia, there are those, such as Noam Chomsky, who perceive conspiracies (or what he would describe as socially detrimental power structures) in a wide range of places and encourage their analysis. Although by no means a denier himself, Chomsky is among those who defend the right of the deniers to free speech.[32] In both instances—the concern with sinister conjunctions of power and the desire for unrestricted expression—credible principles are undermined by what I consider a highly improper application. The Institute for Historical Review abuses these principles in its publications: Mark Weber, the editor of its journal, wrote in one instance: "Revisionists are victims of a legal assault against freedom of speech. . . . Once again, it is worth stressing the hypocritical, even shameful, silence on the part of the American media."[33]

In addition to capitalizing on the commerce in conspiracy theories, deniers exploit our society's high regard for rebels and mavericks, playing off of positive images of the "rugged individualism" of earlier periods or the more contemporary appreciation of the "charming rogue." Perhaps the receptivity these images find reflects the tendency in rich and essentially safe cultural and academic worlds to overvalue that which goes against the grain or is new and challenging. The deniers are aware of the advantages they gain from bold tactics and employ strategies such as posting rewards for those who can prove Jews were killed in gas chambers. To back up its self-declared renegade position, the Institute for Historical Review offered Simon Wiesenthal $50,000 if he could provide such proof. In some quarters, this looks like an admirable willingness to put one's money where one's mouth is.

Finally, this middle generation has proved most adroit at a form of false contextualization. Relativizers such as Ernst Nolte come, in Deborah Lipstadt's words, "dangerously close to validating the deniers. Without offering any proof, he falsely claims that more 'Aryans' than Jews were murdered at Auschwitz."[34] Nolte's notion of multiple victims might be classified as "soft revisionism." Almost as troubling as such frequent inaccuracies are the tinges of racism and antisemitism in deniers' accounts that explain away the "traditional" historiography as biased by Jewish influences. The relativists and the deniers in this middle generation seek a veneer of respectability by claiming that they alone are truly disinterested.[35]

In conclusion, it is evident that Holocaust denial stems from roots, and exhibits rationales, that are as diverse as Western society. The old deniers simply lie about the past because they find it easier to live that way than to confront the truth and their guilt. This inability to confront the past honestly—the failed *Vergangenheitsbewältigung*—stems not only from their behavior during the period 1933–45 but also from the years of lies that followed. The young deniers do not believe that historical truth really matters. They are disenchanted with their lives, and their bitterness finds expression in various forms of rebellion and in pathetic attempts at self-empowerment. They have little compunction about lying or even inflicting bodily harm. Finally, the middle generation has at the core of its *Grundintentionen* a complex cynicism: these deniers embrace conspiracy theories and are prepared to propagate lies, however odious, to gain fortune and publicity.

Recognizing these generational distinctions among deniers may help us not just understand the movement but also combat its influence within our society. As with a physician fighting a disease, one must first understand the agent of infection before one can prescribe a remedy. Generational theory, then, facilitates insight into the deniers' diverse motivations, helps shed light on their networks, and suggests reasons why members of particular societies are susceptible to such fallacies. It is a useful tool for exploring below the surface of the phenomenon and for answering the seldomly asked question as to why they hold such views.

It is indeed difficult to know to what extent the different generations share ideas or participate in the same networks. Clearly, all three blocs subscribe to certain fundamental ideas, such as the nonoccurrence of the Holocaust and the existence of a Jewish conspiracy. Hence, when the director of the Wiesenthal Center in Los Angeles, Rabbi Marvin Hier, gave instructions to Yaron Svoray when the latter traveled to Germany to infiltrate the extreme right wing, he told him: "Look for connections . . . between the old Nazis and the young; one group of skinheads and another; the right-wing parties and the skinheads."[36] However, as I have argued here, there are also age-specific formulations. The old SS soldiers at their reunions do not usually believe that they will effect real change, while the message of the young neo-Nazis in their "oi" music sounds a call to action. Ultimately, as we confront the threat of the Holocaust deniers, it is crucial to preserve distinctions and to create categories. In another instance of categories being useful, the Library of Congress has recently developed a separate call-number prefix for publications by deniers, in order to distinguish them from legitimate scholarly works. Categories based on generations are likewise useful in that they enable us to understand more about the myriad motivations and resources of the deniers.

Geoffrey J. Giles

Blind in the Right Eye: German Justice and Holocaust Denial

ON DECEMBER 1, 1994, A NEW GERMAN LAW CAME INTO EFFECT THAT metes out imprisonment for up to five years to those who deny the Holocaust. The bill was aimed at controlling the rising tide of neo-Nazis.[1] An average of three attacks by right-wing extremists took place *each day* in Germany in 1994, by the admission of the federal authorities, and at least thirty people had been killed during the preceding four years.[2] As one U.S. newspaper put it in August: "After a relatively quiet first half of 1994, German right-wing extremists are again wreaking high-profile havoc. A series of incidents is undermining efforts to shape reunified Germany's twenty-first-century image as a leading force for moderation and stability."[3] The previous maximum prison sentence for such crimes, including the display of Nazi symbols, was three years. The bill had initially been blocked by the opposition Social Democrats on the grounds that its provisions would end the strict separation between the police and the federal intelligence service. A last-minute compromise placed some restrictions on the way covert intelligence is gathered.[4]

The passage of the bill was doubtless aided in the end by a recent court ruling at Mannheim in favor of the Holocaust denier Günther Deckert, which received little coverage in the American press and therefore deserves some attention here. The judge in question, Rainer Ortlet, gave the strong impression that he considered Holocaust denial simply a matter of free speech. He thus sent a coded, but strong and welcome, signal of encouragement to the radical right. His ruling of June 22, 1994 was not released in full until the middle of August. At that time it unleashed a spontaneous torrent of criticism from many Germans, which led to the suspension of the judge.

What is disturbing to me, however, is that such a judgment could be handed down at all in the 1990s, and by a court taking a careful second look at the case, at that. Let me briefly outline the facts of the case, before turning to the wording of the ruling. Günther Deckert was the leader of the extreme right-wing National Democratic party (NPD), which counts some 5,000 members. In November 1991 he invited the notorious Fred Leuchter to give a closed lecture before an invited audience in Mannheim. Deckert translated Leuchter's English comments, and the audience applauded each "proof" about the "lies" and "myths" about the gas chambers. He recorded the whole event on videotape, and subsequently circulated copies of this to interested parties. The state prosecutor stepped in at this point to charge Deckert with neo-Nazi activities. On three occasions during the 1980s charges had been brought against him but with minimal result, apart from a demotion in his position as a schoolteacher of English and French. Now the videotapes provided hard evidence of serious violations, however. The district court at Mannheim sentenced Deckert to one year in prison or a fine of 10,000 marks. Deckert appealed, and the appeals court suspended the sentence on March 15, 1994, sending the case back to the Mannheim district court for reconsideration and revision.

There it landed on the desk of Judge Ortlet, a fierce opponent of the left who had consistently handed down the harshest sentences possible in cases involving left-wing activities. His fanaticism seems to have hampered his career, which advanced rather slowly owing to a reputation that was not appreciated by his more moderate superiors, and he is said to have developed a sort of persecution complex as a result. His aggressive opinions repeatedly had to be restrained by chairmen of the bench.[5]

And now Ortlet, in a triad of judges at Mannheim, was the one given the responsibility of writing this sensitive ruling. Sensitive, because the federal court at Karlsruhe had already been swamped with faxes from American Jews, when Deckert had prematurely trumpeted his acquittal. Ortlet's commentary on the case revealed a certain sympathy for the NPD leader. He admitted that Deckert had clearly violated the law by telling the audience, at the November 1991 session with Leuchter, that the Holocaust was a myth perpetrated by "a parasitic people who were using a historical lie to muzzle and exploit Germany."[6] But Ortlet characterized Deckert as "a universally popular and successful teacher who has never been guilty of any transgression in his job," and went on to describe him thus:

> The accused, who stands on the political right, is not an antisemite in the sense of National Socialist racial ideology, which in the last resort denied Jews their right to life; rather he condemns their deprivation of rights and their persecution. . . . On the basis of his pronounced national standpoint, however, he bitterly resents the Jews' constant insistence on the Holocaust and the financial, political, and moral demands they make of Germany on the basis of this, even almost fifty years after the end of the war. He is of the opinion that a mass murder of the Jews in the National Socialist concentration camps did not take place, at least by means of gassing. . . .
>
> [The plaintiff] finds it necessary to reexamine again and again, by means of research, even those historical theses that are regarded as sound.
>
> One may be of the opinion that the accused pursued a legitimate interest in striving to ward off the claims against Germany regarding the Holocaust that are still made after the passage of almost a half-century. However, he did not employ the requisite and appropriate means for this. . . . It would have been entirely sufficient, in pursuit of his declared aims, to draw attention to the long period that has elapsed since the National Socialist persecution of the Jews, the extent of the atonement already undertaken by Germans, and the unatoned and unrepented mass crimes of other nations.[7]

Let me spell out the messages that these remarks convey. First, Judge Ortlet implies that there is a kind of antisemitism that, if divorced from Nazi racial ideology, is somehow valid and acceptable. Second, he tries to explain away and to excuse Deckert's antisemitism on the grounds of his marked nationalism. Patriotism, it seems, may excuse antisemitic tendencies. Third, the judge implies that fifty years after the war, these incessant demands of "the Jews" are rather unreasonable. After all, other countries have been guilty of mass crimes (he does not actually say "genocide"), and they do not find it necessary to constantly repeat their regrets and act the penitent. And fourth, he suggests that the mass murder of the Jews in gas chambers is merely a historical thesis, not a fact, which it is appropriate to test repeatedly. This, despite the fact that the German Federal Supreme Court had ruled in the past that the murder of the Jews *is* a proven fact that can no longer be challenged.

Indeed, in his ruling Judge Ortlet casts doubt time and again on the veracity of the Holocaust. Instead of stating outright that the Holocaust *did* happen, he uses phrases such as "the generally accepted view on the question of the destruction of the Jews," and elsewhere admits only that "the overwhelming majority of the German population is convinced" that the gassings took place. But that is not total acceptance; that still leaves open a large loophole, which delighted the radical right in Germany.[8]

The revised ruling did impose a $6,500 (10,000 mark) fine on Deckert, but it also threw out the two-year jail sentence the prosecution had sought. In seeking to exonerate the defendant, Judge Ortlet almost showered Deckert with praise, underlining the "good impression" that the latter made in the courtroom and commending him for the vigorous and responsible way in which he defended his sincerely held political convictions. "Finally," Ortlet wrote, "[the court] did not overlook the hard fate of the defendant, who, after a long and successful career as a teacher, had to give up his beloved profession and now faces a miserable existence. . . . The court judges the fact that he did not bring himself, after all this, to take the logical step and cut his ties to the NPD, as the result of a decision based on his conscience, which deserves respect." As a footnote, Ortlet opined that a prison sentence would have little purpose, because it was quite clear that no change could be expected in Deckert's political beliefs or his passionately held views on the Holocaust. Deckert ends up sounding like a martyr, rather than one of Germany's chief inciters to hate crimes.[9]

There was nevertheless a panel of three judges to hear this case, and Ortlet was not even its chair. His superior here, Judge Wolfgang Müller, had developed a reputation for being poorly prepared for cases. His wife was very ill, and he had frequently appeared distracted in court. This in no way excuses his countersignature on the ruling, however, by which he concurred with Ortlet. These two judges were quickly suspended from their posts on the grounds of "extended illness" (which, in a tradition designed to protect the independence of the judiciary, is the only reason for which a judge may be suspended in Germany). The third, female judge, about whom less is known, was not suspended. By the middle of September, however, Judge Müller was back in chambers.[10] Judge Ortlet, apparently unrepentant, was not. In August he defended his ruling in the newsmagazine *Focus,* saying: "If you study the verdict in a factual way, you have to establish that it is in order."[11]

One can see from this episode how necessary it was to have a new anti-denial law on the statute books in Germany, where even some of those charged with administering justice consider the existence of a Holocaust open to debate. How effective the law will be remains to be seen. Fred Leuchter, himself arrested in Germany in October 1993 for delivering a talk in Deckert's hometown of Weinheim, left the country two months later with the permission of the German authorities, after raising $13,000 in bail. In mid-September 1994 the court case against him began, but Leuchter failed to show up and Germany had no idea where he was. His lawyer claimed that Leuchter was refusing to appear because he believed he would not receive a fair trial.[12] The judge suspended the case indefinitely. Leuchter had already been in trouble with the law in the United States, where he was released on two years' probation in June 1991 from a court in Cambridge, Massachusetts, for claiming to be an engineer although he has no degree in engineering.[13] Meanwhile, shots against the new law have already been fired by the senior (one can no longer say respected) historian and professor Ernst Nolte, who has publicly claimed that the law against deniers could mean "a danger for intellectual freedom in Germany."[14]

Neither the judge nor the professor are at all representative of the majority of Germans. Yet they are both important voices in high places, and therefore their pronouncements have to be taken seriously. The German press and the German public were right to express outrage over the Mannheim ruling. Chancellor Kohl himself denounced the ruling, charging that it sent a "bad signal."[15] We, too, should watch vigilantly for such disturbing developments in Germany, as in other countries.

Cases like these have significant and far-reaching effects, in every way more serious than the trivia of the O. J. Simpson trial on which the American press wasted such a shameful amount of time and space in the mid-nineties. The Deckert case is important because it involves a significant historical event. And as one reporter noted: "To show sympathy toward this man, or to suggest that people ought to discuss the case calmly, is to misread history."[16] In the end, the German authorities seemed to have acknowledged this, and Judge Ortlet "retired for health reasons" on May 15, 1995. Then in the summer of 1995, Gary Lauck, the American, self-styled leader of the neo-Nazi movement, was arrested in Denmark at the behest of the German police and extradited to Germany. With the tacit cooperation of the U.S. State Department, Lauck began serving a four-year prison sentence in August 1996 that had been imposed by a Hamburg court. This tightening of the rather slack boundaries of official tolerance for right-wing extremism will be welcomed far beyond the borders of Germany itself.

Notes

Christopher R. Browning, "The Holocaust and History"

1. Steven Katz, *The Holocaust in Historical Context* (Oxford: Oxford University Press, 1994), vol. 1, pp. 128–29.

2. Robert Melson, *Revolution and Genocide: On the Origins of the Armenian Genocide and the Holocaust* (Chicago: University of Chicago Press, 1992).

3. This use of "holocaust" is advocated by Yehuda Bauer, "The Place of the Holocaust in Contemporary History," *Studies in Contemporary Jewry* 1 (1984): 201–24.

4. This exchange took place at a colloquium at the University of Pennsylvania in 1988, the papers of which are published in *Reevaluating the Third Reich,* ed. Thomas Childers and Jane Caplan (New York: Holmes and Meier, 1993). See especially pp. xiii–xv and 234–52.

5. Michael Burleigh and Wolfgang Wippermann, *The Racial State: Germany 1933–1945* (Cambridge: Cambridge University Press, 1991), pp. 1–2.

Alan E. Steinweis, "The Holocaust and Jewish Studies"

1. William H. Honan, "Holocaust Teaching Gaining a Niche, but Method Is Disputed," *New York Times,* April 12, 1995.

2. Sybil Milton, "Point of View: Re-examining Scholarship on the Holocaust," *Chronicle of Higher Education,* April 21, 1993.

3. For historical comparisons see Steven T. Katz, *The Holocaust in Historical Contzext* (New York: Oxford University Press, 1994). Although it argues the "uniqueness" position, Katz's book provides a good introduction to the controversy. Among the comparative studies that focus on the Nazi era, two useful works are Michael Burleigh and Wolfgang Wippermann,

The Racial State: Germany 1933–1945 (Cambridge: Cambridge University Press, 1991), and Michael Berenbaum, ed., *A Mosaic of Victims: Non-Jews Persecuted and Murdered by the Nazis* (New York: New York University Press, 1990).

4. The public debate was triggered by the publication of Richard J. Herrnstein and Charles Murray, *The Bell Curve: Intelligence and Class Structure in American Life* (New York: Free Press, 1994). Useful anthologies documenting the controversy are *The Bell Curve Debate: History, Documents, Opinions* (New York: Times Books, 1995), and *The Bell Curve Wars: Race, Intelligence, and the Future of America* (New York: Basic Books, 1995). For evidence that racialism is no longer taboo even among Jewish scholars of history, see Norman F. Cantor, *The Sacred Chain: The History of the Jews* (New York: HarperCollins, 1994).

5. Important recent works include Robert Proctor, *Racial Hygiene: Medicine under the Nazis* (Cambridge, Mass.: Harvard University Press, 1988); Michael Burleigh, *Death and Deliverance: "Euthanasia," in Germany 1900–1945* (Cambridge: Cambridge University Press, 1994); Henry Friedlander, *The Origins of Nazi Genocide: From Euthanasia to the Final Solution* (Chapel Hill: University of North Carolina Press, 1995).

6. See, for example, Yehuda Bauer, *A History of the Holocaust* (New York: Watts, 1982), which devotes barely a couple of paragraphs to the subject. Leni Yahil, *The Holocaust: The Fate of European Jewry, 1932–1945* (New York: Oxford University Press, 1990), discusses the "euthanasia" in more detail, but only as a preliminary to the "Final Solution."

7. Michael R. Marrus, "'Good History' and Teaching the Holocaust," *Perspectives* (American Historical Association newsletter) 31:5 (May–June 1993).

Gerald E. Markle, "The Holocaust and Sociology"

1. Helen Fein, *Genocide: A Sociological Perspective* (Newbury Park, Cal.: Sage Publications, 1993).

2. Zygmunt Bauman, *Modernity and the Holocaust* (Ithaca: Cornell University Press, 1990).

3. J. Stanley Milgram, *Obedience to Authority* (New York: Harper & Row, 1974). Of all Nechama Tec's books on the Holocaust, the most traditionally "sociological" (in that it attempts to test sociological theory) is *When Light Pierced the Darkness* (New York: Oxford University Press, 1986). For Fred Katz's most recent book, see *Ordinary People and Extraordinary Evil* (Albany: State University of New York Press, 1993). R. Ruth Linden, *Making Stories, Making Selves: Feminist Reflections on the Holocaust* (Columbus: Ohio State University Press, 1993).

4. Raul Hilberg, *Perpetrators, Victims, and Bystanders: The Jewish Catastrophe, 1933–1945* (New York: HarperCollins, 1992).

5. Alvin Gouldner, "The Sociologist as Partisan: Sociology and the Welfare State," *American Sociologist* 3 (1968): 103.

6. Gerald E. Markle, Mary Lagerwey, Todd Clason, Jill Green, and Tricia Mead, "From Auschwitz to Americana: Texts of the Holocaust," *Sociological Focus* 25 (1992): 179–202.

7. Vincent Pecora, "Habermas, Enlightenment and Antisemitism," in *Probing the Limits of Representation: Nazism and the Final Solution,* ed. Saul Friedlander (Cambridge, Mass.: Harvard University Press, 1992), pp. 155–70.

8. Gerald E. Markle, *Meditations of a Holocaust Traveler* (Albany: State University of New York Press, 1995).

9. Bauman, *Modernity and the Holocaust,* p. viii.

10. Quoted in Margaret Canovan, *Hannah Arendt: A Reinterpretation of Her Political Thought* (Cambridge: Cambridge University Press, 1992), p. 20.

11. Primo Levi, *Other People's Trades* (New York: Summit Books, 1989), p. 104.

12. Levi, *The Drowned and the Saved* (New York: Vintage International, 1989), p. 117.

13. Ibid., p. 42.

14. Hannah Arendt, *Eichmann in Jerusalem: A Report on the Banality of Evil* (New York: Viking, 1963), and *The Origins of Totalitarianism* (New York: Harcourt, Brace and Jovanovich), p. 18.

15. Gershom Scholem, *On Jews and Judaism in Crisis* (New York: Schocken, 1976), pp. 299–300.

16. Jean Amery, *At the Mind's Limits* (New York: Schocken, 1990), p. 8.

John K. Roth, "The Holocaust and Philosophy"

1. Elie Wiesel, *Night,* trans. Stella Rodway (New York: Bantam, 1986), p. 3.

2. See Claude Lanzmann, *Shoah: An Oral History of the Holocaust* (New York: Pantheon, 1985), p. 70.

3. Elie Wiesel, foreword to Harry James Cargas, *Shadows of Auschwitz: A Christian Response to the Holocaust* (New York: Crossroad, 1990), p. ix.

Jeffrey M. Peck, "The Holocaust and Literary Studies"

1. John Borneman and Jeffrey M. Peck, *Sojourners: The Return of German Jews and the Question of Identity* (Lincoln: University of Nebraska Press, 1995). The video documentary has the same title.

2. This problem of representation has been raised particularly in postmodernist criticism, especially in literature, history, and anthropology. For a more detailed discussion than I can provide here, see the essays in and especially the introduction to *Probing the Limits of Representation: Nazism and the "Final Solution,"* ed. Saul Friedlander (Cambridge, Mass.: Harvard University Press, 1992).

3. See, for example, Paul Ricoeur's "The Model of the Text: Meaningful Action Considered as a Text," in *Interpretive Science: A Reader,* ed. Paul Rabinow and William M. Sullivan (Berkeley: University of California Press, 1979), pp. 197–221. Almost any of Clifford Geertz's voluminous writings will steer the reader in this textualist direction, but see in particular his essays in *The Interpretation of Culture: Selected Essays* (New York: Basic Books, 1973) and *Local Knowledge: Further Essays in Interpretive Anthropology* (New York: Basic Books, 1983).

4. There are literally hundreds of titles on Holocaust literature. Some of the most prominent critics are Berel Lang, Lawrence Langer, Geoffrey Hartman, David Roskies, and Sidra Ezrahi.

5. On AIDS, see, for example, Sander Gilman, *Disease and Representation: Images of Illness from Madness to AIDS* (Ithaca: Cornell University Press, 1985). On atom bomb representations, see John Whittier Treat, *Writing Ground Zero: Japanese Literature and the Atomic Bomb* (Chicago: University of Chicago Press, 1995).

6. James Young, *The Texture of Memory: Holocaust Memorials and Monuments* (New Haven: Yale University Press, 1993), and Jane Kramer, *The Politics of Memory: Looking for Germany in the New Germany* (New York: Random House, 1996), pp. 254–93.

7. An excellent study is Shoshana Felman and Dori Laub, *Testimony: Crises of Witnessing in Literature, Psychoanalysis, and History* (New York and London: Routledge, 1992). The authors combine their expertise as literary critic and psychoanalyst to deal with "the relation between art and history, between art and memory, between speech and survival" (p. xiii).

8. James Clifford, "Introduction: Partial Truths," in his *Writing Culture: The Poetics and Politics of Ethnography* (Berkeley: University of California Press, 1986), pp. 1–26.

9. David Lowenthal, *The Past Is a Foreign Country* (New York: Cambridge University Press, 1985).

10. My understanding of this point was enriched by Irene Kacandes

and a discussion she led on teaching the Holocaust at the 1996 Lessons and Legacies conference at Notre Dame University, South Bend, Indiana.

Michael Berkowitz, "Beyond 'the Crisis of German Ideology'"

1. Essential texts for treatment of this subject include David Sorkin, *The Transformation of German Jewry, 1780–1840* (New York: Oxford University Press, 1987); Jehuda Reinharz and Walter Schatzberg, eds., *The Jewish Response to German Culture: From the Enlightenment to the Second World War* (Hanover, N.H.: University Press of New England, 1985); George Mosse, *German Jews beyond Judaism* (Bloomington: Indiana University Press, 1985); Steven Lowenstein, *The Berlin Jewish Community: Enlightenment, Family, and Crisis, 1770–1830* (New York: Oxford University Press, 1994); David Bronsen, ed., *Jews and Germans from 1860 to 1933: The Problematic Symbiosis* (Heidelberg: Winter, 1979); and Michael Meyer, *Origins of the Modern Jew: Jewish Identity and European Culture in Germany, 1749–1824* (Detroit: Wayne State University Press, 1984).

2. A more "one-dimensional" view (focusing on the antisemitic elements) is apparent in the "intentionalist" school of Holocaust historiography, for example, Lucy S. Dawidowicz, *The War Against the Jews, 1933–1945* (New York: Bantam, 1978), and most recently Daniel J. Goldhagen, *Hitler's Willing Executioners: Ordinary Germans and the Holocaust* (New York: Knopf, 1994).

3. Michael Meyer, *Response to Modernity: A History of the Reform Movement in Judaism* (New York: Oxford University Press, 1988).

4. See Sorkin, *Transformation of German Jewry.*

5. See, e.g., Leo Spitzer, "Andean Waltz," in *Holocaust Remembrance: The Shapes of Memory,* ed. Geoffrey H. Hartman (New York: Basil Blackwell, 1994), pp. 161–74.

6. Robert L. Koehl, *The Black Corps: The Structure and Power Struggles of the SS* (Madison: University of Wisconsin Press, 1983); Christopher Browning, *Ordinary Men: Reserve Police Batallion 101 and the Holocaust* (New York: HarperCollins, 1992). Some commentators have alleged that these and other efforts at *Alltagsgeschichte* are inherently apologetic.

7. George L. Mosse, *The Crisis of German Ideology: Intellectual Origins of the Third Reich* (New York: Grosse and Dunlap, 1964).

8. See Steven E. Aschheim, "George Mosse—The Man and the Work," and Moshe Zimmerman, "Mosse and German Historiography," in *George Mosse: On the Occasion of His Retirement* (Jerusalem: Hebrew University, 1986), pp. xi–xxi; Seymour Drescher, Allan Sharlin, and David Sabean, eds., *Political Symbolism in Modern Europe: Essays in Honor of George L. Mosse* (New Brunswick, N.J.: Transaction, 1982), pp. 1–15.

9. Dawidowicz, *War Against the Jews.*

10. See Benjamin Ginsberg, *The Fatal Embrace: Jews and the State* (Chicago: University of Chicago Press, 1993).

11. See Goldhagen, *Hitler's Willing Executioners,* which has set off a wide array of responses; most scholarly ones are extremely critical of his methodology and arguments. Among the most thoughtful critical reviews are Christopher Browning, "Daniel Goldhagen's Willing Executioners," *History and Memory* (Spring/Summer 1996): 88–108; Omer Bartov, "Ordinary Monsters," *The New Republic,* April 29, 1996, pp. 32–38; Jacob Heilbrunn, "Ankläger und Rächer," *Der Tagesspiegel,* March 31, 1996, p. 39; and "Primitive Provokation," *Die Woche,* April 19, 1996, p. 43.

12. Henry Feingold, "Bildung: Was It Good for the Jews?" in *The German-Jewish Legacy in America: From Bildung to the Bill of Rights,* ed. Abraham Peck (Detroit: Wayne State University Press), pp. 57–61.

13. Jehuda Reinharz, *Fatherland or Promised Land: The Dilemma of the German Jew, 1893–1914* (Ann Arbor: University of Michigan Press, 1975).

14. James E. Young, "Israel's Memorial Landscape: Sho'ah, Heroism, and National Redemption," in *Lessons and Legacies: The Meaning of the Holocaust in a Changing World,* ed. Peter Hayes (Evanston: Northwestern University Press, 1991), pp. 279–304.

15. Lion Feuchtwanger, *The Oppermanns* (New York: Carroll & Graf, 1983).

16. Gotthold Ephraim Lessing, "Nathan the Wise," trans. Walter Frank Charles Ade (Woodbury, N.Y.: Barron's, 1972), pp. 86–90.

17. David Ellenson, *Rabbi Esriel Hildesheimer and the Creation of a Modern Jewish Orthodoxy* (Tuscaloosa: University of Alabama Press, 1990); Mordechai Breuer, *Modernity within Tradition: The Social History of Orthodox Jewry in Imperial Germany,* trans. Elizabeth Petuchowski (New York: Columbia University Press, 1992); Steven Lowenstein, *Frankfurt on the Hudson: The German-Jewish Community of Washington Heights* (Detroit: Wayne State University Press, 1988).

18. Michael Brenner, *The Renaissance of Jewish Culture in Weimar Germany* (New Haven: Yale University Press, 1998).

19. Jeffrey Grossman, "The Space of Yiddish in the German and German-Jewish Discourse," Ph.D. diss., University of Texas, Austin, 1992; Mark Gelber, "The jungjüdische Bewegung: An Unexplored Chapter in German-Jewish Literary and Cultural History," *Leo Baeck Institute Year Book* 31 (1986): 105–19; David Brenner, "Promoting the Ostjuden: Ethnic Identity, Stereotyping, and Audience in the German-Jewish Cultural Review *Ost und West* (Berlin, 1901–1923)," Ph.D. diss., University of Texas, Austin, 1993.

20. Michael Berkowitz, *Zionist Culture and West European Jewry before the First World War* (Cambridge: Cambridge University Press, 1993), and *Western Jewry and the Zionist Project, 1914–1933* (Cambridge: Cambridge University Press, 1997); Derek Penslar, *Zionism and Technocracy: The Engineering of Jewish Settlement in Palestine, 1870–1918* (Bloomington and Indianapolis: Indiana University Press, 1991); Glen Sharfman, "The Jewish Youth Movement in Germany, 1900–1936: A Study in Ideology and Organization," Ph.D. diss., University of North Carolina, Chapel Hill, 1989; Stephen Poppel, *Zionism in Germany 1897–1933: The Shaping of Jewish Identity* (Philadelphia: Jewish Publication Society of America, 1977); Donald Niewyk, *The Jews in Weimar Germany* (London and Baton Rouge: Louisiana State University Press, 1980), pp. 125–64; Hagit Lavsky, *Beterem puranut: Darkam veyihudam shel tsionei germanyah, 1918–1932* (Jerusalem: Magnes Press, 1990).

21. Steven Aschheim, *The Nietzsche Legacy in Germany, 1890–1990* (Los Angeles and Berkeley: University of California Press, 1994), pp. 102–12.

22. Tom Segev, *The Seventh Million: The Israelis and the Holocaust*, trans. Haim Watzman (New York: Hill and Wang, 1993), pp. 35–64.

23. Abraham Peck, ed., *The German-Jewish Legacy in America;* Donald Fleming and Bernard Bailyn, *The Intellectual Migration: Europe and America, 1930–1960* (Cambridge, Mass.: Harvard University Press, 1969); Lewis Coser, *Refugee Scholars in America: Their Impact and Their Experience* (New Haven: Yale University Press, 1984); Anthony Heilbut, *Exiled in Paradise: German Refugee Artists and Exiles in America from the 1930s to the Present* (New York: Viking, 1983); John Russell Taylor, *Strangers in Paradise: The Hollywood Emigrés, 1933–1950* (New York: Holt, Rinehart, and Winston, 1983); Helmut F. Pfanner, *Exile in New York: German and Austrian Writers after 1933* (Detroit: Wayne State University Press, 1983); Jarrell C. Jackman and Carla M. Borden, eds., *The Muses Flee Hitler: Cultural Transfer and Adaption, 1930–1945* (Washington, D.C.: Smithsonian Institution Press, 1983); Maurice R. Davie, *Refugees in America* (New York: Harper, 1947).

24. See Claus-Dieter Krohn, *Intellectuals in Exile: Refugee Scholars and the New School for Social Research* (Amherst: University of Massachusetts Press, 1993); Martin Jay, *The Dialectical Imagination: A History of the Frankfurt School and the Institute for Social Research, 1923–1950* (Boston: Little and Brown, 1973); Zoltan Tar, *The Frankfurt School: The Critical Theories of Max Horkheimer and Theodor W. Adorno* (New York: John Wiley, 1977); John McCole, Seyla Benhabib, and Wolfgang Bonss, eds., *Max Horkheimer: Between Philosophy and Social Science* (Cambridge, Mass.: MIT Press, 1993).

25. See Eva Reichmann, "Max Horkheimer the Jew: Critical Theory and Beyond," *Yearbook of the Leo Baeck Institute* 19 (1974): 181–95; Martin Jay, "The Jews and the Frankfurt School: Critical Theory's Analysis of Anti-Semitism," in *Permanent Exiles: Essays on the Intellectual Migration from Germany to America* (New York: Columbia University Press, 1985); Dan Diner, "Reason and 'Other': Horkheimer's Reflections on Anti-Semitism and Mass Annihilation," in *Between Philosophy and Social Science,* pp. 335–63.

26. Gabrielle Simon Edgcomb, *From Swastika to Jim Crow: Refugee Scholars at Black Colleges* (Malabar, Fla.: Krieger, 1993).

27. See Steven Aschheim, *Brothers and Strangers: The East European Jew in German and German Jewish Consciousness, 1800–1923* (Madison: University of Wisconsin Press, 1982), and Jack Wertheimer, *Unwelcome Strangers: East European Jews in Imperial Germany* (New York: Oxford University Press, 1987).

28. Hannah Arendt, *Imperialism* [pt. 2 of *The Origins of Totalitarianism*] (New York and London: Harcourt Brace Jovanovich, 1968), pp. 176–82.

29. Marion Kaplan, *The Jewish Feminist Movement in Germany: The Campaigns of the Jüdischer Frauenbund, 1904–1938* (Westport, Conn.: Greenwood, 1979), p. 205.

Karl A. Schleunes, "The Year 1933"

1. Joseph Goebbels, *Goebbels-Reden, 1932–1939,* vol. 1, ed. Helmut Heiber (Düsseldorf: Droste, 1971), p. 62.

2. Joseph Goebbels, *Die Tagebücher: Sämtliche Fragmente,* vol. 2, pt. 1, ed. Elke Frölich (Munich and New York: K. G. Sauer, 1987), p. 361.

3. Thomas Nipperdey, "1933 und Kontinuität der deutschen Geschichte," *Historische Zeitschrift* 227 (1978): 86.

4. Instances of continuity need not be contradictory to the idea of revolution. Obviously, the Nazi revolution of 1933 did not drop suddenly from the skies. Revolutions do have contexts. The generation-long tradition of eugenics in German scientific and social thought is an instance of continuity that finds its fulfillment in the Nazi revolution.

5. This definition of revolution is adapted from Felix Gilbert, "Revolution," *Dictionary of the History of Ideas,* ed. P. Wiener, vol. 4 (New York: Scribners, 1968), p. 158.

6. See, for example, the dozens of index entries for "revolution" in Adolf Hitler, *Sämtliche Aufzeichnung, 1905–1924,* ed. Eberhard Jäckel (Stuttgart: Deutsche Verlags-Anstalt, 1980), pp. 1308–9.

7. Adolf Hitler, *Monologe im Führerhauptquartier, 1941–1944: Die*

Aufzeichnungen Heinrich Heims, ed. Werner Jochmann (Hamburg: A. Kraus, 1980), p. 155.

8. Alfred Rosenberg quoted in Max Weinreich, *Hitler's Professors: The Part of Scholarship in Germany's Crimes against the Jewish People* (New York: YIVO, 1946), p. 101.

9. Reinhart Koselleck, "Revolution, Rebellion, Aufruhr, Burgerkrieg," in *Geschichtliche Grundbegriffe,* ed. Otto Brunner, Werner Conze, Reinhart Koselleck, vol. 5 (Stuttgart: Klett-Cotta, 1984), p. 655.

10. Alan Bullock, *Hitler: A Study in Tyranny* (New York: Harper, 1952), chap. 5.

11. Karl Dietrich Bracher, Wolfgang Sauer, and Gerhard Schulz, *Die nationalsozialistische Machtergreifung* (Cologne: Westdeutscher Verlag, 1960), pp. 31–74.

12. Martin Broszat, *The Hitler State,* trans. John W. Hiden (London: Longman, 1981), p. 308.

13. Alfred Cobban, "The Decline of Political Theory," in *European Intellectual History since Darwin and Marx,* ed. Warren Wager (New York: Harper Books, 1967), p. 193.

14. Gerhard L. Weinberg, "The Nazi Revolution: A War against Human Rights," in his *Germany, Hitler, and World War II* (Cambridge: Cambridge University Press, 1995), pp. 57–67.

15. David Schoenbaum, *Hitler's Social Revolution: Class and Status in Nazi Germany, 1933–1939* (New York: Doubleday, 1966).

16. Hermann Rauschning, *The Revolution of Nihilism: Warning to the West,* trans. E. W. Dickes (New York: Alliance, 1939), p. 64.

17. Horst Möller, "Die nationalsozialistische Machtergreifung: Konterrevolution oder Revolution?" *Vierteljahrshefte für Zeitgeschichte* 31 (1983): 25.

18. Ibid., pp. 44–47.

19. Michael Prinz, "Der Nationalsozialismus—Eine 'Braune Revolution'?" in *Revolution in Deutschland? 1789–1989,* ed. Manfred Hettling (Göttingen: Vandenhoeck & Ruprecht, 1991), pp. 76–77.

20. Arthur Hatto, "'Revolution': An Enquiry into the Usefulness of an Historical Term," *Mind* 58 (1949): 504.

21. Condorcet quoted in Felix Gilbert, "Revolution," p. 157.

22. Hugo von Hofmannsthal, "Das Schriftum als geistiger Raum der Nation" [speech given at the University of Munich on January 10, 1927] in his *Gesammelte Werke, Prosa IV,* ed. Herbert Steiner (Frankfurt am Main: S. Fischer Verlag, 1955), p. 413. See also Klemens von Klemperer, *Germany's New Conservatism: Its History and the Dilemma in the Twentieth Century* (Princeton: Princeton University Press, 1957), p. 9.

23. Hofmannsthal, "Schriftum," p. 409.

24. Fritz Stern, *The Politics of Cultural Despair: A Study in the Rise of the Germanic Ideology* (Berkeley and Los Angeles: University of California Press, 1961).

25. Hans Freyer, *Revolution von Rechts* (Jena: Eugen Diedrichs, 1931), p. 26.

26. Ernst Nolte, *Marxismus und industrielle Revolution* (Stuttgart: Klett-Cotta, 1983), p. 39.

27. Arno J. Mayer, *Dynamics of Counterrevolution in Europe, 1870–1956* (New York: Harper Torchbooks, 1971); see also his *Why Did the Heavens Not Darken? The "Final Solution" in History* (New York: Pantheon, 1988).

28. See also Alfred Rosenberg's article "1789?" *Völkischer Beobachter,* February 22, 1921, repr. in his *Kampf um die Macht: Aufsätze von 1921–1932,* ed. Thilo von Trotha (Munich: Franz Eher, 1942), pp. 17–20.

29. E. B. Wheaton, *The Nazi Revolution, 1933–1935; Prelude to Calamity* (Garden City, N.Y.: Doubleday [Anchor Books], 1969), p. 299.

30. Heinz Hohne, *The Story of Hitler's SS: The Order of the Death's Head,* trans. Richard Barry (New York: Coward-McCann, 1970), p. 85. Nearly all writers on the period note the spontaneous terrorism that followed on the heels of the Nazi seizure of power. For an analysis of how this brutality fit into the Nazi racial revolution, see Robert Gellately, *The Gestapo and German Society: Enforcing Racial Policy, 1933–1945* (Oxford: Clarendon Press, 1990).

31. On Krieck, see Bracher, *Nationalsozialistische Machtergreifung,* p. 308.

32. Eugen Fischer, *Der völkische Staat, biologisch gesehen* [speech given July 29, 1933 at the University of Berlin] (Berlin: Junker und Dünnhaupt, 1933), p. 11.

33. Hans Freyer, *Das politische Semester: Ein Vorschlag zur Universitätsreform* (Jena: Eugen Diedrichs, 1933), pp. 22–26.

34. Martin Heidegger, *Introduction to Metaphysics,* trans. Ralph Mannheim (New Haven: Yale University Press, 1959), p. 199. For Hannah Arendt's speculation on why Heidegger may have left this phrase in later editions of his book, see Elisabeth Young-Bruehl, *Hannah Arendt: For Love of the World* (New Haven: Yale University Press, 1982), p. 443. On Heidegger's attraction to National Socialism, see also Thomas Sheehan, "A Normal Nazi," *New York Review of Books* 40:1–2 (January 14, 1993): 30–35.

35. Milton Mayer, *They Thought They Were Free: The Germans, 1933–1945* (Chicago: University of Chicago Press, 1955), p. 105.

36. Wolfhard Buchholz, *Die nationalsozialistische Gemeinschaft "Kraft durch Freude": Freizeitgestaltung und Arbeiterschaft im Dritten Reich,* Ph.D.

diss., University of Munich, 1976. See especially the section on "Die KdF als Instrument zur Verwirklichung der Volksgemeinschaft," pp. 167–87.

37. George L. Mosse, *The Crisis of German Ideology: Intellectual Origins of the Third Reich* (New York: Grosset & Dunlap, 1964), p. 294.

38. For an overview of the Generalplan Ost, see Czeslaw Madajczyk, "Vom 'Generalplan Ost' zum 'Generalsiedlungsplan,'" in Mechthild Rössler and Sabine Schleiermacher, eds., *Der "Generalplan Ost": Hauptlinien der nationalsozialistischen Planungs- und Vernichtungspolitik* (Berlin: Akademie Verlag, 1993), pp. 12–24; see also Helmut Heiber, "Der Generalplan Ost," *Vierteljahrshefte für Zeitgeschichte* 6 (1958): 281–325.

39. Achim Besgen, *Der stille Befehl* (Munich: Nymphenburger Verlag, 1960), p. 75.

Peter Hayes, "The Deutsche Bank and the Holocaust"

1. See the Hamburger Stiftung für Sozialgeschichte's *OMGUS Ermittlungen gegen die Deutsche Bank—1946/1947* (Nördlingen: Franz Greno, 1985).

2. See Fritz Seidenzahl, *100 Jahre Deutsche Bank* (Frankfurt: Deutsche Bank AG, 1970).

3. The excellent result of the official team's labors is Lothar Gall, Gerald Feldman, Harold James, Carl-Ludwig Holtfrerich, and Hans Büschgen, *Die Deutsche Bank 1870–1995* (Munich: C. H. Beck, 1995). The major East German documentary collections consist of the files of the Deutsche Bank's headquarters in Berlin, located in the Bundesarchiv Potsdam (henceforth BAP) when I used them but now in Berlin-Lichterfelde, and of assorted branch offices, now in the Sächsisches Staatsarchiv Leipzig (henceforth SSAL) and the Sächsisches Hauptstaatsarchiv Dresden (henceforth SHAD).

4. See Gall, *Deutsche Bank,* pp. 282–83.

5. See Christopher Kopper, *Zwischen Marktwirtschaft und Dirigismus: Bankenpolitik im "Dritten Reich" 1933–1939* (Bonn: Bouvier, 1995), pp. 135–39.

6. Gall, *Deutsche Bank,* pp. 339, 342–43, 352–53, and 392–93; but regarding Stauss's ties to the NSDAP, compare with Kopper, *Zwischen Marktwirtschaft und Dirigismus,* p. 28.

7. Gall, *Deutsche Bank,* pp. 394, 401.

8. BAP, 80Ba2, 41/21078, Sitzungen des Rheinisch-Westfälischen Beirats, esp. 26.vii.34, 27.xi.35, 5.v.36, 11.xi.36, 28.x.37, and 31.iii.38.

9. See Hans-Erich Volkmann, "Die NS-Wirtschaft in Vorbereitung des Krieges," in Wilhelm Deist and Manfred Messerschmidt, eds., *Ur-*

sachen und Voraussetzungen der deutschen Kriegspolitik (Stuttgart: Deutsche Verlags Anstalt, 1979), pp. 177–368.

10. Gall, *Deutsche Bank,* pp. 317–20.

11. For overviews of what happened, see BAP, 80Ba2, 55/21082, especially Urbig's memo dated "Ende Juli 1933"; Gall, *Deutsche Bank,* pp. 336–39; and Kopper, *Zwischen Marktwirtschaft und Dirigismus,* pp. 132–35.

12. For examples, see, most recently, Heinz Hoehne, *Die Zeit der Illusionen* (Düsseldorf: Econ, 1992), pp. 69–72, 99–101.

13. See Gall, *Deutsche Bank,* pp. 280–81, 300–306.

14. Quoted in ibid., pp. 337–38.

15. Ibid., pp. 339–41; Kopper, *Zwischen Marktwirtschaft und Dirigismus,* p. 135.

16. Quoted in Gall, *Deutsche Bank,* p. 337.

17. For what follows, see BAP, 80Ba2, 2169/16165, especially the file note by Boner, 28.iv.33; Sijpesteijn to Boner, 28.iv.33; draft and final versions of the minutes of the meeting of the Personnel and Finance Committee, 8.v.33; and minutes of the meeting of the same committee, 28.vi.33.

18. The following accounts derive primarily from BAP, 80Ba2, 2372/14732, 2389/14725, 2390/14728, and 2391/14735 (on Jesserich); 2316/15318 (on Hochtief); and 2330/16938, 2349/16954, and 2353/16953 (on Holzmann).

19. On the following, see BAP, 80Ba2, 4295/18184, Urbig, Porz. L. Hutschenreuther AG, Allgemeines, especially Bl. 96, Schweisheimer to Urbig, 15.xi.33, and Bl. 237–39, Urbig to Schweisheimer, 17.xi.34, where the quoted passages appear; and 4332/18168, Urbig, Hutschenreuther Personalia, Bl. 170 and 172–73.

20. See BAP, 80Ba2, 1186/16675 (Hirsch Kupfer); 2671/17496, 2677/17495, and 2681/17494 (Orenstein & Koppel); 3188/16317 (Daimler-Benz); 5183/19529 (Leonard Tietz); and 5214/16892 (Hertie); as well as Hans Pohl, Stephanie Habeth, and Beate Brüninghaus, *Die Daimler-Benz AG in den Jahren 1933 bis 1945* (Wiesbaden: Steiner, 1986), pp. 42–45.

21. For one courageous instance, concerning Kurt Joachimssohn at BMW, see BAP, 80Ba2, 3109/15387; for an example of the reference letters, 1610/15002, Bl. 19–20, Emil Georg von Stauss to S. Tauss, 19.viii.33; and on the purge at Loewe, 3455/16833, Bl. 260, Kimmich's secretary to Benz, 28.v.37.

22. BAP, 80Ba2, 5200/14641, Stauss, AWAG, Allgemeines, 17.iii.33–10.xi.37, esp. Bl. 24, "Information zu diskreter Verwendung," n.d.; Bl. 52–53, Aktennotiz, 29.vii.35; Bl. 61–62, Aktenvermerk, 22.xi.35;

Bl. 67, unsigned note to Stauss, 18.xii.35; and Bl. 181, Pohl of the Economics Ministry to Wertheim AG, 8.vii.37.

23. BAP, 80Ba2, 2078/19682, Sippell, Zellstofffabrik Waldhof, Allgemeines, 17.iv.36–23.i.38, Bl. 1, Aktenvermerk by Sippell, 17.iv.36.

24. BAP, 80Ba2, 3188/16317, Stauss, Daimler-Benz AG, Allgemeines, 11.i–9.xi.33, esp. Bl. 212, memo for the Generalsekretariat, 5.vii.33; and 3455/16833, Kimmich, Gesfürel, Allgemeines, 11.vi.34–23.ii.38, esp. Bl. 75–82, file note by Solmssen, 5.vi.36.

25. BAP, 80Ba2, 5183/19529, Kimmich, Westdeutsche Kaufhof AG, Allgemeines, 18.viii.34–23.ii.39, esp. Bl. 129–32, Notizen für Herrn Dr. Kimmich, Berlin, betr. die personellen u. besonderen Geschäftsverhältnisse der Westd. Kaufhof AG, 25.vi.35.

26. BAP, 80Ba2, 3416/16560, Kiehl, Elektrische Licht- u. Kraftanlagen, Allgemeines, 12.ix.34–?, esp. Bl. 50–54, memo by Kiehl, 7.x.35 (on Cassirer); and 3481/16933, Rummel, Heliowatt-Werke Elektrizitäts AG, Allgemeines, 17.x.35–18.xii.44, esp. Bl. 5, a list of stockholders as of 15.xi.35; Bl. 8, memorandum concerning Manfred Aron, 16.xi.35; and Bl. 9, Rummel to Ebbecke, 18.xi.35. Manfred Aron may have been induced to sell by repeated arrests and incarceration in a concentration camp, but there is no evidence that the Deutsche Bank instigated these events; see Hamburger Stiftung's *OMGUS/Deutsche Bank,* p. 171.

27. BAP, 80Ba2, 1288/17894, Kronprinz AG f. Metallindustrie, Solingen, esp. Bl. 29–30, Deutsche Bank to Kronprinz, 16.v.36.

28. See Johannes Ludwig, *Boykott, Enteignung, Mord* (Hamburg: Facta Oblita Verlag, 1989), pp. 11–89; Kopper, *Zwischen Marktwirtschaft und Dirigismus,* p. 278; and Hans G. Meyen, *120 Jahre Dresdner Bank: Unternehmens-Chronik 1872 bis 1992* (Frankfurt: Frankfurter Societäts-Druckerei GmbH, 1992), p. 118.

29. See Hayes, "Big Business and 'Aryanization' in Germany, 1933–1939," *Jahrbuch für Antisemitismusforschung* 3 (1994): 260–61.

30. Ibid., p. 268.

31. For a fuller discussion of Hitler's and Göring's actions and motives, see ibid., pp. 265–66.

32. See Raul Hilberg, *The Destruction of the European Jews* (New York: Holmes & Meier, 1985), vol. 1, p. 100. I believe Kopper understates the value of this sort of business to the large banks (*Zwischen Marktwirtschaft und Dirigismus,* p. 277). On their motivations, see SSAL, Deutsche Bank, Filiale Leipzig, no. 623, Vorstand to Branch Directors, February 11, 1938; and Dresdner Bank, Filiale Leipzig, no. 167, Direktion Berlin to Branch Directors, July 2, 1938; and no. 168, Frankfurt Branch to Leipzig Branch, August 5, 1938.

33. For example, see Generallandesarchiv Karlsruhe (henceforth GLAK), Abt. 505: Arisierungen, no. 218, Badische Bank to Badische Finanz- und Wirtschaftsministerium, July 1, 1938.

34. BAP, 80Ba2, 1293/17772, Bl. 146–47, Aktenvermerk by Rösler, April 14, 1938. The Deutsche's share came to 200,000 marks. To carry out the takeover, the Deutsche loaned Mannesmann some 15.2 million of the purchase price of 17.7 million marks.

35. See SHAD, Firmenbestand 222, Altbanken Chemnitz, no. A4/21/15, A. Reich to Commerzbank Zentrale Berlin, September 1, 1941; and no. A7/21/46–47, Deutsche Bank Zentrale to Karl Goeritz, March 30, 1938; and account reports of March 1 and August 21, 1939.

36. SSAL, Deutsche Bank, Filiale Leipzig, no. 623, Vorstand to Branch Directors, January 14, 1938; Rundschreiben des Filialbüros Berlin, January 25, 1938.

37. Ibid., Vorstand to Branch Directors, signed by Kimmich and Rummel, February 11, 1938.

38. Kopper, *Zwischen Marktwirtschaft und Dirigismus,* p. 279; SSAL, Deutsche Bank, Filiale Leipzig, no. 623, Rundschreiben des Filialbüros, March 7, 1938–January 10, 1939; and BAP, 80Ba2, 41/21708, Sitzungen des Rheinisch-Westfälischen Beirats, Bl. 126, minutes of the meeting of November 2, 1938. The Bachmann takeover appears to have yielded the bank some 50,000 marks on the buying and selling of the stock alone; see BAP, 80Ba2, 3688/14828. For Adler & Oppenheimer, such profits came to 189,000 marks on the shares owned personally by the namesake families; see Hamburger Stiftung, *OMGUS/Deutsche Bank,* pp. 397–99.

39. Kopper, *Zwischen Marktwirtschaft und Dirigismus,* pp. 279–80.

40. Ibid., pp. 268–72, 273–75.

41. For the sum, see Gall, *Deutsche Bank,* p. 351.

42. On the means by which the regime collected the proceeds, see Hilberg, *Destruction,* vol. 1, pp. 134–38. Note, however, that his estimate of the state's total receipts must be revised upward by at least 50 percent in light of the postwar tabulation recently discovered in the files of the Oberfinanzdirektion Berlin; see Stefan Mehl, *Das Reichsfinanzministerium und die Verfolgung der deutschen Juden 1933–1943* (Berlin: Zentralinstitut für sozialwissenschaftliche Forschung der Freien Universität, 1990), pp. 44, 78, 85, 97. As for the fate of prices paid for large firms, in the case of Gebr. Heine, the biggest textile mail-order house in Germany at the time of its takeover in 1938–39, the state confiscated some 60–65 percent of the proceeds of c. 8 million Reichsmarks from the sellers in the period surrounding their emigration and probably most of the residual later; see SSAL, Devisenstelle Leipzig, nos. 849–51, Betr. Erlös aus dem Verkauf der Fa. Gebr. Heine. On the receipts on stock market transactions, see, for

example, the figures for April 1939: BAP, 25.01, 3088, Bl. 100, DBZ, no. 122, May 28, 1939.

43. See BAP, 80Ba2, 10562/261, Rechts-Abteilung, Antijüdische Gesetzgebung, 1934–39, esp. Bl. 149–50, 156–58.

44. See Gall, *Deutsche Bank,* p. 349; and BAP, 31.01, Reichswirtschaftsministerium, Bd. 15515.

45. See Bundesarchiv Koblenz (henceforth BAK), R2: Reichsfinanzministerium, Akte 13532, Böhmische Union Bank, 1.ii–25.xi.39, esp. Bl. 98–99, Economics Ministry to Deutsche Bank Sekretariat, 1.vi.39.

46. See Hamburger Stiftung, *OMGUS/Deutsche Bank,* pp. 169–70.

47. See Mehl, *Reichsfinanzministerium und Verfolgung,* pp. 68 (on the fuel plants) and 186 (on the revenues).

48. For a good overview of the way the Aryanization machinery in Holland turned almost all Jewish wealth into government revenue, see A. J. van der Leeuw, "Der Griff des Reichs nach dem Judenvermögen" and "Reichskommissariat und Judenvermögen in den Niederlanden," in A. H. Paape, ed., *Studies over Nederland in oorlogstijd,* vol. 1 ('s-Gravenhage: Martinus Nijhoff, 1972), pp. 211–36 and 237–49.

49. See Kopper, *Zwischen Marktwirtschaft und Dirigismus,* pp. 292–304, 313; Gall, *Deutsche Bank,* pp. 381–82; and, for examples of such transactions, Oesterreiches Staatsarchiv Wien (henceforth OSAW), 06R105/1, Akten 40395/38 and 55145/38. On the "Aryanization" machinery that largely excluded the Deutsche Bank, see OSAW, 04R001/1, box 73, Akte 2160/00, vol. 2, Bürckel's undated memo [mid-1938]. That the Deutsche Bank was well aware of the economic unfairness of the takeover process is clear from SSAL, Deutsche Bank, Filiale Leipzig, Akte 623, Zentrale Filialbüro to Leipzig branch, 14.v.38, enclosing a letter from Prokurist Osterwind in Vienna.

50. BAP, 80Ba2, 11709/23355, Bl. 32–33, Zweigstelle Bielitz to HTO Kattowitz, 20.xii.40; and Bl. 147, newspaper clipping announcing the confiscation, 28.iv.40.

51. See SHSA, Dresden, Firmenbestand 222a, Akte 4/01/1/5.

52. See BAP, 80Ba2, 6853/252, Rösler, Böhmische Union Bank, Allgemeines, 5.ix.39–20.i.41, Bl. 245, excerpt from Dr. Zahn to Director Pohle, 26.x.40.

53. BAP, 80Ba2, 7268/11097A, Holländische Geschäfte, 1936–44, esp. Bl. 19–21, correspondence between the Deutsche Bank and Albert de Bary, 13–23.viii.40; and Bl. 64–65, Deutsche Bank to Albert de Bary, 24.iv.41, and Deutsche Bank to Devisenabteilung, Bielefeld branch, 19.v.41.

54. Kopper, *Zwischen Marktwirtschaft und Dirigismus,* p. 277; BAP, 80Ba2, 4138/17811, Abs, Nordd. Lederwerke, Allgemeines, 30.iv.38–

23.vi.40; and 4147/31, Rechtsabteilung, Adler & Oppenheimer/Nordd. Lederwerke.

55. For good overviews, see Kopper, *Zwischen Marktwirtschaft und Dirigismus,* pp. 315–48, and Gall, *Deutsche Bank,* pp. 368–77.

56. BAK, R2/13532, esp. Bl. 15–17, 47–49, and 140–41; R2/13535, esp. Bl. 300–303; R2/13536; and Gall, *Deutsche Bank,* pp. 369–70.

57. See Kopper, *Zwischen Marktwirtschaft und Dirigismus,* p. 341; BAK, R2/13532, esp. Bl. 98–99, Economics Ministry to Deutsche Bank Sekretariat, 1.vi.39.

58. BAP, 80Ba2, 46/23287, Schriftwechsel von Halt, 1937–44, Bl. 30–31, Sabathil to von Halt, 22.v.40, enclosing report of Hirschmann's activities in Prague; and Bl. 40, handwritten memo by von Halt, 15.i.40.

59. BAP, 80Ba2, 6855/34, Rösler, BUB, Allgemeines, 10.iv.42–?, Bl. 179–79a, file note by Director Kaiser, 20.vii.43.

60. SSAL, Deutsche Bank Filiale Leipzig, Akte 623, Rösler and Kaiser to Direktionen unserer Filialen, 21.vi.39, and Zentrale to Direktionen, 10.ii.40.

61. Kopper, *Zwischen Marktwirtschaft und Dirigismus,* p. 339.

62. Gall, *Deutsche Bank,* pp. 370–71; BAK, R2/13536, esp. Bl. 63–69, 86–99, 170.

63. BAP, 80Ba2, 6854/37, Rösler, BUB, 22.i.41–?, Bl. 126–30, BUB Direktion to Oswald Rösler, 17.vi.41.

64. BAK, R2/13536, esp. Bl. 140–41; SSAL, Deutsche Bank Filiale Leipzig, vol. 623, esp. BUB to Regierungspräsident, Aussig, 15.vi.39; and Kopper, *Zwischen Marktwirtschaft und Dirigismus,* p. 344.

65. BAP, 80Ba2, 6942/15119, Sekretariat, Berghütte, Teschen, 1940–45, especially Bl. 123, calculations enclosed with BUB to Kehrl, 10.ii.41.

66. For a partial tabulation of "aryanizations" by the BUB, see Statni ustredni archiv v Praze [State Archives, Prague], 109–4: Staatssekretär des Reichsprotectors, Akte 1259, SD Leitabschnitt Prag to Gies, 16.vii.41. On the resale of Jewish-owned stock, see BAP, 80Ba2, 6854/37, esp. Bl. 123–24, BUB to Rösler, 9.vi.41, and 6875/69, esp. Bl. 534–35, Deutsche Bank to Freiherr von Falkenhausen, Paris, 6.xi.43; Kopper, *Zwischen Marktwirtschaft und Dirigismus,* pp. 337, 339–40; and Gall, *Deutsche Bank,* pp. 373–76.

67. Gall, *Deutsche Bank,* p. 376; BAP, 80Ba2, 11013/60, Zusammenstellungen der liquiden Mittel der BUB, 30.xi.43–31.i.45, esp. Bl. 44 and 102.

68. See Gall, *Deutsche Bank,* pp. 376–77.

Henry L. Mason, "Accommodations and Other Flawed Reactions"

1. The Dutch use the verb *verwerken* and the noun *verwerking* for "coping," "coming to terms" (e.g., with aspects of the past). Better known, of course, are the German *Vergangenheitsbewältigung* and *Umgang mit der Vergangenheit.*

2. E. H. Kossmann, "Commentaar," in David Barnouw et al., eds., *1940–1945: Onverwerkt verleden?* (Utrecht: HES, 1985), p. 50. In the same publication, also see H. Daalder, "De Tweede Wereldoorlog en de binnenlandse politiek," pp. 27–44. In his inaugural address at the University of Amsterdam in December 1983, J. C. H. Blom provided a challenging presentation of this issue: "In de ban van goed of fout? Wetenschappelijke geschiedschrijving over de bezettingstijd in Nederland," reprinted in his *Crisis, bezetting en herstel* (Rotterdam: Universitaire Pers, 1989), pp. 102–20.

3. See Blom's brief discussion of "accommodation" and other such terms in his preface to Gerhard Hirschfeld, *Bezetting en collaboratie* (Haarlem: H. J. W. Becht, 1991), pp. 9–10.

4. A. van den Houten, *Geslagen mensen* (The Hague: Omniboek, 1991), p. 40; A. H. Paape, "Veertig jaar Rijksinstituut voor Oorlogsdocumentatie," in Barnouw, *Onverwerkt verleden?* p. 19.

5. See Blom, *Crisis, bezetting en herstel,* pp. 102–20.

6. Hirschfeld, *Bezetting en collaboratie,* p. 111.

7. Approximately 1 percent of government employees were Jewish.

8. J. P. A. François used the term "pathological" in the 1950 edition of his textbook on international law. At that time he confirmed his wartime position on the Jewish dismissals as depicted above. See the comments by Isaak Kisch in L. de Jong, *Het Koninkrijk der Nederlanden in de Tweede Wereldoorlog* (The Hague: SDU, 1991), pt. 14, vol. 1, p. 240. See also Henry L. Mason, "Jews in the Occupied Netherlands," *Political Science Quarterly* (Summer 1984): 320–21.

9. Mason, "Jews in the Occupied Netherlands," pp. 326–27. See also various comments in de Jong, *Het Koninkrijk,* pt. 14, vol. 1, pp. 253–54.

10. Hirschfeld, *Bezetting en collaboratie,* pp. 113, 116, 118, 121, 125. (The German historian Gerhard Hirschfeld is not related to the wartime Dutch secretary-general H. M. Hirschfeld.) See also Kisch's comments in de Jong, *Het Koninkrijk,* pt. 14, vol. 1, p. 239.

Recent research by Jos Scheren and Friso Roest pays close attention to the wartime behavior of local government officials in Amsterdam, exploiting previously unused local archives. They have discovered, for example, that Amsterdam city employees on their own developed a map indicating the density of Jewish inhabitants and Jewish-owned shops in various sections of the city. These data were made available to the Germans before they demanded them—before the Germans had decided whether to create a Jewish ghetto in Amsterdam. (Ultimately, the Germans decided not to establish a ghetto in Amsterdam, nor anywhere else in Western and Central Europe.) Surely the Amsterdam officials pushed their accommodation to the outer limits of "toleration."

11. Hirschfeld, *Bezetting en collaboratie,* p. 136.

12. Mason, "Jews in the Occupied Netherlands," p. 319; Hirschfeld, *Bezetting en collaboratie,* pp. 142–43.

13. Hirschfeld, *Bezetting en collaboratie,* pp. 146–48.

14. Ibid., pp. 145, 149–50. One factor in the survival of relatively large numbers of Jews in Paris and Budapest in 1944 was the last-minute refusal of police in these cities to collaborate with the Germans in the roundup of Jews—after years of splendid collaboration in this sphere. Evidently, the number of Jews saved in the Netherlands as a result of uncooperative police was very few. Guus Meershoek, a historian at the University of Amsterdam, is currently completing extensive research on the Amsterdam police in wartime, particularly its role in the persecution and deportation of Jews. His first article on this topic appears in the Third Yearbook (1992) of the Institute for War Documentation.

15. Hirschfeld, *Bezetting en collaboratie,* pp. 154, 157, 159.

16. Ibid., pp. 160, 170–77, 181, 256.

17. Hans Knoop, *De Joodsche Raad; het drama van Abraham Asscher en David Cohen* (Amsterdam: Elsevier, 1983), pp. 17, 82–83. See also Mason, "Jews in the Occupied Netherlands," pp. 332–35.

18. Knoop, *De Joodsche Raad,* pp. 85–86.

19. Ibid., pp. 154–56.

20. Ibid., pp. 131–35, 175–77; Mason, "Jews in the Occupied Netherlands," pp. 332–33.

21. The Honor Board did exclude Asscher and Cohen from taking on any Jewish public offices or functions for the rest of their lives. Knoop, *De Joodsche Raad,* pp. 42, 89, 183, 191, 221–23, 243–45. The complexities and ambiguities of the Honor Board's deliberations on the Joodsche Raad are discussed in N.K.C.A. in 't Veld, *De Joodse Ereraad* (The Hague: SDU, 1989).

22. Knoop, *De Joodsche Raad,* pp. 93, 205. As Knoop points out, much of the leadership of the postwar Jewish community in the Netherlands had to come from former leaders or officials of the *Joodsche Raad;* there were hardly any other survivors. For example, three of the first five editors of the main postwar Jewish weekly in the Netherlands, the *Nieuw Israëlietisch Weekblad,* were *Joodsche Raad* survivors. (See pp. 177–78.)

23. Blom, *Crisis, bezetting en herstel,* p. 135.

24. Comments by E. B. Locher-Scholten in de Jong, *Het Koninkrijk,* pt. 14, vol. 2, p. 839. Rudy Kousbroek, *Het Oostindisch kampsyndroom* (Amsterdam: Meulenhoff, 1992), pp. 296–305, 309–11.

25. Kousbroek, *Kampsyndroom,* pp. 326–27.

26. C. Fasseur, "Het verleden tot last. Nederland, de Tweede Wereldoorlog en de dekolonisatie van Indonesië," in Barnouw, *Onverwerkt Verleden,* pp. 133, 144, 152. Kousbroek, *Kampsyndroom,* pp. 240, 244. De Jong, *Het Koninkrijk,* pt. 14, vol. 2, p. 983.

27. Fasseur, "Het verleden tot last," p. 150. However, a remarkably *verwerkt* book on the "police actions" and the entire issue of decolonization did appear in 1970: J. A. A. van Doorn and W. J. Hendrix, *Ontsporing van geweld* (Rotterdam: Universitaire Pers, 1970).

28. Ed van Thijn, *Nog één nacht slapen?* (Nijmegen: SUN, 1995), pp. 40–41.

29. Dienke Hondius, *Terugkeer—Antisemitisme in Nederland rond de bevrijding* (The Hague: SDU, 1990); G. L. Durlacher, *Strepen aan de hemel* (Amsterdam: Meulenhoff, 1985), pp. 87–88; van den Houten, *Geslagen mensen,* pp. 27, 47, 53–54; Herman Musagh, in Barnouw, *Onverwerkt verleden,* pp. 68–69; Evelien Gans, *Gojse nijd & joods narcisme* (Amsterdam: Arena, 1994), pp. 30–33; van Thijn, *Nog één nacht slapen?* pp. 41–43. For the essence of Hondius's book, in English, see her article "A Cold Reception: Holocaust Survivors in the Netherlands and Their Return," *Patterns of Prejudice* 28:1 (1994): 47–65.

30. Kousbroek, *Kampsyndroom,* pp. 304–5; van Thijn, *Nog één nacht slapen?* pp. 44–46.

31. Van Thijn, *Nog één nacht slapen?* pp. 40–41.

32. Ibid., pp. 37–38.

33. Friso Wielenga, *Schaduwen van de Duitse geschiedenis* (Amsterdam: Boom, 1993), pp. 13–16, 53–55, 64–70.

34. Hans Daudt, my colleague at the University of Amsterdam during 1973–74, reminded me of the title of Arend Lijphart's classic work on the Dutch political system: *The Politics of Accommodation: Pluralism and Democracy in the Netherlands* (Los Angeles: University of California Press, 1968). How useful were the profound experiences of the Dutch with pluralism and democracy when a Nazi occupation required accommodation?

NOTE: Peter Romijn's innovative article on the *verwerking* of collaboration appeared too late for me to consider here. See Romijn, "The Image of Collaboration in Post-War Dutch Society," *Bulletin of the International Committee for the History of the Second World War* 27/28 (1995): 311–24.

Debórah Dwork, "Custody and Care of Jewish Children in the Postwar Netherlands"

This study was supported by an anonymous donor and by the New Land Foundation, and I express my warmest thanks to both parties. It was written during the tenure of a Guggenheim Foundation Fellowship, for which I am grateful. Finally, I acknowledge the enormous help of Dr. Dick van Galen-Last and Dr. David Barnouw of the Rijksinstituut voor Oorlogsdocumentatie, who cheerfully sent material by fax and express.

For the convenience of the reader, all books translated into English will be cited in the English version, even though the quality of the translations varies greatly. Robert Jan van Pelt of the University of Waterloo, Canada, and I have translated all other texts, oral histories, and archive documents. Page numbers are given for the interview transcripts, even though neither the tapes nor texts are held in a public repository. It is my hope that eventually they will be made available, so I have provided specific citations with that in mind.

1. Philip Gerrit (Gerry) Mok, interview with the author, Amsterdam, June 11, 1986, p. 13.

2. Ibid., pp. 23–24, 25.

3. It is not known precisely how many of the Jewish children living in the Netherlands in 1940 (both Dutch citizens and refugees from other countries, especially Germany) were still alive in 1945. Figures are even less accurate as to how many Jewish children were hidden (briefly or for long periods) in the Netherlands, and what percentage of these youngsters survived. The *oorlogspleegkinderen* figures are rather certain, because these children were registered after the war. See E. C. Lekkerkerker, "Oorlogspleegkinderen," *Maandblad voor de Geestelijke Volksgezondheid* 1 (October 1946): 228. Jacob Presser, the great historian of the destruction of Dutch Jewry, has slightly different figures, but this may be due to the time from which he dates his numbers: Lekkerkerker's figures are from early autumn of 1946; Presser's are a good six months later. "In the spring of 1947 it appeared that of the 3,481 OPK children [on the register as of what date?], 1540 were reunited with their parents." Jacob Presser, *Ashes in the Wind* (Detroit: Wayne State University Press, 1988), p. 542. This translation is particularly poor, losing the tone and sometimes even the meaning of Presser's original text, *Ondergang* (The Hague: Staatsuitgeverij, 1965).

4. Piet Meerburg, interview with the author, Amsterdam, June 27, 1986, p. 22.

5. The assertion by Joseph Goldstein, Anna Freud, and Albert Solnit that "the Dutch Parliament decreed that the children would be returned to their parents, thereby not leaving the outcome to case-by-case determi-

nation by the courts," is incorrect; see their *Beyond the Best Interest of the Child* (New York: Free Press, 1973), pp. 107–8. More accurate is Jacob Presser's remark that "there were quite a few cases in which judges saw fit to set aside the natural right of parents, as though their suffering during the war had not been more than most people could bear"; *Ashes in the Wind,* pp. 542–43. The *Vrij Nederland* journalist Elma Verhey investigated the postwar experiences of the *oorlogspleegkinderen* in her book *Om het joodse kind* (Amsterdam: Nijgh and van Ditmar, 1991) and noted that, when confronted with the biological parents, "the foster parents, no matter how difficult it must have been to give up the children, have always given them back to the parents, so far as we know" (p. 84). This has nothing to do with the role of OPK but concerns the direct, personal interaction between the two sets of parents. Verhey's book appeared just as the now–adult hidden children were bringing their private history into the public realm with the first international meeting of The Hidden Child organization in New York in May 1991. The publicity surrounding this event brought new cases to light, about which Verhey has spoken publicly and written. Her revised assessment corroborates Presser with regard to OPK, and she now believes that at least a few foster parents obstructed the postwar reunion of their foster child with the biological family.

6. Interview with Piet Meerburg, p. 22.

7. Ibid.

8. Verhey, *Om het joodse kind,* p. 44. Verhey adds a sixth person, Gesina van der Molen, but my research leads me to believe that although van der Molen became the leading personality later on, she was not present at this meeting. There are, of course, no contemporary documents in the public record about this.

9. See Debórah Dwork, *Children With A Star* (New Haven: Yale University Press, 1991), pp. 40–41, 51–52.

10. Interview with Piet Meerburg, pp. 3–4.

11. Dwork, *Children With A Star,* pp. 49–50.

12. Virrie Oudkerk-Cohen, interview with the author, Amsterdam, June 19, 1986, pp. 2–3.

13. Joel S. Fishman, "The War Orphans Controversy in the Netherlands: Majority-Minority Relations," in *Dutch Jewish History,* ed. Jozeph Michman and Tirtsah Levie (Jerusalem: Institute for Research on Dutch Jewry, 1984), p. 423.

14. Interview with Piet Meerburg, p. 22; Verhey, *Om het joodse kind,* p. 71.

15. Rijksinstituut voor Oorlogsdocumentatie, doc. no. E.1/44, "Wet houdende Voorzieningen inzake Oorlogs-Pleeg-Kinderen," p. 1, arts. 1–2.

16. Ibid., section on "De Kring der Betrokkenen," p. 1.

17. Bert-Jan Flim's painstakingly researched doctoral dissertation, *Omdat hun hart sprak* (Groningen University, September 1995), traces the history of the Dutch child rescue organizations. Among other discoveries, he found that An der Waard had contemporary documents pertaining to the committee's discussions in 1944, and I rely on his interpretation of these papers here. Flim's study was published in the Netherlands as *Omdat hun hart sprak* (Den Haag: Kok Kampen, 1996), pp. 354–63.

18. Rijksinstituut voor Oorlogsdocumentatie, doc. no. E.1/44, p. 2, art. 11.

19. Ibid., section on "De Kring der Betrokkenen," p. 2.

20. Verhey, *Om het joodse kind,* pp. 74–75.

21. Joel Fishman, "The Reconstruction of the Dutch Jewish Community and Its Implications for the Writing of Contemporary Jewish History," *Proceedings of the American Academy for Jewish Research* 45 (1978): 71–74, 84; idem, "Jewish War Orphans in the Netherlands—The Guardianship Issue 1945–1950," *Wiener Library Bulletin* 27 (1973–74): 31. See also idem, "The Jewish Community in Post-War Netherlands," *Midstream* (January 1976): 44–45.

22. Josef Michman, "The Problem of the Jewish War Orphans in Holland," in *She'erit Hapletah, 1944–1948: Rehabilitation and Political Struggle,* ed. Yisrael Gutman and Avital Saf (Jerusalem: Yad Vashem, 1990), pp. 195–96.

23. *Staatsblad van het Koninkrijk der Nederlanden* (no. F 137), Besluit van 13 Augustus 1945, art. 3, clause 2.

24. Ibid., art. 4, clause 1.

25. Rijksinstituut voor Oorlogsdocumentatie, doc. no. E.1/44, section "Toelichting" p. 2. Note, however, that while the authors state that there were two alternatives, only the first is included in the surviving document; page 3 of this section has been lost. Therefore we can only partially understand the perspectives and opinions of, and the options offered by, the authors of the bill.

26. Ibid., section "Voogdijcommissie van oorlogspleegkinderen," p. 2.

27. Paul Scholten, *Asser's Handleiding tot de Beoefening van het Nederlandsch Burgerlijk Recht,* Eerste deel-Personenrecht, Eerste stuk-Familierecht (Zwolle: Uitgevers-Maatschappij W. E. J. Tjeenk Willink, 1936), pp. 412, 419. See the relevant sections of the civil code (Burgerlijk Recht): art. 413, clauses 3–5.

28. Besluit van 13 Augustus 1945, p. 3.

29. Fishman, "The Reconstruction of the Dutch Jewish Community," pp. 81–82; idem, "Jewish War Orphans," p. 32; see also Reine Friedman-van der Heide, *Het Joodse Oorlogspleegkind* (Amsterdam: Jewish Coordinating Committee, 1946), pp. 34–36.

30. Verhey, *Om het joodse kind,* p. 99.
31. Caroline Eitje, "De Joodse Jeugd," *De Groene Amsterdammer,* September 1, 1945, pp. 4–5.
32. Interview with Piet Meerburg, pp. 22–23.
33. "De Joodsche Oorlogspleegkinderen," *Trouw,* June 13, 1945, pp. 1–2.
34. Gesina van der Molen, "Diefstal van JOODSE KINDEREN?" *Trouw,* May 25, 1946, p. 1.
35. Verhey, *Om het joodse kind,* p. 100.
36. Michman, "Jewish War Orphans," p. 199.
37. "Een rechterlijke dwaling," *Nieuw Israelitisch Weekblad,* August 5, 1949.
38. Jozeph Melkman, "Hannie Morpurgo," *Nieuw Israelitisch Weekblad,* April 15, 1949.
39. Text is quoted in full in Friedman-van der Heide, *Het Joodse Oorlogspleegkind,* p. 10.
40. See Bert-Jan Flim's discussion of van der Molen's analysis of the children's position in the column-based social structure of the Netherlands. *Omdat hun hart sprak* (dissertation version), p. 313.
41. Ibid., pp. 7–8.
42. Abraham de Jong, "Het Joodse Oorlogspleegkind," *Nieuw Israelitisch Weekblad,* November 8, 1946, pp. 1–2.
43. Daniel L. Schorr, "The Netherlands," *American Jewish Year Book 5708* (Philadelphia: Jewish Publication Society, 1947), pp. 342–43.
44. Interview with Gerry Mok, pp. 35, 39.
45. Goldstein, Freud, and Solnit, *Beyond the Best Interest of the Child,* p. 107.
46. Max Arian, interview with the author, Amsterdam, June 11 and 14, 1986, pp. 29, 32. See also, among Max Arian's many publications, "Het grote kinderspel" and "Een gesprak met Semmy Riekerk," *De Groene Amsterdammer,* May 4, 1987, pp. 5–7, 9, and 10–11; and "Internationale bijeenkomst van ondergedoken kinderen in New York," *ICODO Info* (July 1991): 5–17. ICODO is the acronym for the Stichting Informatie- en Coordinatieorgaan Dienstverlening Oologsgetroffenen.
47. Interview with Gerry Mok, p. 33.
48. Max Gosschalk, interview with the author, Deventer, The Netherlands, August 1, 1987, pp. 16–17.
49. For a discussion of these issues, see Dwork, *Children With A Star,* chap. 3, "In Secret," pp. 68–109.
50. Maurits Cohen, interview with the author, The Hague, June 9, 1986, p. 3.
51. Ibid., p. 7.

52. Ibid., pp. 10, 11.

53. Bertha (Betty) Evelyn Beatrice Knoop, interview with the author, Naarden, The Netherlands, July 3, 1986, transcript p. 3.

54. Ibid., p. 4.

55. Ibid., pp. 5–6.

56. Interview with Gerry Mok, p. 35.

57. Ibid., p. 38.

58. Ibid., p. 39.

59. Interview with Max Arian, pp. 38, 39.

60. Ibid., p. 43.

61. Ibid., p. 49.

62. Ibid., pp. 46, 47, 52.

63. Ibid., p. 52.

64. Ibid., p. 53.

65. Interview with Betty Knoop, p. 4.

66. Ibid., p. 7.

67. Interview with Maurits Cohen, p. 13.

68. Ibid., p. 12.

69. Ibid., p. 13.

Harold Marcuse, "Dachau"

1. In this essay I use "holocaust" with a small *h* in a broad sense to designate atrocities committed in the National Socialist empire against any unarmed people, especially those in concentration camps, extermination centers, and prisoner-of-war camps. In common usage today the capitalized "Holocaust" means the Nazi program of extermination of Jews; specialists also include certain other groups targeted for extermination, such as Sinti and Roma (Gypsies) and homosexuals.

2. On the term "collective memory" it has become fashionable to cite the work of the French sociologist Maurice Halbwachs, who introduced it to modern academic discourse. Although Halbwachs's writings are indeed stimulating, his argument that all remembering is socially conditioned is not especially relevant to this analysis of commemoration. See also the discussion of the term in the December 1997 *AHR* special forum "History and Memory," especially Susan Crane, "Writing the Individual Back into Collective Memory," *AHR* 102 (1997), 1372–85, 1376 ff.

3. The documentation of most of the memorials discussed here is scant and inaccessible. Existing published materials are cited in the notes below; beyond that, readers are referred to my dissertation: Harold Marcuse, *Nazi Crimes and Identity in West Germany: Collective Memories of the Dachau Concentration Camp, 1945–1990* (Ann Arbor: University Micro-

films #9308392, 1992), and my forthcoming monograph *Legacies of Dachau: The Uses and Abuses of a Concentration Camp, 1933–2000* (Cambridge University Press).

4. The present usage of the term "identity" can be traced back to the work of Erik Erikson, *Identity: Youth and Crisis* (New York: W. W. Norton, 1968). For a recent discussion of its utility, see Richard Handler, "Is 'Identity' a Useful Cross-Cultural Concept?" in *Commemorations: The Politics of National Identity,* ed. John Gillis (Princeton: Princeton University Press, 1994), pp. 27–40. My own use of it is influenced by Jürgen Habermas, "Können komplexe Gesellschaften eine vernünftige Identität ausbilden?" in his *Zur Rekonstruktion des historischen Materialismus* (Frankfurt: Suhrkamp, 1976), pp. 92–126. Habermas cites literature on identity as it is used in psychoanalysis, sociology, and developmental psychology; see p. 121, n. 3.

5. See Harold Marcuse, "The Politics of Memory: Nazi Crimes and Identity in West Germany, 1945–1990," *Working Paper Series* 45, Center for European Studies, Harvard University, 1993, pp. 5 ff.

6. For a brief overview in English, see Deborah Lipstadt, *Denying the Holocaust: The Growing Assault on Truth and Memory* (New York: Plume, 1994), esp. pp. 49–64.

7. Johannes Tuchel has written the best scholarly analyses of this period: "Herrschaftssicherung und Terror: Zu Funktion und Wirkung nationalsozialistischer Konzentrationslager 1933 und 1934," *Occasional Papers,* FU Berlin Fachbereich Politikwissenschaft 7 (1983); and *Konzentrationslager: Organisationsgeschichte und Funktion der "Inspektion der Konzentrationslager," 1934–1938* (Boppard: Harold Boldt, 1991) (Schriften des Bundesarchivs 39).

8. See Primo Levi, *Survival in Auschwitz,* to cite only one of the better known examples. The standard scholarly treatment is still Raul Hilberg, *The Destruction of the European Jews* (Chicago: Quadrangle, 1961; rev. ed. New York: Holmes & Meier, 1985).

9. Enno Georg, *Die wirtschaftlichen Unternehmungen der SS* (Stuttgart: DVA, 1963); Hermann Kaienburg, *"Vernichtung durch Arbeit": Der Fall Neuengamme: Die Wirtschaftsbestrebungen der SS und ihre Auswirkungen auf die Existenzbedingungen der KZ-Gefangenen* (Bonn: Dietz, 1991).

10. See Robert Abzug, *Inside the Vicious Heart: Americans and the Liberation of Nazi Concentration Camps* (New York and Oxford: Oxford University Press, 1985).

11. See Johannes Neuhäusler, *What Was It Like in the Concentration Camp at Dachau?* (Munich: Manz, 1960; 10th ed., n.d.), esp. pp. 50–80.

12. See Karl-Klaus Rabe, *Umkehr in die Zukunft: Die Arbeit der Ak-*

tion Sühnezeichen/Friedensdienste (Bornheim-Merten: Lamuv, 1983); also Clemens Vollnhals, *Evangelische Kirche und Entnazifizierung, 1945–1949: Die Last der NS-Vergangenheit* (Munich: Oldenbourg, 1989).

13. I am referring specifically to an exchange between Martin Broszat and Saul Friedländer in what has become known as the "historians' debate." See Martin Broszat and Saul Friedländer, "A Controversy about the Historicization of National Socialism," *New German Critique* 44 (Spring–Summer 1988): 85–126. See also Norbert Frei, "Farewell to the Era of Contemporaries: National Socialism and Its History en Route into History," in *Passing into History: Nazism and the Holocaust beyond Memory,* ed. Gulie Ne'eman Arad, *History and Memory* special issue 9 (Fall 1997), 59–79.

14. For a detailed discussion of the contradictory reports about these early projects, see Marcuse, *Nazi Crimes,* pp. 258 ff.

15. The cross can be seen in contemporary photographs and drawings, for instance in an ink sketch published in the Christmas 1947 issue of *Der Ausblick,* a magazine created by the Germans interned in the postwar Dachau camp.

16. Survivor Richard Titze told me that the yellow-painted star of David was fashioned from a swastika that the SS had erected on the site. A photograph of this temporary memorial was published in "Neues KZ-Massengrab entdeckt," *Neue Zeitung,* September 9, 1949.

17. Marcuse, *Nazi Crimes,* p. 318.

18. A sketch of this design can be found in Josef Wiedemann's blueprint of the memorial site, November 16, 1960, Kohlhofer papers, Dachau Memorial Site Archive. See also Stefan Schwarz, memo about a meeting in the Finance Ministry, March 9, 1962, Landesentschädigungsamt Munich.

19. See Thomas Nipperdey, "Nationalidee und Nationaldenkmal in Deutschland im 19. Jahrhundert," *Historische Zeitschrift* 206 (1968): 539–85, esp. 578–81; and Volker Plagemann, "Bismarck-Denkmäler," in *Denkmäler im 19. Jahrhundert: Deutung und Kritik,* ed. Hans-Ernst Mittig and Thomas Nipperdey (Munich, 1972), pp. 217–52, illustrations pp. 417–42. New York City's Statue of Liberty (1876) is a non-German example of this tradition.

20. See Knappe to Schwalber, July 1960, Bavarian Main State Archive (henceforth BayHsta), Joseph Schwalber papers, no. 89. Excerpts from the letter were published in *Münchner Merkur/Dachauer Nachrichten,* July 30, 1960. Six- by eight-inch photographs of the model can be found in the Dachau county governor's office, Landratsamt file Dachau 064–2. In 1991 the model could no longer be located.

21. Union of Munich Architects (Ungelehrt, Döllgast, Haeusser),

"'Das Befreiungsmal von Dachau': Offener Brief an den Bürgermeister von Dachau," *Süddeutsche Zeitung,* November 13, 1945; "Das Dachauer Gedächtnis- und Befreiungsmal," *Der Baumeister* 1 (1946): 24.

22. Klaus Wegmann, *Mahn- und Gedenkstätten in der Deutschen Demokratischen Republik* (Berlin: Volk und Wissen, 1969), pp. 1–31.

23. Heinz Koch, *Nationale Mahn- und Gedenkstätte Buchenwald: Geschichte ihrer Entstehung* (Weimar: n.p., 1988), 9–11; Volkhard Knigge, "Zur Geschichte der KZ-Gedenkstätten in der DDR," in *Erinnerung: Zur Gegenwart des Holocaust in Deutschland West und Deutschland Ost* (Frankfurt: Haag and Herchen, 1993), 67–77, 69 ff; Knigge, "Vom Reden und Schweigen der Steine: Zu Denkmalen auf dem Gelände ehemaliger nationalsozialistischer Konzentrations- und Vernichtungslager," in *Fünfzig Jahre danach: Zur Nachgeschichte des Nationalsozialismus,* ed. Sigrid Weigel and Birgit Erdle (Zurich: Hochschulverlag, 1996), pp. 193–235.

24. For collections of photographs of many such memorials, see Adolf Rieth, *Den Opfern der Gewalt: KZ-Opfermale der europäischen Völker* (Tübingen: Wasmuth, 1968); Harold Marcuse, Frank Schimmelfennig, and Jochen Spielmann, *Steine des Anstosses: Nationalsozialismus und Zweiter Weltkrieg in Denkmalen, 1945–1985* (Hamburg: Museum für Hamburgische Geschichte, 1985); Sybil Milton and Ira Nowinski, *In Fitting Memory: The Art and Politics of Holocaust Memorials* (Detroit: Wayne State University Press, 1991); and James E. Young, *The Texture of Memory: Holocaust Memorials and Meaning* (New Haven: Yale University Press, 1993).

25. On the Auschwitz competition, see Jochen Spielmann, *Entwürfe zur Sinngebung des Sinnlosen—Der Wettbewerb für ein Denkmal für Auschwitz* (Ph.D. dissertation, Free University Berlin, 1990), microfiche.

26. On Koelle, see the Germanisches Nationalmuseum Nürnberg's *Dokumente zu Leben und Werk des Bildhauers Fritz Koelle (1895–1953),* no. 4, Sonderausstellung des Archivs für Bildende Kunst (exhibition catalog, n.p.p., n.d.). The 1.44-meter-high Dachau sculpture from 1946 is depicted on page E29. For biographical information, see Hans Vollmer, *Allgemeines Lexikon der Bildenden Künstler des XX. Jahrhunderts* (Leipzig: E. A. Seemann, 1956), vol. 3, p. 79.

27. The Rot statue is in the garden of the town's famed Baroque monastery; the 1946 Dachau poster was published in *Concentration Camp Dachau: Album* (n.p.p.: n.p., n.d. [1946]), copies held by archive of the Dachau Memorial Site. On the publication date see Marcuse, *Nazi Crimes,* p. 277, n. 88. Rapoport's sculpture is depicted and discussed in detail in Young, *Texture of Memory,* pp. 155–84.

28. A picture of the sculpture was printed on an invitation to a September 1949 commemorative ceremony and appeal for donations distrib-

uted by Auerbach's office. See Auerbach to Mayor Wimmer, August 30, 1949, Munich City Archive, BuR 2277, and Auerbach, printed Call for Donations, September 1, 1949, BayHsta, MSo 134.

29. For Auerbach's biography, see Constantin Goschler, "Der Fall Philipp Auerbach: Wiedergutmachung in Bayern," in *Wiedergutmachung in der Bundesrepublik Deutschland,* ed. Ludolf Herbst and Constantin Goschler (Munich: Oldenbourg, 1989).

30. Dachau survivor Hans Schwarz wrote to French survivors that the sculpture was "universally condemned" because it "immortalized the horrors." Letter from Schwarz to Noe Vilner and others, December 2, 1949, Institut für die Geschichte der Arbeiterbewegung (now in the Bundesarchiv, Potsdam), V 278/2/161.

31. See Robert Sigel, *Im Interesse der Gerechtigkeit: Die Dachauer Kriegsverbrecherprozesse, 1945–1948* (Frankfurt: Campus, 1992); also Frank Buscher, *The U.S. War Crimes Trial Program: 1946–1955* (New York and Westport, Conn.: Greenwood, 1989).

32. See John Gimbel, *The American Occupation of Germany: Politics and the Military, 1945–1949* (Stanford: Stanford University Press, 1968).

33. See Marcuse, *Nazi Crimes,* pp. 124–27; also Christa Schick, "Die bayerischen Internierungslager," in *Von Stalingrad zur Währungsreform: Zur Sozialgeschichte des Umbruchs in Deutschland,* ed. Martin Broszat, Klaus-Dietmar Henke, and Hans Woller (Munich: Oldenbourg, 1988), pp. 301–25.

34. See Ulrich Brochhagen, *Nach Nürnberg: Vergangenheitsbewältigung und Westintegration in der Ära Adenauer* (Hamburg: Junius, 1994), pp. 240–50. Although these men were no longer officially prisoners of war, and although some of them had been arrested after the war, "prisoners of war" (*Kriegsgefangenen*) was the term used in popular and official West German parlance. See also Norbert Frei, *Vergangenheitspolitik: Die Anfänge der Bundesrepublik und die NS-Vergangenheit* (Munich: Beck, 1996), pp. 155, 158, 234.

35. See Marcuse, *Nazi Crimes,* 198 ff. Other examples include the generous reinstatement of former army officers and Nazi officials under the "131 law," and the concurrent practice of marginalizing survivors attempting to collect benefits under compensation and restitution programs.

36. Ibid., pp. 148–52.

37. Ibid., pp. 156–59.

38. Hoegner to Gen. Walter J. Muller, Director of the Office of Military Government for Bavaria, March 23, 1946, BayHsta Stk 113623.

39. The English translation is taken in part from Pfister to Steener/ Fine Arts, April 15, 1946, BayHsta Stk 113623.

40. See "Ausschreibungsunterlagen zum Wettbewerb auf der Leiten,"

June 5, 1946, BayHsta Stk 113623; "Dachau bei München: Denkmal im Konzentrationslager," *Baumeister-Rundschau* 5 (1946): 62; "Denkmal im Konzentrationslager Dachau," *Neue Bauwelt* 17 (1946): 12.

41. For a detailed account of the "Leiten affair," see Marcuse, *Nazi Crimes,* pp. 169–84.

42. See Marcuse, *Nazi Crimes,* pp. 183 f, 279 f. This exhibition is very scantily documented.

43. "Staatsregierung und Landtag auf dem Leitenberg: Landrat Junker mit der Ausgestaltung betraut," *Münchner Merkur/Dachauer Nachrichten,* December 3–4, 1949.

44. Ehard to Land Commissioner Bolds, February 1, 1950, BayHsta Stk 113625. See also "Wettbewerbsausschreibung einer Gedächtnishalle," *Bayerischer Staatsanzeiger,* February 11, 1950, and *Süddeutsche Zeitung,* February 11, 1950.

45. "Urkunde zur Grundsteinlegung auf der Leiten bei Dachau," April 29, 1950, BayHsta Stk 113628. A photocopy of the document, which was published in the *Abendzeitung* of May 2, 1950, is held by the Dachau memorial site.

46. See Llew Gardner, "So Stark the Memories—But They Say 'Let's Forget,'" *Sunday Express* (London), January 10, 1960; reprinted as "How Can Germany Forget?" *Washington Daily News,* January 18, 1960, p. 14.

47. Wolfgang Petzet, "Das Ergebnis des Leitenberg-Wettbewerbs," *Münchner Merkur/Dachauer Nachrichten,* May 4, 1950.

48. Dieter Sattler, minutes of the first meeting of the jury for the Leiten competition, April 25, 1950, BayHsta Stk 113627. This document lists the artists and describes the nine best entries.

49. Dieter Sattler, report about the third meeting of the jury on May 19 and 20, 1950, and memo by Gummpenberg, June 14, 1950, BayHsta Stk 113627. The design by Roth and Hiller was a high, twelve-sided building crowned by a beehivelike cupola supported by twelve interior columns. Prismatic glass vaulting at the apex brightened the interior. A "solemn" bronze sculpture was positioned in the axis of the entrance, and plaques with the coats of arms of forty nations were mounted under bronze candleholders in the colonnade. See H. Fischer, "Gedächtnishalle auf dem Leitenberg bei Dachau," *Die Bauzeitung* (Stuttgart), January 1951, pp. 17–23, in which plans and sketches of the other two winning entries are also published.

50. See Erich Preuss, report about the construction project on the Leiten, February 3, 1951, BayHsta Stk 113627, and Preuss/Landesentschädigungsamt, memo regarding the repositioning of the cornerstone, February 15, 1951, BayHsta Stk 113626. At that time the projected costs were about 630,000 Deutschmarks.

51. Marcuse, *Nazi Crimes,* pp. 263–67; also Meinhold Lurz, "Die Heldenhaine und Totenburgen des Volksbundes deutsche Kriegsgräberfürsorge," *Arch+* 71 (October 1983): 66–70. Tannenberg was erected 1924–27 near Allenstein in what is now Poland; see *Festschrift zur Einweihung des Tannenberg-Denkmals am 18. September 1927* (Königsberg: n.p., 1927). The Annaberg (Austria) monument was built to commemorate the counterrevolutionary forces of 1919. Wilhelm Kreis, who had won a competition for a model Bismarck tower early in the century, designed even larger but formally similar structures for Warsaw and Stalingrad in the 1940s as well.

52. Marcuse, *Nazi Crimes,* pp. 276–81. A number of pictures in the series are published in Ludo Vaneck, *Le Livre des Camps* (Leuven: Kritak, 1979), p. 63.

53. Marcuse, *Nazi Crimes,* pp. 206–18.

54. Ibid., pp. 218–24. For a brief contemporary summary, see Gaston Coblentz, "Dachau Crematorium Is Kept as Memorial," *New York Herald Tribune,* March 8, 1954, p. 1.

55. Marcuse, *Nazi Crimes,* pp. 291–308.

56. I have made this argument in greater detail in another essay: Harold Marcuse, "Die museale Darstellung des Holocaust an Orten der ehemaligen Konzentrationslager in der Bundesrepublik, 1945–1990," in Moltmann et al., eds., *Erinnerung: Zur Gegenwart des Holocaust,* pp. 79–98.

57. This inscription was removed at the latest by 1948, when the camp was converted into a settlement for refugees from the East. I have been unable to determine whether the inscription was visible while the Nazi suspects were interned in the camp by U.S. military authorities. Presumably it was removed or painted over in 1945; otherwise it would have been noted in contemporary descriptions.

58. Eugen Kogon et al., eds., *Nazi Mass Murder: A Documentary History of the Use of Poison Gas* (New Haven: Yale University Press, 1995), chap. 8, section "Dachau."

59. For a sketch of Holocaust denial regarding Dachau, see Barbara Distel, "Dachau," in *Legenden, Lügen, Vorurteile: Ein Wörterbuch zur Zeitgeschichte,* ed. Wolfgang Benz (Munich: Deutscher Taschenbuchverlag, 1992), pp. 49–53.

60. The red granite cornerstone is still visible today, under plexiglass in front of the international memorial. Its inscription reads: "Primus lapis monumenti in victimarum nazismii memoriam errigendi quae in carceribus dachauae intra annos 1933–1945 mortem subier positus est A.D. IV id Sept 1956." [This first stone of a monument to be erected in the memory of the victims of Nazism who died in the Dachau prisons in the years 1933–1945 was set here on September 4, 1956.]

61. For more details, see Marcuse, *Nazi Crimes,* pp. 308 ff.

62. The triangles are reminiscent of the monument in the Weimar city cemetery designed by Walter Gropius in 1923. It commemorated the trade unionists who fell in March 1919 defending the new German republic against counterrevolutionary forces. See Dietrich Schubert, "Das Denkmal der Märzgefallenen in Weimar," *Jahrbuch der Hamburger Kunstsammlungen* 21 (1976): 199 ff.

63. A blueprint of this plan is held by the Bauamt in Dachau. I thank Prof. Detlef Hoffmann for sharing a copy of the plan.

64. Marcuse, *Nazi Crimes,* pp. 316–18.

65. Neuhäsler, *What Was It Like,* inside back cover. I have modified the translation slightly to bring it closer to the original German.

66. Marcuse, *Nazi Crimes,* pp. 323–27.

67. The archive of the Archbishopric of Munich denied me access to Neuhäusler's papers, and I have been unable to find the reasons for the modified suggestion in other sources. Presumably Neuhäusler's recognition that the Catholic chapel should not dominate to such an extent prompted the change.

68. Marcuse, *Nazi Crimes,* pp. 342 ff., 348–54; Stefan Schwarz, *Die jüdische Gedenkstätte in Dachau* (Munich: Landesverband, 1972).

69. Marcuse, *Nazi Crimes,* pp. 357–68.

70. For the full text of the call, see Kurt Scharf, "Spendenaufruf für den Bau einer Evangelischen Kirche in Dachau," Kirchenamt Hannover to all parishes, May 20, 1964, Evangelisches Zentralarchiv Berlin (henceforth EZB), file 6172/8a.

71. The early discussion is summarized in Wilm to Scharf, April 19, 1963, EZB, file 6172/5.

72. See the draft of the protocol of the meeting of the working committee of the Evangelische Kirche Deutschlands, January 20, 1964, EZB, file 6172/9.

73. See the minutes of the working committee, January 20, 1964, EZB, file 6172/5. The architects were A. Zamstra (Amsterdam), Friedhelm Amslinger (Munich), Egon Eiermann (Karlsruhe), Johann Ludwig (Munich), Dieter Oesterlen (Hannover), Helmut Striffler (Mannheim), and Hans Christoph Müller (Berlin).

74. See D. Scharf, Dr. Luskey, A. L. Bouman, "Versöhnungskirche im Lager Dachau," four-page brochure (Berlin, 1965); and Helmut Striffler, "The Building," in Christian Reger, *Protestant Church of Reconciliation in the former Concentration Camp at Dachau* (n.p.p.: n.p., n.d. [ca. 1968]) [brochure available at the Protestant church in the Dachau memorial site].

75. The German reads: "Zuflucht ist unter dem Schatten Deiner Flügel."

76. Reger, *Protestant Church of Reconciliation.*

77. The living quarters were deemed too small, so no cleric ever actually lived in the memorial building.

78. Ludger Bült, "Dachau—15.10.89 / 10 Jahre ASF," eleven-page manuscript in Dachau Memorial Site Archive. ASF volunteers already assisted during construction of the chapel in 1966, but not as part of a continuing program.

79. For the development of this position and the discussion of related issues, see the newsletter of the ASF, *Zeichen: Mitteilungen der Aktion Sühnezeichen/Friedensdienste,* e.g. the special issue "Erinnern, nicht vergessen: Gedenkstätten in der Bundesrepublik," 11:3 (September 1983), passim. The *Gedenkstättenrundbrief* (Memorial Site Circular), which was sponsored from 1985 to 1993 by the ASF, has become the central journal for all German memorial sites. Through it the developments of the 1990s can best be traced.

80. The German and English editions of the catalog were published in May 1978. See *Mitteilungen der Lagergemeinschaft Dachau,* November 1978.

81. See Marcuse, *Nazi Crimes,* pp. 399, 413.

82. These buildings were torn down in 1985 by the Bavarian Riot Police, who were stationed in the former SS barracks after the U.S. Army moved out in 1971.

83. The villa was torn down without prior public notification in 1987, after being considered for housing an international youth center. See "Photo-report," *Süddeutsche Zeitung/Dachauer Neueste,* May 23, 1987; "Spuren wurden vernichtet" (joint letter to the editor), *Süddeutsche Zeitung/Dachauer Neueste,* June 3, 1987.

84. The importance of local grassroots support groups for the existence of West German concentration camp memorial sites was noted, for instance, in the national parliamentary hearing on the future of such sites after the unification of East and West Germany in 1989. See Deutscher Bundestag, Innenausschuss, "Stellungnahmen der Sachverständigen und Verbände zur öffentlichen Anhörung des Innenausschusses zu dem Thema 'Beteiligung des Bundes an Mahn- und Gedenkstätten,'" Bonn, Ausschussdrucksache 12/67 (February 22, 1994).

85. For examples of these discussions, see *Dachauer Hefte* 3 (1987), *Frauen: Verfolgung und Widerstand,* and 10 (1994), *Täter und Opfer.* Additionally, prior to the 1990s local historian Sybille Steinbacher would not have been able to access the most important source material for her pathbreaking study of relations between the town and the camp, *Dachau: Die Stadt und das Konzentrationslager in der NS-Zeit* (Frankfurt: Peter Lang, 1993).

86. The initiative, which began in 1977, is documented in a file in the Comité International de Dachau papers given to the Dachau Archive in 1992.

87. See *Jahresbericht der Gedenkstätte Buchenwald,* 1994, pp. 48 ff.

Michael R. Marrus, "The Future of Auschwitz"

This essay has appeared in a similar form in the following: "The Future of Auschwitz: A Case for the Ruins," in *A User's Guide to German Studies,* ed. Scott Denham, Irene Kacandes, and Jonathan Petropoulos (Ann Arbor: University of Michigan Press, 1997), pp. 357–66.

1. On questions of conflicting memories see Jonathan Webber, *The Future of Auschwitz: Some Personal Reflections,* Frank Green Lecture (Oxford: Oxford Centre for Postgraduate Hebrew Studies, 1992); James E. Young, *The Texture of Memory: Holocaust Memorials and Meaning* (New Haven, Conn.: Yale University Press, 1993), chap. 5; Debórah Dwork and Robert Jan van Pelt, "Reclaiming Auschwitz," in *Holocaust Remembrance: The Shapes of Memory,* ed. Geoffrey H. Hartman (Oxford: Blackwell, 1994), pp. 232–51.

2. The best historical orientation to Auschwitz is Debórah Dwork and Robert Jan van Pelt, *Auschwitz: 1270 to the Present* (New York: Norton, 1996). See also Yisrael Gutman and Michael Berenbaum, eds., *Anatomy of the Auschwitz Death Camp* (Bloomington: Indiana University Press, 1994), and especially the articles by Jean-Claude Pressac and Robert Jan van Pelt. For a chronological account, drawn from archival sources, see Danuta Czech, *Kalendarium der Ereignisse im Konzentrationslager Auschwitz-Birkenau 1939–1945* (Reinbek bei Hamburg: Rowohlt, 1989). For a bibliographic collection, see Opracowala Anna Malcowna, *Bibliographia KL Auschwitz za lata 1942–1980* (Oświęcim: Wydawnictwo Państwowego Muzeum w Oświęcimiu, 1991).

3. United Nations Educational, Scientific and Cultural Organization, nomination of Auschwitz-Birkenau National Museum to the World Heritage List, Warsaw, May 2, 1978. For important details see Jean-Claude Pressac, *Auschwitz: Technique and Operation of the Gas Chambers* (New York: Beate Klarsfeld Foundation, 1989). There is an excellent collection of photographs in the book by Theresa Swiebocka, with Jonathan Webber and Connie Wilsack, eds., *Auschwitz: A History in Photographs* (Bloomington: Indiana University Press, 1993).

4. Franciszek Piper, "Estimating the Number of Deportees and Victims of the Auschwitz-Birkenau Camp," *Yad Vashem Studies* 21 (1991): 49–99. See also Wolfgang Benz, *Dimensions des Volkermords: Die Zahl der jüdischen Opfer des Nationalsozialismus* (Munich: Oldenbourg, 1991).

5. For an account of some of these issues and the various perspectives on them, see Timothy W. Ryback, "Evidence of Evil," *The New Yorker,* November 15, 1993, pp. 68–81.

6. See Wladyslaw T. Bartoszewski, *The Convent at Auschwitz* (New York: George Braziller, 1990).

7. James Young, "Reflections on the Conservation at Auschwitz-Birkenau," unpublished paper prepared for the conference "The Future of Auschwitz: Should the Ruins Be Preserved?" in August 1993, p. 2.

Nathan F. Cogan, "A Commentary on the Video-Documentary The Last Remnants of Lithuanian Jewry"

1. For detailed accounts of the genocide in Lithuania, 1941–44, see Avraham Tory, *Surviving the Holocaust: The Kovno Ghetto Diary* (Cambridge: Harvard University Press, 1990); Yitzhak Arad, *Ghetto in Flames* (New York: 1985); Dov Levin, *Fighting Back: Lithuanian Jewry's Armed Resistance against the Nazis* (New York: Holmes & Meier, 1985); Sol Littman, *War Criminal on Trial: The Rauca Case* (Toronto: 1983); and Martin Gilbert, *The Holocaust: A History of the Jews of Europe during the Second World War* (New York: Henry Holt, 1985).

2. Lawrence Langer, *Holocaust Testimonies: The Ruins of Memory* (New Haven: Yale University Press, 1991), particularly chap. 1, "Deep Memory: The Buried Self."

3. The typescript (MSW4) of Dora's testimony taken September 6, 1991, runs 14 pages.

4. Shmuel "Sam" Mikelovich, a schoolteacher in Baltipai (a suburb of Vilnius) and the son of Litvak survivors of the gulag, used that term in interviews October 1992. He indicated there were 100,000 "shooters," some of whom were accidentally "exonerated" by the government in 1992.

5. Jana Ran Carny's testimony, taken December 2–4, 1992, is corroborated by her personal memoir, published in Russian in Vilnius in 1993.

6. Louis Begley, *Wartime Lies* (New York: Ballantine, 1991), p. 97.

7. Sarah Neshamit, "Rescue in Lithuania during the Nazi Occupation," in *Rescue Attempts during the Holocaust,* Proceedings of the Second Yad Vashem International Conference (Jerusalem: Yad Vashem, 1973), pp. 289–332.

Scott Denham, "Schindler Returns to Open Arms"

This chapter appeared in a slightly different form as *"Schindler's List* in Germany and Austria: A Reception Study," *German Politics and Society* 13 (Spring 1995): 135–46.

1. Marion Dönhoff, "Dissent on *Schindler's List,*" letter to the editor, *New York Review of Books,* June 9, 1994, p. 60.

2. James O. Jackson, "Schindler Schock: Spielberg's Film Stuns the Two Lands of the Holocaust, Germany and Israel, Annoying Some Critics but Overwhelming Viewers," *Time,* March 14, 1994, p. 53 (European edn.); Andrew Nagorski, "*Schindler's List* Hits Home," *Newsweek,* March 14, 1994, p. 77.

3. Craig R. Whitney, "Tears and Praise at German Premiere of *Schindler's List,*" *New York Times,* March 2, 1994, pp. B1, B6 (national edn.).

4. Dönhoff, "Dissent."

5. Ludwig Heinrich, "Bei Spielberg fehlt keiner," *Oberösterreichische Nachrichten,* February 16, 1994; "Hoffnung statt Hoffnungslosigkeit: Benefizgala von 'Schindlers Liste' in Wien," *Wiener Zeitung,* February 18, 1994.

6. Andreas Kilb, "Warten, bis Spielberg kommt," *Die Zeit,* January 28, 1994, p. 1 (foreign edn.).

7. Ibid.

8. Christoph Stopka, "Ich bin Frau Schindler," interview with Emilie Schindler, *Bunte,* February 17, 1994, pp. 22–25.

9. Nagorski, "Hits Home."

10. "Vom grossen Morden," *Der Spiegel,* February 21, 1994, p. 168.

11. See Dönhoff, "Dissent"; Bascha Mika, "Schindler und die Schüler: Geschichtsunterricht im Kino," *Tageszeitung,* March 15, 1994; Christian Neuwirth, "Uneinigkeit über Gratis-Kinokarten," *Salzburger Nachrichten,* March 5, 1994.

12. Stopka, "Ich bin Frau Schindler."

13. Niklas Frank, "Der Deutsche, der uns rettete," *Stern,* March 1994, pp. 197–205.

14. "Grenze für Greuel," *Der Spiegel,* March 14, 1994, pp. 192–206.

15. Frank Schirrmacher, "Schindlers Liste," *Frankfurter Allgemeine Zeitung,* March 1, 1994, p. 1.

16. Sylke Tempel, "Handeln im rechten Moment," *Die Wochenpost,* February 24, 1994, p. 21; Sabine Horst, "'We Couldn't Show That,'" *Konkret,* March 1994, pp. 40–42.

17. Tempel, "Handeln."

18. Gerd Gemünden, "I No Longer Trust the Power of Images: A Conversation with Wim Wenders," unpublished interview, March 1, 1994.

19. Claude Lanzmann, "Holocauste, la représentation impossible," *Le Monde,* March 3, 1994, Arts & Spectacles section, pp. i, vii; also appeared as "Ihr sollt nicht weinen: Einspruch gegen *Schindlers Liste,*" *Frankfurter Allgemeine Zeitung,* March 5, 1994, and in a slightly different form

as "Man hat kein Recht, den Holocaust zu zeigen," *Der Standard,* March 4, 1994.

20. Sigrid Löffler, "Kino als Ablass: Spielbergs misslungener Holocaust-Film," *Die Wochenpost,* February 24, 1994.

21. Will Tremper, "Indiana Jones im Ghetto von Krakau," *Die Welt,* February 26, 1994; Günther Rühle, "Nachruhm," *Tagesspiegel,* March 10, 1994. For U.S. reviews, see, for example, J. Hoberman et al., "*Schindler's List:* Myth, Movie, and Memory," *Village Voice,* March 29, 1994; Jason Epstein, "A Dissent on 'Schindler's List,'" *New York Review of Books,* April 21, 1994, p. 65; Philip Gourevitch, "A Dissent on 'Schindler's List,'" *Commentary* 97:2 (1994): 49–52; and "Two Cheers for Schindler," *Tikkun* 9:2 (March–April 1994): 7–9.

22. Henryk Broder, "Kritik der dummen Kerls: Spielbergs Widersacher," *Frankfurter Allgemeine Zeitung,* March 15, 1994, p. 33.

23. On this see Verena Leuken, "Die Wiederverwertung der Betroffenheit: 'Hitlerjunge Salomon': Verlogener Streit um einen schlechten Film," *Frankfurter Allgemeine Zeitung,* January 29, 1992, p. 27.

24. Henryk Broder, "Deutsche Ausreden," *Die Woche,* March 3, 1994.

25. Ibid.

26. Broder, "Kritik."

27. Ibid.

28. Namely by Elisabeth Bauschmid, "Kronzeuge Himmler: Der neue Relativismus der geistigen Welt: Schindler, Spielberg und die Zumutung des Erinnerns," *Süddeutsche Zeitung,* March 3, 1994, and by Michael Wolffsohn, "Gute Deutsche?" *Die Welt,* March 4, 1994.

29. Broder, "Kritik."

30. Jan Gympel, "Das Kino ist keine moralische Waschanlage: Will Tremper und der immer heftigere Streit um den Film 'Schindlers List,'" *Tagesspiegel,* March 20, 1994; see also Moritz Rinke, "Schindlers Hühner: Über das Scheitern einer Deutschen Diskussion," *Baseler Zeitung,* May 2, 1994.

31. Michael Wolffsohn, "Der eingebildete Antisemit: Die Kritiker von 'Schindlers Liste' gehören nicht in die rechte Ecke," *Frankfurter Allgemeine Zeitung,* March 19, 1994.

32. Ibid.

33. Klaus Rainer Röhl, "Broders Liste," *Die Wochenpost,* March 30, 1994, p. 12.

34. Andreas Kilb, "Stichelei: Noch einmal zu *Schindlers Liste,*" *Die Zeit,* April 1, 1994, p. 13 (foreign edn.).

35. Ibid. (my emphasis).

36. Yizhak Ahren et al., eds., *Das Lehrstück "Holocaust": Zur Wir-*

kungspsychologie eines Medienereignesses (Opladen: Westdeutscher Verlag, 1982), p. 11.

37. See Andrew Nagorski, "Spielberg's Risk: The Director Takes a Chance with a Holocaust Drama Shot in Black and White," *Newsweek,* May 24, 1993, pp. 60–61, and Wilfried Mommert, "Brauner verlor gegen Spielberg," *Leipziger Volkszeitung,* March 4, 1994.

38. Nagorski, "Schindler."

Judith E. Doneson, "Is a Little Memory Better than None?"

1. Elie Wiesel spoke at St. Louis's Temple Shaare Emeth on November 14, 1993.

2. Since the time Elie Wiesel appeared with Oprah Winfrey, Ms. Winfrey has dramatically altered the format of her hour-long show. She has toned down the sensationalism and moved toward issues that concern a mass audience in the contemporary world. She now delves into such subjects as menopause, family violence, fashion, and suggested books for the audience to read.

3. *New York Times,* April 4, 1993. The *Oprah Winfrey Show* was viewed on NBC/TV in St. Louis, Missouri, on July 7, 1993.

4. *New York Times,* May 20 and 27, 1994, and July 8, 1994.

5. One is reminded of the debates between Elie Wiesel and Gerald Green, script writer of *Holocaust,* over the nine-and-one-half-hour watershed docudrama televised on NBC/TV, which helped to plant the Final Solution in the public mind. Wiesel's scathing attacks and Green's responses took place over several weeks in the Arts and Leisure section of the *New York Times.* See Elie Wiesel, "Trivializing the Holocaust: Semi-Fact and Semi-Fiction," *New York Times,* April 16, 1978, for the first in the cycle. Or see Elie Wiesel, "Trivializing Memory," in his *From the Kingdom of Memory* (New York: Summit Books, 1990), pp. 165–72.

6. Saul Friedlander, *Memory, History, and the Extermination of the Jews of Europe* (Bloomington: Indiana University Press, 1993), p. 43.

7. See Judith E. Doneson, *The Holocaust in American Film* (Philadelphia: Jewish Publication Society, 1987).

8. George L. Mosse, *Germans and Jews* (New York: Grosset & Dunlap, 1970), p. 76.

9. The *Sally Jessy Raphael Show,* seen on KSD/TV (NBC) in St. Louis, October 21, 1993. About disc jockeys, see *St. Louis Post Dispatch,* January 26, 1993; re Dolly Parton, see *St. Louis Post Dispatch,* February 20, 1994; re professor at William Paterson College, see *New York Times,* February 13, 1994; re Khalid Abdul Muhammad, see Paul Berman, "The Other and the Almost the Same," *New Yorker,* February 28, 1994, p. 61; re Farrakhan,

New York Times, February 21, 1994. The *Arsenio Hall Show* was seen on KMOV/TV (CBS) in St. Louis, February 25, 1994. Re public access channels, see *New York Times,* May 23, 1993; and re young revisionist, Timothy W. Ryback, "Evidence of Evil," *New Yorker,* November 15, 1993, p. 78.

10. Deborah Lipstadt, *Denying the Holocaust* (New York: Free Press, 1993), p. 2.

11. Walter Reich, *New York Times Book Review,* July 11, 1993.

12. *Oprah Winfrey Show,* July 15, 1993.

13. Elie Wiesel appeared on *Charlie Rose,* a popular conversational program on public television, on August 10, 1994.

14. Michael Marrus, "The Use and Misuse of the Holocaust," in *Lessons and Legacies: The Meaning of the Holocaust in a Changing World,* ed. Peter Hayes (Evanston: Northwestern University Press, 1991), p. 117.

15. Wiesel, "Trivializing Memory," p. 171.

16. Elie Wiesel appeared on *Later,* seen on NBC/TV, 1 A.M. in the Central time zone, on two consecutive evenings, January 13 and 14, 1992, and more recently on *Charlie Rose,* appearing on PBS also in the late-night venue, August 10, 1994. Interestingly, a random if unscientific survey showed that several local bookstores in St. Louis sold out of Elie Wiesel's *Night* following the Oprah interview.

17. *Nightline,* ABC/TV, 10:30 A.M. Central time, December 28, 1993.

18. For an overview of some works related to representations and popularizations of the Holocaust, see Leon A. Jick, "The Holocaust: Its Use and Abuse within the American Public," *Yad Vashem Studies* 14 (Jerusalem: Yad Vashem, 1981): 303–18; Annette Insdorf, *Indelible Shadows: Film and the Holocaust* (1st ed., 1983; Cambridge: Cambridge University Press, 1990); Alvin Rosenfeld, *Imagining Hitler* (Bloomington: Indiana University Press, 1985); Judith E. Doneson, *The Holocaust in American Film* (Philadelphia: Jewish Publication Society of America, 1987); Anton Kaes, *From Hitler to Heimat: The Return of History as Film* (Cambridge, Mass.: Harvard University Press, 1989); Saul Friedlander, ed., *Probing the Limits of Representation* (Cambridge, Mass.: Harvard University Press, 1992); and idem, *Memory, History, and the Extermination of the Jews of Europe* (Bloomington: Indiana University Press, 1993).

19. *Charlie Rose* is seen on public television stations. About Mengele, see "Now It Can Be Told," January 6, 1992. The *Jerry Springer Show* was seen on KDS/TV (NBC) in St. Louis at 10 A.M., February 8, 1994; the *Oprah Winfrey Show* on July 15, 1993.

20. Omer Bartov, "Intellectuals on Auschwitz," *History and Memory* 5:1 (Spring–Summer 1993): 92–93.

21. The speaker was sponsored by the Aish HaTorah organization of St. Louis, Missouri, and delivered at the city's Jewish Community Center in November of 1993.

22. Jane Perlez, "At Warsaw Ghetto, Poles and Jews Bound by Hope," *New York Times,* April 20, 1993.

23. *Travel & Leisure,* April 1993.

24. Wiesel, *From the Kingdom of Memory,* pp. 169–70.

25. On MacKinnon, see Michiko Kakutani, "Pornography, the Constitution and a Fight Thereof," review of Catherine A. MacKinnon's *Words, New York Times,* October 29, 1993; on Pope John Paul II, see "Pope Spreads 'Gospel of Life,'" *St. Louis Post Dispatch,* August 16, 1993; for Tom Hanks, see *The Golden Globe Awards,* broadcast on TNT Television January 23, 1994.

26. Leon A. Jick, "The Holocaust: Its Use and Abuse," pp. 315–16.

27. For example, see chap. 4, "Television and the Effects of *Holocaust,*" in Doneson, *The Holocaust in American Film;* Judith E. Doneson, "American Films on the Holocaust: An Aid to Memory or Trivialization?" *Annals of the American Academy of Political and Social Science* (November 1996); Kaes, *From Hitler to Heimat;* and Siegfried Zielinski, "History as Entertainment and Provocation: The TV Series 'Holocaust' in West Germany," in *Germans and Jews since the Holocaust,* ed. Anson Rabinbach and Jack Zipes (New York: Holmes & Meier, 1986).

28. *Nightline,* December 28, 1993.

29. Both Mr. Bukiet and Ms. Maslin appeared on *Charlie Rose,* PBS/TV, January 11, 1994.

30. David Margolick, "Schindler's Jews Find Deliverance Again," *New York Times,* February 13, 1994.

31. Ibid.

32. Keith Stone, "'Operation Grow Hair' Changes Some Skinheads," *St. Louis Post Dispatch,* January 1, 1994.

33. *St. Louis Post Dispatch,* March 1, 1994.

34. Craig R. Whitney, "Tears and Praise at German Premiere of 'Schindler's List,'" *New York Times,* March 2, 1994.

35. Michael Kammen, *Mystic Chords of Memory* (New York: Alfred A. Knopf, 1991), p. 534. "Disney Plans New Park with Historical Theme," *St. Louis Post Dispatch,* November 12, 1993. See William Styron, "Slavery's Pain, Disney's Gain," *New York Times,* August 4, 1994, for an opposing view of the Disney theme park, which was indeed rejected at the proposed site.

36. Saul Friedlander, *Memory, History, and the Extermination,* pp. xii–xiii.

37. Rebroadcast as part of *Nightline,* April 21, 1993, regarding the situation in Bosnia.

38. *Nightline,* December 28, 1993.

39. Robert Jay Lifton, "Can Images of Bosnia's Victims Change the World?" *New York Times,* August 23, 1992.

40. Walter Goodman, "First the TV Images, Then the Policy," *New York Times,* February 14, 1994.

41. Jeffrey Schmalz, "Whatever Happened to AIDS?" *New York Times Magazine,* November 28, 1993.

42. Leon Wieseltier, "After Memory," *The New Republic,* May 3, 1993, p. 18.

43. *Nightline,* December 28, 1993.

44. Christopher Browning, *Ordinary Men* (New York: Harper-Collins, 1992).

45. Kammen, *Mystic Chords of Memory,* p. 688.

46. Carl L. Becker, "What Is Evidence?" in *The Historian as Detective,* ed. Robin W. Winks (New York: Harper Colophon, 1970), p. 7.

Lawrence Baron, "Holocaust Awareness and Denial in the United States"

This chapter is a revised and updated version of a paper written in the summer of 1993 and first presented on March 7, 1994, at the Annual Scholars' Conference on the Holocaust and Church Struggle held at Rider College, Lawrenceville, New Jersey. It was published under the title "What Do Americans Know about the Holocaust? Putting the American Jewish Committee's Survey in Perspective," in *The Holocaust: Lessons for the Third Generation,* ed. Dominick A. Iorio, Richard L. Libowitz, Marcia S. Littell (Lanham: University Press of America, 1997), pp. 13–22. I thank Alan Berger, Christopher Browning, and Hubert Locke for their feedback on that draft.

1. Jennifer Golub and Renae Cohen, *What Do Americans Know About the Holocaust?* (New York: American Jewish Committee, 1993).

2. Ibid., p. 13.

3. Joseph Polakoff, "Survivors Are Shocked by Holocaust Ignorance," *San Diego Jewish Press Heritage,* May 7, 1993, p. 3.

4. Interview of Elie Wiesel, *Oprah Winfrey Show,* July 1993. This fear that the Holocaust denial movement might achieve greater success once the survivors have died was recently reiterated by Deborah E. Lipstadt, "A Clear and Future Danger," *Tikkun* 10:3 (May–June 1995): 17.

5. For examples of this phenomenon, see Michiko Kakutani, "When

History and Memory Are Casualties: Holocaust Denial," *New York Times,* April 30, 1993; Edward Norden, "Yes and No to Holocaust Museums," *Commentary* 96:2 (August 1993): 29; Marina Rust, "Youth and the Truth," *Vogue,* August 1993, p. 172; Deborah E. Lipstadt, *Denying the Holocaust: The Growing Assault on Truth and Memory* (New York: Plume, 1994), p. xi; Diet Eman with James Schaap, *Things We Couldn't Say* (Grand Rapids, Mich.: William B. Eerdmans, 1994), p. 377.

6. David W. Moore and Frank Newport, "Misreading the Public: The Case of the Holocaust Poll," *Public Perspective,* March–April 1994, pp. 28–29.

7. John Kifner, "Pollsters Find Error on Holocaust Doubts," *New York Times,* May 20, 1994; "Holocaust Poll Analyzer Named," *New York Times,* May 27, 1994; "Definitive Report Shows Less Than 2 Percent of Americans Are Hard-Core Holocaust Deniers," American Jewish Committee press release (July 11, 1994), which in this chapter I refer to as the second AJC poll; Tom Smith, *Holocaust Denial: What the Survey Data Reveal* (New York: American Jewish Committee, 1995), pp. 9–17, 22, 50.

8. Harold Quinley, "America Views the Holocaust," *Dimensions: A Journal of Holocaust Studies* 6:2 (1991): 4–7. Despite the Anti-Defamation League study, the authors of the first AJC poll claim that their study was the first systematic survey of what Americans know and think about the Holocaust. See Golub and Cohen, *What Do Americans Know,* pp. 1, 12.

9. Lawrence Baron, "Building Tolerance Project: Results for 1994–95."

10. Quinley, "America Views," pp. 4–7.

11. Diane Ravitch and Chester E. Finn, *What Do Our 17-Year-Olds Know? A Report on the First National Assessment of History and Literature* (New York: Harper and Row, 1987), pp. 1–42; Golub and Cohen, *What Do Americans Know,* pp. 12–13.

12. Ravitch and Finn, *What Do Our 17-Year-Olds Know?* pp. 61–63. For an overview of these results, see Smith, *Holocaust Denial,* pp. 37–38.

13. Baron, "Building Tolerance Project."

14. Elly Dlin and Sharon Gillerman, "Education on the Holocaust: The United States and Israel," in *The Encyclopedia of the Holocaust,* ed. Israel Gutman, vol. 2 (New York: Macmillan, 1990), pp. 420–23.

15. Stacy Weiner, "Teaching the Unteachable: Public Schools Teach the Holocaust," *Jewish Monthly,* April 1992, p. 35.

16. Donald Schwartz, "Who Will Tell Them After We're Gone? Reflections on Teaching the Holocaust," *History Teacher* 23:2 (February 1990): 99.

17. Weiner, "Teaching the Unteachable," pp. 35–39; Adam Hauck, "Teaching of Holocaust Gaining Tenure in Public Schools," *Daily Aztec*, San Diego State University, September 12, 1994, p. 1.

18. These sorts of issues are what stalled the recent adoption of a Holocaust requirement in New Jersey's public schools.

19. Weiner, "Teaching the Unteachable," p. 35. For the enrollment figures for American high schools in 1988 and 1989, see *Digest of Education Statistics* (Washington, D.C.: U.S. Department of Education, 1991), pp. 55, 68. According to these tables, 11,370,646 students were enrolled in public and 896,478 in private high schools.

20. Golub and Cohen, *What Do Americans Know*, p. 17.

21. Smith, *Holocaust Denial*, pp. 7–8.

22. Golub and Cohen, *What Do Americans Know*, pp. 24–34.

23. Section 27-20-3, *Illinois School Code*, January 1, 1990.

24. Weiner, "Teaching the Unteachable," p. 36.

25. Diane Ravich, "The Plight of History in American Schools," in *Historical Literacy: The Case for History in American Education*, ed. Paul Gagnon and the Bradley Commission on History in Schools (New York: Macmillan, 1989), pp. 65–66; Glenn S. Pate, "The United States of America," in *The Treatment of the Holocaust in Textbooks: Federal Republic of Germany, Israel, and the United States of America*, ed. Randolph L. Braham (New York: Columbia University Press, 1987), p. 271.

26. Golub and Cohen, *What Do Americans Know*, pp. 38–47.

27. Quinley, "America Views," p. 6.

28. Weiner, "Teaching the Unteachable," p. 38.

29. Elena Neuman, "Whither Jewish Studies?" *The Forward*, August 24, 1990, pp. E1, E5; Edward Alexander, "The Attack on Holocaust Studies," *Holocaust Studies Annual* 1 (1983): 1–6.

30. Norden, "Yes and No," pp. 23–32; "United States Holocaust Memorial Museum: The First Year 1993–1994," (Washington, D.C.: U.S. Holocaust Memorial Museum, 1994).

31. See letter insert mailed with the booklet "United States Holocaust Museum: The Year in Review 1994–1995" (Washington, D.C.: U.S. Holocaust Memorial Museum, 1995) and the article "Bringing the Lessons Home" on page 5 of the booklet itself. (United States Holocaust Memorial Museum Honoring Five Years, http://www.ushmm.org).

32. *Books in Print 1993–1994: Subject Guide*, vol. 2 (New Providence: R. R. Bowker, 1993), pp. 3840–45. Smith also includes a table on the numbers of articles on the Holocaust appearing in major American newspapers from 1990 until 1994. In 1990 an average of .96 articles appeared daily in each major newspaper; the figure rose to a daily average of 1.32 by the first six months of 1994. See Smith, *Holocaust Denial*, p. 43.

33. Hauck, "Teaching of Holocaust," p. 1. For information on the Schindler's List Project, see "Schindler's List Project," fact sheet of the Office of the Governor of California Pete Wilson, April 11, 1994.

34. Smith, *Holocaust Denial,* pp. 4–5. The television broadcast of *Schindler's List* was viewed by 65 million people. "Lawmaker Criticizes 'Schindler's List' Airing Wednesday," February 26, 1997. http://www.english.upenn.edu/~afilreis/holocaust/schindler-on-tv.html.

35. James E. Young, *The Texture of Memory: Holocaust Memorials and Meaning* (New Haven: Yale University Press, 1993), p. 284; Helen Fein, "The Holocaust—What It Means, What It Doesn't," *Present Tense* 15:1 (November–December 1987): 24–29; David Frolick, "Teaching Children about Children in the Holocaust or Why I Am Confused About Holocaust Education in the Public Schools," *Shofar* 10:2 (Winter 1992), pp. 108–12; Weiner, pp. 36–39.

36. Golub and Cohen, *What Do Americans Know,* p. 17. The first AJC poll found that 50 percent of American adults learned about the Holocaust from television and 24 percent from movies. Those figures rose to 58 percent and 33 percent in the AJC poll taken in 1994. See Smith, *Holocaust Denial,* p. 46.

37. "Survey Finds 21% in US Uninformed about Holocaust," *San Diego Union-Tribune,* April 23, 1998, p. A-10.

38. For a brief overview of the high quality of much of the history written about the Holocaust, see Michael R. Marrus, "Good History and Teaching the Holocaust," *Perspectives: The American Historical Association Newsletter* 31:5 (May–June 1993): 1, 6–12.

39. On the problem of equating the Holocaust with persecutions of other groups, see Steven T. Katz, *The Holocaust in Historical Context: The Holocaust and Mass Death before the Modern Age* (New York: Oxford University Press, 1994), pp. 1–63. For a variety of viewpoints on the comparability and uniqueness of the Holocaust, see *Is the Holocaust Unique? Perspectives on Comparative Genocide,* ed. Alan S. Rosenbaum (Boulder: Westview Press, 1996).

Jonathan Petropoulos, "Holocaust Denial"

I thank Peter Hayes for his helpful editorial suggestions. Christopher Jackson and Scott Denham also provided close readings and merit my sincere thanks.

1. Sun Tzu, "The Art of War" (c. 500 B.C.): "Know the enemy and know yourself." Peter Tsouras, ed., *Warriors' Words: A Quotation Book from Sesostris III to Schwarzkopf* (London: Cassell Arms and Armour, 1992), p. 156.

2. Deborah Lipstadt, *Denying the Holocaust: The Growing Assault on Truth and Memory* (New York: Free Press, 1993).

3. H. H. Gerth and C. Wright Mills, *From Max Weber: Essays in Sociology* (New York: Overview Press, 1946), pp. 59–60.

4. Robert Wohl, *The Generation of 1914* (Cambridge, Mass.: Harvard University Press, 1979), p. 5.

5. Ibid., pp. 80–81.

6. Mannheim paraphrased by Wohl, ibid., p. 78.

7. Gerald Posner, *Hitler's Children: Sons and Daughters of Third Reich Leaders Talk about Themselves and Their Fathers* (New York: Berkeley Books, 1992), p. 208.

8. Ibid., p. 211.

9. In 1995 a "major magazine" entitled *Marco Polo* (circulation 200,000) was shut down by the "prestigious" publishing house Bungei Shunju for featuring an article claiming that the gas chambers at Auschwitz were a myth. *Baltimore Sun,* February 2, 1995, p. A1. See also David Goodman and Masanori Miyazawa, *Jews and the Japanese Mind: The History and Uses of a Cultural Stereotype* (New York: Free Press, 1994).

10. Rena Giefer and Thomas Giefer, *Die Rattenlinie: Fluchtwege der Nazis. Eine Dokumentation* (Frankfurt: Anton Hain, 1991), p. 233. See also Allan Ryan, *Quiet Neighbors* (New York: Harcourt Brace Jovanovich, 1984).

11. Manfred Jenke, *Verschwörung von Rechts? Ein Bericht über den Rechtsradikalismus in Deutschland nach 1945* (Berlin: Colloquium Verlag, 1961), p. 312.

12. Ibid., p. 317.

13. Yaron Svoray and Nick Taylor, *In Hitler's Shadow: An Israeli's Amazing Journey inside Germany's neo-Nazi Movement* (New York: Doubleday, 1994), pp. 91–110.

14. Jenke, *Verschwörung von Rechts?* pp. 342–95. See also David Clay Large, "Reckoning without the Past: The HIAG of the Waffen-SS and the Politics of Rehabilitation in the Bonn Republic, 1950–1961," *Journal of Modern History* 59 (1987): 79–113; Kurt Tauber, *Beyond Eagle and Swastika: German Nationalism since 1945* (Middletown, Conn.: Wesleyan University Press, 1967), pp. 332–62; and James Diehl, *The Thanks of the Fatherland: German Veterans after the Second World War* (Chapel Hill: University of North Carolina Press, 1993).

15. Anna Merritt, *Public Opinion in Occupied Germany: The OMGUS Surveys, 1945–1949* (Urbana: University of Illinois Press, 1970); and Anna Merritt and Richard Merritt, *Public Opinion in Semisovereign Germany: The HICOG Surveys, 1949–1955* (Urbana: University of Illinois Press,

1980). See also Michael Kater, "Problems of Political Reeducation in West Germany, 1945–1960," *Simon Wiesenthal Center Annual* (1987): 99–123.

16. Merritt and Merritt, *Public Opinion in Semisovereign Germany.*

17. Ibid.

18. Bruce Pauley, *From Prejudice to Persecution: A History of Austrian Anti-Semitism* (Chapel Hill: University of North Carolina Press, 1992), pp. 305–7.

19. Eric Santner, *Stranded Objects: Mourning, Memory, and Film in Postwar Germany* (Ithaca and London: Cornell University Press, 1990), p. 35.

20. Posner, *Hitler's Children,* p. 211.

21. "Pope Denies Claim of Help to Nazis," *Boston Globe,* February 20, 1992. For more on the rat-line, see Giefer and Giefer, *Die Rattenlinie.*

22. Ciaran O'Maolain, *The Radical Right: A World Directory* (Essex: Longman, 1987), p. 307. "A Network of Neo-Nazis?" *International Herald Tribune,* August 30, 1993, p. 1.

23. Marie-Luise Gättens and David Schwarz, "Affirmation and Denial of History in German Oi Music," paper presented at the German Studies Association Conference, Dallas, October 1, 1994.

24. "A Network of Neo-Nazis?"

25. *Der Spiegel* 46 (1993): 108. "Der Yuppie-Nazi steht im Konzentrationslager und darf vortragen, warum dort, technisch gesehen, keine Juden umgebracht worden sein können: 'Sie haben all überlebt und kassieren jetzt Geld von uns."

26. Svoray and Taylor, *In Hitler's Shadow,* p. 173.

27. Douglas Coupland, *Generation X: Tales for an Accelerated Culture* (New York: St. Martin's, 1991).

28. "Call to Action to the Academic World," *Response* 15:2 (Summer 1994): 8.

29. Ortega paraphrased by Wohl, *Generation of 1914,* p. 151.

30. For an overview of prominent deniers, see Sol Littman, *Holocaust Denial: Bigotry in the Guise of Scholarship. A Simon Wiesenthal Center Report* (Los Angeles: Simon Wiesenthal Center, 1994).

31. Svoray and Taylor, *In Hitler's Shadow,* pp. 259–60.

32. Noam Chomsky, "The Faurisson Affair: His Right to Say It," *Nation,* February 28, 1991, p. 231.

33. Mark Weber, "From the Editor," *Journal of Historical Review* 13:2 (March–April 1993): 3.

34. Ibid., p. 215.

35. Similarly, there are some in the Middle East who deny the Holo-

caust largely on account of their anti-Zionist views, although they, too, are not always open about their political motivations.

36. Svoray and Taylor, *In Hitler's Shadow,* p. 40.

Geoffrey J. Giles, "Blind in the Right Eye"

1. The law also extends the ban on the use of Nazi symbols to include anything even resembling Nazi emblems or slogans. Robin Gedye, "Denying the Holocaust Is a Crime in Germany," *Daily Telegraph,* September 22, 1994.

2. Calculated from figures in the Associated Press report "German Law Targets Neo-Nazis," September 21, 1994.

3. Justin Burke, "Germany Shudders as Neo-Nazism Rekindles," *Christian Science Monitor,* August 19, 1994.

4. Reuters, "Germany Approves Jail Terms for Denying Holocaust," September 23, 1994.

5. Hanno Kühnert, "Mit Blindheit geschlagen," *Die Zeit,* August 26, 1994 (overseas edn.).

6. Craig R. Whitney, "Judge's Slap in the Face for Holocaust Victims," *International Herald Tribune,* August 11, 1994.

7. "Politische Herzenssache," *Die Zeit,* August 26, 1994 (overseas edn.).

8. Kühnert, "Mit Blindheit geschlagen."

9. "Politische Herzenssache."

10. Reuters, "Judge at Center of Holocaust Ruling Row Returns," September 26, 1994.

11. Reuters, "Judge in Neo-Nazi Ruling Sees No Problem," August 14, 1994.

12. Reuters, "U.S. Nazi Apologist Fails to Attend German Trial," September 14, 1994.

13. *Jerusalem Post,* October 30, 1993.

14. Gunter Hoffmann, "Eine Obsession," *Die Zeit,* September 2, 1994 (overseas edn.).

15. Agence France Presse, "'Nazi Theory' Judge Reinstated," September 19, 1994.

16. Robert B. Goldmann, "Don't Be Calm About the Holocaust," *International Herald Tribune,* August 17, 1994.

Notes on Contributors

LAWRENCE BARON (Ph.D., University of Wisconsin) is the director of the Lipinsky Insitute for Judaic Studies and Nasatir Professor of Modern Jewish History at San Diego State University. He served as the historical consultant and chapter writer for Pearl and Sam Oliner's *The Altruistic Personality: Rescuers of Jews in Nazi Europe.* He is the president of the Western Jewish Studies Association.

MICHAEL BERKOWITZ (Ph.D., University of Wisconsin), reader in Modern Jewish History at University College, London, is the author of two books on Zionism in the West and, most recently, a study of the emergence of Jewish-identity politics, *The Jewish Self-Image in the West, 1881–1939.*

CHRISTOPHER R. BROWNING (Ph.D., University of Wisconsin), Distinguished University Professor of History at Pacific Lutheran University, is the author of a number of leading works on the history of the Holocaust, including *The Path to Genocide* and *Ordinary Men.*

NATHAN F. COGAN (Ph.D., University of California at Berkeley) is a professor of English at Portland State University and the producer of the video-documentary *The Last Remnants of Lithuanian Jewry.*

SCOTT DENHAM (Ph.D., Harvard University) teaches German at Davidson College, specializing in modernism, Weimar culture, and German film. A co-editor of *A User's Guide to German Cultural Studies,* he is currently writing a critical history of Walter Gropius and the Bauhaus.

JUDITH E. DONESON (Ph.D., Hebrew University of Jerusalem) has taught at Tel Aviv and St. Louis Universities and has been a fellow of the Center for Jewish Studies (formerly Annenberg Institute) at the University of Pennsylvania. She is the author of *The Holocaust in American Film* and of numerous contributions to edited collections and journals. She is currently the director of the Holocaust Museum and Learning Center in St. Louis and teaches at Washinton University.

DEBÓRAH DWORK (Ph.D., University of London), Rose Professor of Holocaust History at Clark University, is the author of *Children With a Star* and *Auschwitz: 1270 to the Present* (with Robert-Jan van Pelt).

GEOFFREY J. GILES (Ph.D., Cambridge), associate professor of history and codirector of the Center for Modern German Studies at the University of Florida, is the author of *Students and National Socialism in Germany.* He is president of the Friends of the German Historical Institute in Washington, D.C., and academic coordinator of the Holocaust Educational Foundation's Eastern European Study Seminars, which visit Holocaust sites in Central and Eastern Europe.

PETER HAYES (Ph.D., Yale University) is a professor of history at Northwestern University and the author or editor of four books, including the prizewinning *Industry and Ideology: IG Farben in the Nazi Era* and *Lessons and Legacies: The Meaning of the Holocaust in a Changing World.* His essay in this volume represents part of a larger work in preparation on German big business and the Holocaust. In 1997–98, he was the J. B. and Maurice C. Shapiro Senior Scholar-in-Residence at the U.S. Holocaust Memorial Museum in Washington, D.C.

HAROLD MARCUSE (Ph.D., University of Michigan) is an assistant professor of history at the University of California, Santa Barbara.

GERALD E. MARKLE (Ph.D., Florida State University) is the author of numerous books, including *Meditations of a Holocaust Traveler.* His two most recent books are novels set in World War II.

Michael R. Marrus (Ph.D., University of California at Berkeley) is a professor of history and dean of the graduate school at the University of Toronto. He is the author of *The Holocaust in History.*

Henry L. Mason (Ph.D., Columbia University) is a professor of political science at Tulane University. He has written several monographs and articles on Dutch experiences during World War II.

Jeffrey M. Peck (Ph.D., University of Calfiornia at Berkeley) is a professor of German at Georgetown University.

Jonathan Petropoulous (Ph.D., Harvard University) is an associate professor of history at Loyola College in Maryland. He is the author of *Art as Politics in the Third Reich* and *The Faustian Bargain: The Art World in Nazi Germany* and co-editor of *A User's Guide to German Cultural Studies.*

John K. Roth (Ph.D., Yale University) is Russell K. Pitzer Professor of Philosophy at Claremont McKenna College and the author and editor of numerous works, including *Different Voices: Women and the Holocaust* (with Carol Rittner) and *Holocaust: Religious and Philosophical Implications* (with Michael Berenbaum).

Karl A. Schleunes (Ph.D., University of Minnesota) is a professor of history at the University of North Carolina at Greensboro and the author of the classic study *The Twisted Road to Auschwitz.*

Alan E. Steinweis (Ph.D., University of North Carolina) is an associate professor of history and Judaic studies at the University of Nebraska, Lincoln. He is the author of *Art, Ideology,* and *Economics in Nazi Germany,* as well as numerous essays, and is currently researching the subject of Nazi "knowledge" of Jews and Judaism.

Elie Wiesel (Ph.D.) received the Nobel Peace Prize in 1986. He is a university professor and Andrew W. Mellon Professor in the Humanities at Boston University.